A BIBLIOGRAPHIC GUIDE TO
POPULATION GEOGRAPHY

A BIBLIOGRAPHIC GUIDE TO POPULATION GEOGRAPHY

DEPARTMENT OF GEOGRAPHY

RESEARCH PAPER NO. 80

By

WILBUR ZELINSKY

Southern Illinois University

GREENWOOD PRESS, PUBLISHERS
WESTPORT, CONNECTICUT

Library of Congress Cataloging in Publication Data

Zelinsky, Wilbur, 1921-
   A bibliographic guide to population geography.

   Reprint of the ed. published by the Dept. of Geography,
University of Chicago, in series: Research paper no. 80.
   1. Demography--Bibliography. 2. Population--Bibliog-
raphy. I. Title. II. Series: Chicago. University.
Dept. of Geography. Research paper ; no. 80.
Z7164.D3Z44 1976 [HB881] 016.30132 75-36518
ISBN 0-8371-8645-5

Originally published in 1962 by the Department of Geography,
The University of Chicago, Chicago, Ill.

Reprinted with the permission of Research Papers-University of Chicago

Reprinted in 1976 by Greenwood Press,
a division of Williamhouse-Regency Inc.

Library of Congress Catalog Card Number 75-36518

ISBN 0-8371-8645-5

Printed in the United States of America

I N T R O D U C T I O N

A Bibliographic Guide to Population Geography is a list of all the
significant writings -- a total of 2,588 items -- that could be located by
the compiler on all phases of population geography, as defined for the purposes of this bibliography, published throughout the world since the begin-
ning of specialized work in this discipline in the latter half of the Nine-
teenth Century through mid-1961. This work is intended primarily as a
convenience for the scholarly investigator; but, although a finding list
with no attempt to provide descriptive or critical annotations, it is also
inevitably a crude sort of inventory. The reader can draw some interesting
conclusions as to relative coverage of topics and areas without much diffi-
culty and will note serious regional gaps in the literature of population
geography. If this work can facilitate or stimulate research on the many
phases of the subject that clamor for attention, then the effort that has
gone into its compilation will have been amply repaid.

This volume is the first comprehensive bibliography devoted exclu-
sively to population geography. It might be considered as a successor to
Hans Dörries, "Siedlungs- und Bevölkerungsgeographie (1908-1938)," (5)
except for the fact that this earlier work, the first retrospective bibliography to give population geography any particular notice, was mainly concerned with publications in settlement geography. There is only a moderate
amount of overlap in coverage between it and the present work; less than
30 percent of the titles cited here fall within the time period handled by
Dörries, and many of these were not included in his list.

THE FIELD OF POPULATION GEOGRAPHY

This work cannot be used effectively without understanding the limits
that have been set in its topical coverage and thus something of the nature of
population geography. Because it is one of the youngest of the geographic
specialities, the contents, functions, and limits of population geography have
not yet become crystallized in theory or practice. Tentatively, the subject
can be defined rather cumbersomely, but with some precision, as the science
that deals with the extent and ways in which the total, unique geographic
character of places is formed by and, in turn, reacts upon a set of population phenomena which vary within it through both space and time as they follow
their own behavioral laws and interact with numerous nondemographic phenomena.
'Place' in this context may be a territory of any extent from a few acres up
to the entire inhabited surface of the earth. It is a matter of more than incidental interest that this same definition might suffice for almost any other
systematic division of geography with suitable substitutions for the terms
'population' and 'nondemographic.' In the simplest terms, the population
geographer studies the ways in which spatial differences in population are
related to spatial differences in the aggregate nature of places. Note that
the essential purpose of this field is far broader and deeper than the ele-
mentary task of stating where how many of what sort of people reside. As in
all other branches of geography, the simple 'whereness' of things cannot be
accepted as an adequate definition of the scope and purpose of population
geography. Although the term 'geographic' is commonly and erroneously used
as a synonym for 'locational,' no analysis enters the realm of geography until
it seeks out the interrelatedness of things that vary in space and probes the
complex flux of cause and effect among two or more sets of features that endow
given places at given times with unique personalities. It is this primary
concern with the nature of places that distinguishes population geography from
demography, the discipline whose ultimate concern is the understanding of the

nature of population phenomena _per se_, even though the two fields share much
of their subject matter and methodology.

We find that the population geographer is concerned with three distinct
and ascending levels of discourse, as follows: 1) the simple description of
the location of population numbers and characteristics; 2) the explanation of
the spatial patterns of these phenomena; and 3) the geographic analysis of
population features -- in short, the interrelations among areal differences
in population and other aspects of the geographic totality of the study area.
Since population geography has so recently appeared on the scene, a dispro-
portionate number of the items listed in this bibliography are devoted to a
setting forth of the basic distributional facts; it can be anticipated that a
greater number of explanatory and analytical studies will appear as the field
achieves greater maturity. The quite severe quantitative and qualitative limi-
tations in the basic population information available for most of the world
until very recent years have greatly inhibited the development of population
geography and demography and are, in fact, largely responsible for the late-
ness of their advent as serious intellectual endeavors. The rapidly growing
quantities of official demographic data in scores of nations and the considerable improvement in detail and reliability offer us the prospect that geographers may soon be able to exploit population materials much more widely and
effectively as part of their central strategy in analyzing a great variety of
problems. Indeed the interplay between demographic phenomena and many of the
other topics within the geographer's orbit is so richly varied and sensitive
that the population approach may prove as fruitful as any for general regional
analysis and for many important aspects of human geography. As this fact of
the deep, multiple bonds between population and much of the rest of the geographer's universe is more fully recognized and as more and better raw facts
accumulate and superior methods for utilizing them are invented, we have
every right to expect that population geography will shift from its present,
rather peripheral standing to a commanding position within the discipline.

Precisely which demographic phenomena does the geographer map, explain, and interpret? If we define 'population' in the broadest terms, then the range of phenomena treated by the demographer and the population geographer would include anything pertaining to human beings and would run the entire gamut of the social sciences. Such a mass of social, economic, psychological, cultural, and political detail would obviously exceed the grasp of any single group of specialists; and thus it is necessary to circumscribe fairly sharply, if arbitrarily, the field of population studies. For all practical purposes, we can equate the resulting list of human characteristics with those appearing in the census enumeration schedules and vital registration systems of the more statistically advanced nations. These, in turn, are such facts as can be quickly and reliably collected from individual respondents by enumerators or registrars with only a moderate amount of training. For the most part, then, these are characteristics readily perceptible in individuals or families; other equally important facts that can be discerned only by skillful or protracted observation of the larger group or intensive study of individuals lie beyond the bounds of population geography and are largely the responsibility of the social or anthropogeographer.

The demographic characteristics studied by the population geographer can be grouped into three broad classes: absolute numbers; physical, social, and economic characteristics; and population dynamics. It is always assumed, of course, that locational facts are available for whatever topic is under scrutiny. In this brief statement no more than a brief listing of characteristics can be provided; their relative importance, implications, and interrelations are subjects that call for extended essays. The absolute size of a population (along with its areal distribution) is obviously a matter of basic concern for the geographer. Because of the relative abundance of data and widespread interest in the matter, this is the population characteristic that has been dealt with more often than any other. The extremely diverse group of characteristics that define the kind of community under consideration can be conveniently divided into those that are essentially biological and those that are economic, social, or cultural in causation. The biological traits are determined by the facts of birth or heredity or the physiological behavior of individuals, and are largely beyond the control of the group or individual. They include sex, age, and -- if we assume that there are adequate, objective criteria for its recognition -- race. Morbidity (the prevalence and kinds of disease) and cause of death might also be added, even though there are social and cultural factors affecting these phenomena. The socially determined population facts are much more numerous. We have here residence, occupation, marital status and history, family size, composition, and relationships, socio-economic class and caste, income, literacy, educational status and attainment, reproductive history, migrational history, religion, language, ethnic group, and nationality. Each of these items can be subdivided into quite detailed categories, so that the resulting number of possible combinations of characteristics is almost limitless. Finally, there are the dynamic characteristics of a population: net change, fertility, mortality, and migration in all its many forms.

LIMITATIONS IN COVERAGE

Population geography has been defined for our purposes as the study of the differences in the population characteristics of places and, more particularly, the ways in which these differences, interacting among themselves and with many nondemographic phenomena, have affected, and been affected by, the total character of the inhabited earth, helping create the almost infinitely complex variations that can be observed from region to region: i.e., population as an element in the total geographic context. In addition to studies that fall within this definition, it has seemed reasonable to include certain other ancillary items, such as bibliographies and works on population mapping.

In practice, it has been necessary to apply a rather narrow interpretation of
population geography in selecting items for inclusion, since a liberal definition, however justifiable on methodological grounds, would have meant extend-
ing this compilation into several zones bordering on quite active neighboring
disciplines and thus expanding it beyond all reasonable dimensions.

Certain of the "cut-off points" between disciplines that have been
observed in this compilation must be specified, but with the comment that all
are quite arbitrary. Within the broad overlap between population and urban
geography, it was decided to exclude almost all studies of individual cities
or metropolitan areas but to include treatments of the urban population or
networks of regions and nations. There is also the problem of the extensive
geographic literature dealing with colonization and the process of settlement.
Although this subject might logically be regarded as falling well within the
field of population geography, it has become a distinct entity, one deserving
separate treatment, and, with some rare exceptions, all titles in this field
have been excluded. Also omitted are studies that deal principally with the
morphology of settlement and thus the ultimate details of population distribution, even though many of these are of demographic interest; and, again, nearly
all publications on medical and religious geography have been excluded. It has
been especially difficult to mark off the limits of population geography in
those sectors bordering on social geography and anthropogeography; and here
each case has been weighed individually. One of the largest groups of such
items are those studies dealing with ethnic minorities. Almost the entirety
of the voluminous literature on minorities within European nations has been
omitted; and it is a moot point whether these publications can best be cate-
gorized as social, political, or population geography. On the other hand, in
non-European areas, particularly those for which the population literature is
relatively scanty, most of the items concerned with ethnic minorities have
been admitted. There are also a number of works in economic and political

geography which might equally well be classified as population geography, and, again, individual scrutiny has been necessary.

One important modification of the rules for inclusion should be noted: criteria were applied with greater strictness and most narrowly in areas with an abundance of population literature, and the limits of eligibility were stretched for territories which have been poorly studied. These flexible standards result in quite different kinds of coverage for such areas as, say, Ethiopia or Bolivia as compared with France or Italy. In the many marginal cases that appeared, consideration was given both to the authorship and to the auspices under which a work was published. Thus, the benefit of the doubt was usually given to publications by professional geographers on population topics whether appearing in geographic or nongeographic media (although a number of items had to be omitted because they clearly failed to meet the criteria noted above); generally, most marginal items appearing in geographic periodicals or volumes were included even though they may have been written by nongeographers.

In a number of cases, nongeographic works of major importance or unusual scope that are basic to the geographer in his study of a population topic or region have been included. Most of these works fall within the fields of demography, sociology, and anthropology. The huge literature on migration has posed especially difficult editorial problems: only those publications have been included which are distinctly geographic in their approach or provide data on areas relatively neglected by the population scholar. Statistical publications, census bulletins, compendia of statistics, and the like have all been omitted, except for the indispensable Demographic Yearbook (6) and a few items that include a significant amount of interpretive material; but bibliographies of population statistics are cited.

This bibliography is restricted almost wholly to verbal materials. Single population maps, whether issued as separate publications or as incidental items in books and articles, are not noted; but the few atlases, such as 28, 122, or 2485, which give population topics strong emphasis, have been

listed. Aside from such serial bibliographies of maps as the Bibliographie

Cartographique Internationale, Referativnyi Zhurnal (8), various national

series, and incidental notes in the major demographic and geographic biblio-

graphic series, the most complete listing of recent population maps is a

mimeographed compilation entitled Population Maps Exhibited at the XIXth IGU

Conference, Stockholm August 1960 and edited by William William-Olsson, Depart-

ment of Geography, Stockholm School of Economics. Most of the many excellent

national atlases that have appeared in recent years contain one or more plates

on population phenomena and are of major significance to population students

investigating the nations in question. Citations of these atlases have been

omitted for two reasons:[1] most of the nations concerned are relatively fully

covered in the general and geographic literature on population, and the atlases

are described in two recent analytical works -- Polish Academy of Sciences,

Institute of Geography, National Atlases; Sources, Bibliography, Articles

(Dokumentacja Geograficzna, Zeszyt 4), Warszawa, 1960 and Academy of Sciences

of the U.S.S.R., National Committee of Soviet Geographers, Atlas Nationaux;

Histoire, Analyse, Voies de Perfectionnement et d'Unification (published on

behalf of the commission on National Atlases of the International Geographi-

cal Union), Moskva and Leningrad, 1960.

A brief glance at this volume will disclose the fact that only those

materials have been listed that can be described as scholarly in intent and

substantial in form. Ephemeral matter, items in newspapers and popular maga-

zines, manuscripts and other essentially private documents, and very brief

publications have been excluded. Thus there are no pamphlets, broadsides,

mimeographed matter (with a very few exceptions), book reviews (except for

---

[1]The one exception (1461) is for a series of atlas plates accompanied
by copious commentary and describing a population for which other materials
are difficult to come by.

review articles or unusually extensive reviews), or short notices of publications. Most of the titles cited in this bibliography can be located in the
larger geographical libraries of the United States and other nations or can
be obtained through interlibrary loan. The decision to include master's
theses and doctoral dissertations is based on the fact that almost all such
documents can be consulted either by interlibrary loan or by microfilm.

Within the limits stated above, this bibliography is all-embracing,
without any attempt at selectivity. Items of weak scholarship or questionable
value are in no way distinguished from works of outstanding merit. Such critical evaluation may be possible in future editions of this volume.

METHOD OF COMPILATION

The bulk of the titles cited in this volume were obtained by a thorough
review of five major bibliographic sources: Bibliographie Géographique Internationale (1), covering the period 1891-1958; Bibliotheca Geographica, herausgegeben von der Gesellschaft für Erdkunde zu Berlin (2), covering the period,
1891-1912; Hans Dörries, "Siedlungs- und Bevölkerungsgeographie (1908-1938),"
(5); Population Index (3), covering the period 1935-1961; and Current Geographical Publications (4), covering the period 1938-1961. It is a matter of great
regret that the Referativnyi Zhurnal (8), which has provided unusually broad
coverage of geographical publications since 1954, is indexed in such a way as
to be of quite limited utility in collecting titles in population geography.
Important as these basic sources may be, they do not provide complete coverage
for the field of population geography, either singly or in combination. The
fact that there is no major bibliographic source for the years preceding 1891
is not a serious annoyance because of the paucity of eligible items during this
early period. The search was extended by examining bibliographic citations in
the more important publications on the subject and by methodical scanning of
the stacks in the libraries of Southern Illinois University and the University
of Chicago and by rather more limited searches in other university libraries.

It is in the nature of bibliographies always to remain incomplete; and
in spite of conscientious efforts to make this list as comprehensive as possible, I should conservatively estimate that at least ten percent of the items
eligible for inclusion have not been located. Regionally, the coverage for
Anglo-America is reasonably complete, and only a small percentage of the
appropriate publications for western and southern Europe are missing. The
coverage for Tropical Africa, while not impressive in its bulk, is known to
be virtually complete by dint of another thoroughgoing search in the period
1952-1954 in addition to the present one. The materials on Latin America and
Asia outside the Chinese and Soviet areas are less complete. The region of
greatest uncertainty includes portions of eastern Europe, the Soviet Union,
and China where the problem of language and the inaccessibility of bibliographic sources make it almost certain that a significant number of items have
been overlooked.

Of the four general types of items included here -- books, monographs
and other numbered items in geographical series, periodical articles, and
chapters or other extracts from books and monographs -- the listing of books
and monographs is probably most nearly complete. It has proved more difficult to track down all relevant periodical literature; but the most grievous
lacunae are undoubtedly those within the category of extracts pertaining to
population geography within volumes devoted principally to other topics. Such
publications are seldom analyzed fully enough in the major demographic and
geographic bibliographies, and it has not been possible to examine more than
a few thousand of the multitude of volumes that might contain usable material.

ARRANGEMENT AND CITATION OF MATERIAL

The material in this bibliography is grouped into two principal sec-
tions. The first, and by far the briefer, contains general studies and study
aids, including systematic treatments of the field of population geography or

segments thereof and studies of specific aspects of population geography that
are worldwide in scope or essentially unlocalized. Most of the titles appear
in Part II where they are arranged by region. Any regional classification is
necessarily arbitrary; but the one adopted here, the numerical system worked
out by the Library of Congress for map cataloging, has the merit of relatively
logical territorial progression and considerable areal detail. The numbers
and sequence have been borrowed from the publication Library of Congress,
Subject Cataloging Division, Classification; Class G; Geography, Anthropology,
Folklore, Manners and Customs, Recreation, third edition, Washington, 1954,
pp. 30-172, except for a few regions not recognized in the Library of Congress
classification, for which appropriate numbers were improvised, e.g., Former
German Territory (6099) and Monsoon Asia (7402).

     Current international boundaries are the only ones recognized in
arranging regional studies within national categories, except for a few
extinct, but convenient, political entities such as Austria-Hungary and
French Indo-China. Thus, for example, publications on Alsace-Lorraine that
appeared while that territory was under German rule will be found listed
under France rather than Germany.

     For areas and nations having a large number of citations, studies deal-
ing with the entire territory are grouped separately from regional, i.e.,
local, studies. For those nations having especially extensive coverage,
namely the United States, Great Britain, France, Germany, Italy, and the
Union of Soviet Socialist Republics, the regional section has been further
subdivided into appropriate regional segments. Cross-references are provided for studies dealing with more than a single area. The user should not
limit his search for material on a given region to those titles listed or
cross-referenced under that region, but should always investigate the more
inclusive areal category into which the region might fall. Thus, for example,

material on Burma might appear not only under Burma but under Southeast Asia (Indochina) and Monsoon Asia or even Asia.

It might be noted parenthetically that despite the flexible standards used for admitting literature on different portions of the world, those nations having a particularly abundant supply of population statistics and geographers are greatly overrepresented in this bibliography. Thus we find that some of the more important nations within the "Atlantic Community" (the United States, Canada, the United Kingdom, Eire, Sweden, the Netherlands, Belgium, France, Germany, Austria, Switzerland, and Italy) account for 40.2 percent of the titles in Part II even though they contain less than 17 percent of the world's population.

Within each area, national, or subnational category, titles are arranged firstly by order of year of publication and then within any given year alphabetically by name of author. It is a matter of more than passing interest to note the chronological distribution of citations. (Because of the time lag between publication and citation in bibliographic sources, not only are most 1961 titles missing but also a large number of those for 1960 and even 1959.)

No date	1	1893	10	1910	11	1927	26	1944	27
1856	1	1894	2	1911	19	1928	29	1945	38
1866	1	1895	7	1912	19	1929	23	1946	39
1872	1	1896	7	1913	16	1930	36	1947	48
1874	1	1897	9	1914	3	1931	33	1948	55
1875	1	1898	7	1915	8	1932	38	1949	89
1876	1	1899	4	1916	11	1933	21	1950	66
1878	1	1900	10	1917	11	1934	56	1951	60
1880	1	1901	9	1918	11	1935	40	1952	110
1882	1	1902	11	1919	15	1936	36	1953	90
1884	1	1903	10	1920	15	1937	52	1954	108
1885	1	1904	12	1921	18	1938	88	1955	110
1886	1	1905	11	1922	16	1939	36	1956	125
1888	1	1906	11	1923	21	1940	31	1957	120
1890	2	1907	14	1924	10	1941	42	1958	126
1891	2	1908	12	1925	24	1942	40	1959	134
1892	3	1909	15	1926	22	1943	38	1960	105
								1961	41

Even if ample allowance is made for the more complete coverage of the past quarter century that can be attributed to superior bibliographic resources and the simple matter of immediacy, there still has been a striking growth in

the literature of population geography in recent years,[1] a trend that bodes

well for the future of this infant discipline.

The form of citation is largely self-explanatory. For all four general

types of entry, the name of the author is given on the first line and the title

of the work on the second, along with the edition and number of volumes, when

such information is called for. Titles are given in the original language for

material appearing in English, French, German, Italian, Portuguese, and Spanish;

for other languages a literal translation and a statement of the original tongue

is given. The reader should realize that in numerous instances, particularly

for periodical literature, summaries of the material are provided in one or

more languages other than that of the original; but no attempt has been made

in this bibliography to note the presence or absence of such summaries. Even

though there is some unavoidable bias inherent in the character of the major

bibliographic sources, the following list of number of entries, by language,

will be of interest to those concerned with the sociology of knowledge:

Language	Count	Language	Count
English	1,042	Czech	12
French	461	Rumanian	8
German	442	Danish	6
Italian	154	Hungarian	6
Spanish	118	Slovenian	6
Dutch	63	Bulgarian	4
Portuguese	56	Norwegian	4
Swedish	56	Afrikaans	3
Russian	51	Turkish	3
Japanese	29	Estonian	2
Polish	26	Flemish	1
Chinese	18	Georgian	1
Serbian	15	Indonesian	1

Citations of books include author, title, and, on the last line, place

of publication, publisher, and date. When it is relevant, additional biblio-

graphic information, such as the name of the sponsoring agency or the series

in which the volume appears, are included on a third line. Monographs and

other separately bound works appearing in numbered series are listed in much

---

[1]The median year of the citations in this volume is 1948.

the same way as ordinary books, except that the series name and number are
given on the third line of the entry. In the case of periodical articles, the
name of the periodical, volume number and, when necessary, number of issue
within the volume, and pagination are given on the last line of the entry.
The authority consulted for titles and other details of geographical serials,
both regular and irregular, has been Chauncy D. Harris and Jerome D. Fellmann,
International List of Geographical Serials, University of Chicago, Department
of Geography, Research Paper No. 63, Chicago, 1960. The last type of entry,
the extract from a larger work, includes pagination with the title on the
second line and concludes with a citation of the book or monograph concerned
that is identical in form with the entries already described for books and
monographs. In a few instances when bibliographic sources have afforded only
partial data and the publications were not available for inspection, incomplete
citations have been included.

The compilation of this work would not have been possible without the
aid rendered by Southern Illinois University. I wish to acknowledge gratefully
the released time granted for the project by the University and the financial
support received through its Graduate School.

I should greatly appreciate receiving corrections of errors in citations and items qualifying for inclusion not appearing in the present list for
insertion in subsequent editions. After June, 1963, correspondence should be
addressed to Department of Geography, Pennsylvania State University, University
Park, Pennsylvania.

Wilbur Zelinsky

Carbondale, Illinois

TABLE OF CONTENTS

Table of Contents   xxiv

KEY TO ABBREVIATIONS

AAAG   Annals of the Association of American Geographers

AG   Annales de Géographie

BSGI   Bollettino, Società Geographica Italiana

CRCIG   Comptes Rendus, Proceedings, etc., Congres International de
              Géographie (International Geographical Congress)

EG   Economic Geography

GR   Geographical Review (New York)

GJ   Geographical Journal

PM   Petermanns Geographische Mitteilungen, or antecedent series

RGA   Revue de Géographie Alpine

RGI   Rivista Geografica Italiana

SGM   Scottish Geographical Magazine

TEG; TESG   Tijdschrift voor Economische Geographie; Tijdschrift voor
              Economische en Sociale Geographie

PART I

GENERAL STUDIES

A. BIBLIOGRAPHIES AND GENERAL AIDS

1 Association de Géographes Français
   Bibliographie géographique internationale, 64 vols.
   Paris, 1892-1961 (Covers period 1891-1958)

2 Baschin, Otto, ed.
   Bibliotheca geographica, herausgegeben von der Gesellschaft
   für Erdkunde zu Berlin, 19 vols.
   Berlin, Kühl, 1895-1917 (Covers period 1891-1912)

3 Office of Population Research, Princeton University and Population
   Association of America
   Population index, quarterly
   Princeton, 1935-

4 American Geographical Society
   Current geographical publications, 10 issues a year
   New York, 1938-

5 Dörries, Hans
   "Siedlungs- und Bevölkerungsgeographie (1908-1938),"
   Geographisches Jahrbuch, 55(1940), 3-380

6 United Nations, Statistical Office
   Demographic yearbook
   New York, 1949-

7 United Nations Educational, Scientific and Cultural Organization,
   International Committee for Social Sciences Documentation
   International bibliography of sociology, annual
   Paris, UNESCO, 1953-

8 U.S.S.R., Akademiia Nauk, Institut Nauchnoi Informatsii
   Referativnyi zhurnal. Geografiia, 12 issues a year
   Moskva, 1954-

9 United Nations Educational, Scientific and Cultural Organization,
   International Committee for Social Sciences Documentation
   International bibliography of economics, annual
   Paris, UNESCO, 1954-

10 United Nations, Statistical Office
   Bibliography of recent official demographic statistics.
   Statistical Papers, Series M, No. 18
   New York, 1954

11 Camargo, José Francisco de
   "Pequeno vocabulario de demografia para uso dos geografos,"
   Boletim Paulista de Geografia, No. 25(1957), 22-30

12 United Nations Educational, Scientific and Cultural Organization,
   International Committee for Social Sciences Documentation
   International Bibliography of social and cultural anthropology, annual
   Paris, UNESCO, 1957-

13   United Nations, Department of Economic and Social Affairs
     Multilingual demographic dictionary. English section
     Population Studies, No. 29
     New York, 1958

14   Eldridge, Hope T.
     The materials of demography: a selected and annotated bibliography.
     International Union for the Scientific Study of Population and
       the Population Association of America
     New York, Columbia University Press, 1959

B. GENERAL STUDIES OF POPULATION GEOGRAPHY AND GENERAL
WORKS ON DEMOGRAPHY OF GEOGRAPHICAL SIGNIFICANCE

15   Krebs, Norbert
     Die Verbreitung des Menschen auf der Erdoberfläche (Anthropogeographie)
     Leipzig and Berlin, Teubner, 1921

16   Ratzel, Friedrich
     Anthropogeographie. Vol. II. Die geographische Verbreitung des Menschen
     Stuttgart, Engelhorn, 1922

17   Knibbs, Sir George H.
     "The geography of population,"
     Queensland Geographical Journal, N.s. 39(1923-24), 46-62

18   Pearson, Sidney Vere
     The growth and distribution of population
     New York, Wiley, 1935

19   Vidal de la Blache, P.
     "La répartition des hommes sur le globe," pp. 17-95 in:
     Principes de géographie humaine
     Paris, Colin, 1941

20   Almagià, Roberto
     "La densità della popolazione e la sua distribuzione," pp. 410-429 in:
     Fondamenti di geografia generale
     Roma, Perrella, 1945

21   Biasutti, Renato
     Geografia della popolazione e delle sedi
     Firenze, 1945

22   Lefèvre, Marguerite A.
     "Groupements des hommes à la surface de la terre," pp. 39-79 in:
     Principes et problèmes de géographie humaine
     Bruxelles, Wauthoz, 1945

23   Phillips, Mary Viola
     "Unit III. Population, for course in global geography,"
     Journal of Geography, 45(1946), 142-148

24 Hettner, Alfred
    "Wanderungen und Ausbreitung des Menschen und seiner Kultur," pp. 100-112
    and "Die Bevölkerung," pp. 294-298 in:
    Allgemeine Geographie des Menschen. I. Band. Die Menschheit;
       Grundlegung der Geographie des Menschen
    Stuttgart, Kohlhammer, 1947

25 George, Pierre
    Introduction à l'étude géographique de la population du monde
    Institut National d'Études Démographiques, Cahiers de "Travaux et
    Documents," No. 14
    Paris, Presses Universitaires de France, 1951

26 Taviani, Paolo E.
    Distribuzione geografica e struttura della popolazione, a traverso la
       storia e nel tempo
    Torino, Giappichelli, 1953

27 Woytinsky, W. S. and Woytinsky, E. S.
    World population and production; trends and outlook
    New York, Twentieth Century Fund, 1953

28 Burgdörfer, Friedrich, ed.
    World atlas of population, issued serially
    Hamburg, Falk, 1954-

29 James, Preston E.
    "The geographic study of population," pp. 106-122 in:
    Preston E. James and Clarence F. Jones, eds.
    American geography: inventory and prospect
    Syracuse, Syracuse University Press, 1954

30 Kirsten, Ernst, et al.
    Raum und Bevölkerung in der Weltgeschichte. Band I. Urgeschichte und
       Altertum. Band II. Mittlere, neuere und neuste Zeit
    Würzburg, Ploetz, 1955-56

31 Schwarz, Gabriele
    Dichtezentren des Menschheit
    Die bewohnte Erde, Einführungen in der Kulturgeographie, No. 2
    Hannover, Schroedel, 1955

32 Beaujeu-Garnier, Jacqueline
    Géographie de la population, 2 vols.
    Paris, Librairie de Médicis, 1956 and 1958

33 Trewartha, Glenn T.
    "Population," pp. 501-537 in:
    V. C. Finch, G. T. Trewartha, A. H. Robinson, and E. H. Hammond
    Elements of geography, physical and cultural, 4th ed.
    New York, McGraw-Hill, 1957

34 Villey, Daniel
    Leçons de démographie: introduction aux problèmes de la population,
       initiations aux outils statistiques et aux theories fondamentales de
       la démographie générale et de la démographie économique, la répartition
       géographique de la population
    Paris, Montchristien, 1957

35 Witthauer, Kurt
    Die Bevölkerung der Erde; Verteilung und Dynamik
    Ergänzungsheft Nr. 265 zu Petermanns Geographischen Mitteilungen
    Gotha, Haack, 1958

36 Ackerman, Edward A.
    "Population and natural resources," pp. 621-648 and "Geography and
        demography," pp. 717-727 in:
    Philip M. Hauser and Otis D. Duncan, eds.
    The study of population: an inventory and appraisal
    Chicago, University of Chicago Press, 1959

37 Biasutti, Renato, et al.
    Le razze e i popoli della terra, 3rd ed., 4 vols.
    Torino, Tipografico Editrice, 1959

38 George, Pierre
    Questions de géographie de la population
    Institut National d'Études Démographiques, Cahiers de "Travaux et
        Documents," No. 34
    Paris, Presses Universitaires de France, 1959

39 Veyret-Verner, Germaine
    Population: mouvements, structures, répartition
    Paris, Arthaud, 1959

40 Migliorini, Elio
    "La distribuzione degli uomini sulla terra," pp. 30-134 and "Popolamento
        della terra," pp. 135-182 in:
    La terra e gli uomini; lezioni di geografia umana, 3rd ed.
    Napoli, Pironti e Figli, 1960

41 Smith, T. Lynn
    "The number and geographic distribution of the population," pp. 41-71 in:
    Fundamentals of population study
    New York, Lippincott, 1960

41a Stamp, L. Dudley
    "The geographical study of population," pp. 26-36 and "The interpretation
        of the population and land-use pattern," pp. 51-60 in:
    Applied geography
    London, Penguin Books, 1960

                    C. UNLOCALIZED STUDIES OF SPECIFIC ASPECTS
                            OF POPULATION GEOGRAPHY

                    C-1. Philosophy and General Methodology

42 Aurousseau, Marcel
    "The distribution of population: a constructive problem,"
    GR, 11(1921), 563-592

43 Aurousseau, Marcel
    "The geographic study of population groups,"
    GR, 13(1923), 266-282

44 Tulippe, Omer
    Considerations sur la géographie du peuplement
    Liège. Université. Séminaire de Géographie. Travaux 33
    Liège, 1932

45 McCarty, Harold H.
    "A functional analysis of population distribution,"
    GR, 32(1942), 282-293

46 MacLean, Donald A.
    "Geography of population. The problem of national, racial and religious
        minorities,"
    American Journal of Economics and Sociology, 3(1944), 479-497

47 Chatelain, Abel
    "Démographie et démogéographie,"
    Les Études Rhodaniennes, 20, Nos. 3 and 4(1945)

48 Hofstee, Evert W.
    /"Regional forecasts of population applied to the social sciences"_7
        (in Dutch)
    TEG, 38(1947), 297-312

49 Roselli, Bruno
    "Pour une étude des types d'agglomeration et de dispersion de la popula-
        tion dans le cadre de l'unité anthropogéographique minimum," pp. 443-
        449 in:
    CRCIG, Lisbonne, 1949, Vol. 3

50 George, Pierre
    "Géographie de la population et démographie,"
    Population, 5(1950), 291-300

51 Veyret-Verner, Germaine
    "Les différents types de régimes démographiques; essai d'interprétation
        géographique,"
    RGA, 40(1952), 547-566

52 Trewartha, Glenn T.
    "The case for population geography,"
    AAAG, 43(1953), 71-97

53 Gachon, Lucien
    "Histoire, géographie, démographie,"
    Norois, 2(1955), 281-316

54 Dziewoński, Kazimierz
    /"Geography of population and settlement; achievements, theoretical bases
        and plan for research,"_7 (in Polish)
    Przegląd Geograficzny, 28(1956), 721-764

55 Veyret-Verner, Germaine
    "Un nouvel indice démographique, l'indice de vitalité; son application
        en géographie,"
    RGA, 46(1958), 333-342

56 Bogue, Donald J.
    "Population distribution," pp. 383-399 in:
    Philip M. Hauser and Otis D. Duncan, eds.
    The study of population: an inventory and appraisal
    Chicago, University of Chicago Press, 1959

57 Halbwachs, Maurice
    "Spatial conditions," pp. 81-117 in:
    Population and society; introduction to social morphology
    Glencoe, Ill., Free Press, 1960

58 Hooson, David J. M.
    "The distribution of population as the essential geographical expression,"
    Canadian Geographer, No. 17(1960), 10-20

C-2. Sources of Data

59 Fraccaro, P.
    "I censimenti nell'antichità,"
    La Geografia, 18(1930), 44-55

60 United Nations, Department of Economic and Social Affairs, Population Division
    Population census methods
    Population Studies No. 4
    New York, 1949

61 George, Pierre
    "Materiaux pour l'étude géographique de la population,"
    AG, 62(1953), 321-346

62 Warntz, William
    "Macrogeography and the census,"
    Professional Geographer, 10, No. 6(1958), 6-10

63 Lopez, José Eliseo
    "El problema de las fuentes para el estudio geográfico de la poblacion,"
    Rivista Geográfica (Universidad de los Andes, Merida), 1(1959), 125-154

C-3. World Distribution of Population

64 Behm, E.
    "Area und Bevölkerung aller Länder der Erde,"
    Geographisches Jahrbuch, 1(1866)

65 Behm, E. and Wagner, H.
    Die Bevölkerung der Erde
    Ergänzungsheftes zu Petermanns Geographischen Mitteilungen, Gotha
    I. (Nr. 33), 1872; II. (Nr. 35), 1874; III (Nr. 41), 1875; IV. (Nr. 46),
        1876; V. (Nr. 55), 1878; VI. (Nr. 62), 1880; VII. (Nr. 69), 1882

66 Wagner, H. and Supan, A.
    Die Bevölkerung der Erde
    Ergänzungsheftes zu Petermanns Geographischen Mitteilungen, Gotha
    VIII. (Nr. 101), 1891; IX. (Nr. 107), 1893

67 Supan, A.
    Die Bevölkerung der Erde
    Ergänzungsheftes zu Petermanns Geographischen Mitteilungen, Gotha
    X. (Nr. 130), 1899; XI. (Nr. 135), 1901; XII (Nr. 146), 1904; XIII. (Nr.
       163), 1909

68 Vidal de la Blache, P.
    "Le repártition des hommes sur le globe,"
    AG, 26(1917), 241-254

69 Vidal de la Blache, P.
    "Les grandes agglomérations humaines,"
    AG, 26(1917), 401-422, 27(1918), 92-101, 124-187

70 Williamson, E. and Adams, E.
    "Density distribution in the earth,"
    Washington Academy of Sciences, 13(1923), 413-428

71 Passarge, Siegfried
    "Die Bevölkerungsdichte der Erde," pp. 128-145 in:
    Die Erde und ihr Wirtschaftsleben
    Hamburg and Berlin, Hanseatische Verlag, 1926

72 Demangeon, Albert
    "La population de la terre,"
    AG, 41(1932), 291-294

73 Dodge, Stanley D.
    "World distribution of population: preliminary survey and tentative
       conclusions,"
    Papers of the Michigan Academy of Science, Arts and Letters, 18(1933),
       137-142

74 Rudolphi, H.
    "Die Verteilung des Menschen auf der Erde und ihre Umgruppierung,"
    Geographische Wochenschrift, 3(1935), 331-340

75 Penck, Albrecht
    "Die Stärke der Verbreitung des Menschen,"
    Geographische Gesellschaft in Wien, Mitteilungen, 85(1942), 241-269

76 Toniolo, Antonio Renato
    "Distribuzione degli uomini sulla superficie terrestre," pp. 291-301 in:
    Compendio di geografia generale
    Milano, Principato, 1943

77 Fawcett, C. B.
    "The numbers and distribution of mankind,"
    Scientific Monthly, 64(1947), 389-395

78 Thaning, O.
    /"The population of the world and its distribution,"/ (in Swedish)
    _pp. 674-701 in:
    /The world's lands and people after the First World War/ Vol. I
    Stockholm, 1947

79 Franke, Wilhelm
    "Die Bevölkerung der Erde um 1949,"
    Die Erde, 3-4(1949-50), 233-237

80   Sander, Erich
     "Verbreitung des Menschen über die Erde,"
     Geographische Rundschau, 1(1949), 330-334

81   Veyret-Verner, Germaine
     "Quelques précisions sur la population actuelle du globe,"
     RGA, 38(1950), 555-558

82   Zavatti, S.
     "Il nuovo limite settentrionale dell'ecumene,"
     RGI, 60(1953), 379-384

83   Zavatti, S.
     "Il nuovo limite australe dell'ecumene,"
     BSGI, Serie 8, 7(1954), 497-504

84   Witthauer, Kurt
     "Die Bevölkerung der Erde Anfang 1956,"
     PM, 100(1956), 57-61

85   Staszewski, Jozef
     Vertical distribution of world population
     Polish Academy of Sciences, Institute of Geography, Geographical Studies,
          No. 14
     Warszawa, State Scientific Publishing House, 1957

     Also: Czasopismo Geograficzne, 31(1960), 307-315 (in Polish)

86   Witthauer, Kurt
     "Bevölkerungszahlen 1957 und ihr potentielles Gewicht,"
     PM, 101(1957), 51-60

87   Staszewski, Jozef
     "Die Verteilung der Bevölkerung der Erde nach dem Abstand vom Meer,"
     PM, 103(1959), 207-215

88   Zierhoffer, August
     /"Some problems of the global distribution of population,"/ (in Polish)
     Czasopismo Geograficzne, 30(1959), 393-414

89   Papy, Louis
     "La répartition de la population dans le monde,"
     Société de Géographie Commerciale de Bordeaux, Bulletin, N.s. 3(1960), 3-9

89a Staszewski, Jozef
     /"Distribution of the world population on the basis of density; a pre-
          liminary communication,"/ (in Polish)
     Przeglad Geograficzny, 32(1960), 335-342

     (Also see Section B)

C-4.   World Population Change, Past, Present, and Future

90   Woeikow, A.
     "Die natürliche Vermehrung der Bevölkerung, ihre geographische Verteilung,
          Vergangenheit und Zukunft,"
     Geographische Zeitschrift, 13(1907), 657-676

91   Fischer, Alois
     "Die Bevölkerungsentwicklung 1925-28,"
     Zeitschrift für Geopolitik, 5(1928), 335-343

92   Sölch, Johannes
     "Die Frage der zukünftigen Verteilung des Menschheit,"
     Geografiska Annaler, 11(1929), 105-146

93   Carr-Saunders, Alexander Morris
     World population: past growth and present trends
     Oxford, Royal Institute of International Affairs, 1936

94   Revelli, Paolo
     La densità della popolazione nella storia della geografia
     Comitato Italiano per lo Studio dei Problemi della Popolazione,
       Pubblicazioni, Serie I, Vol. VI
     Roma, Operaia Romana, 1936

95   Fawcett, C. B.
     "The changing distribution of population,"
     SGM, 53(1937), 361-373

96   Fawcett, C. B.
     "Whither population? Distribution and trends of movement,"
     Geography, 22(1937), 14-22

97   Staszewski, Jozef
     /"World population from 1750 to 1950,"7 (in Polish)
     Przeglad Geograficzny, 23(1951), 95-112

98   Veyret-Verner, Germaine
     "Note sur l'évolution démographique mondiale depuis 1945,"
     RGA, 43(1955), 213-219

99   Witthauer, Kurt
     "Bevölkerungszunahme der Erde 1920-1953 nach Regionen und Ländern,"
     PM, 99(1955), 225-228

100 Witthauer, Kurt
     "Regionale Unterschiede der natürlichen Bevölkerungsentwicklung im
       ersten Nachkriegsjahrzent,"
     PM, 101(1957), 291-296

101 Bacon, Philip
     "Population growth and its impact on geographic education,"
     Journal of Geography, 57(1958), 111-118

102 United Nations, Department of Economic and Social Affairs
     The future growth of world population
     Population Studies, No. 28
     New York, 1958

103 George, Pierre
     "Rythme d'accroisement de la population mondiale,"
     AG, 68(1959), 459-461

104 Witthauer, Kurt
     "Zur geographischen Differenzierung der Bevölkerungsdynamik,"
     PM, 103(1959), 289-296

105 Schlier, Otto
     "Dezentralisation und Konzentration der Erdbevölkerung in den vergangene
        sechzig Jahren,"
     Geographische Rundschau, 12(1960), 337-344

     (Also see 30, 35, 204)

106 Witthauer, Kurt
     "Geographische Differenzierung der Bevölkerungsentwicklung 1920-1960 und
        Bevölkerungszahlen 1960," pp. 249-263 in:
     Emil Meynen, ed.
     Geographisches Taschenbuch und Jahrweiser zur Landeskunde 1960/61
     Wiesbaden, Steiner, 1960

                    C-5. World Distribution of Specific Populations or
                          Population Characteristics

107 Descamps, P.
     "L'agglomeration de la population chez les peuples chasseurs,"
     AG, 32(1923), 506-519

108 Mori, Attilio
     "Gl'italiani all'estero,"
     RGI, 35(1928), 169-179

109 Burgdörfer, Friedrich
     "Entwicklung der Erdbevölkerung und des Deutschtums in der Welt,"
     Zeitschrift für Geopolitik, 8(1931), 125-132

110 Fawcett, C. B.
     "Areas of concentration of population in the English-speaking countries,"
     Population, 1(1934), 4-13

111 Penck, Albrecht
     "Die Ausbreitung des Menschengeschlechts,"
     Gesellschaft für Erdkunde zu Leipzig, Mitteilungen, 55(1937), 5-25

112 Ferenczi, Imre
     "La population blanche dans les colonies,"
     AG, 47(1938), 225-236

113 Mauco, Georges
     "Les étrangers dans le monde,"
     AG, 47(1938), 1-8

114 Rónai, András
     "Distribution of Hungarian settlements over the world,"
     Bulletin International de la Société Hongroise de Géographie, 66(1938),
        38-62

115 Jonasson, Olaf
     /"The Swedish element in world population,"_7 (in Swedish)
     Svensk Geografisk Årsbok, 18(1942), 395-409

116 Fleure, Herbert John
     "The geographical distribution of the major religions,"
     Société Royale de Géographie d'Egypte, Bulletin, 24(1951), 1-18

117   International Labour Office
      "Numbers, types and geographical distribution," pp. 28-86 in:
      Indigenous peoples; living and working conditions of aboriginal popula-
          tions in independent countries
      Geneva, 1953

118   May, Jacques M.
      "Human starvation,"
      Focus, 4, No. 9(1954)

119   Sedlmeyer, Karl Adalbert
      "Die Neger und ihre geographische Verbreitung,"
      Geographische Rundschau, 6(1954), 374-378

120   Veyret-Verner, Germaine
      "La répartition des adultes dans le monde,"
      RGA, 43(1955), 239-254

121   Scott, Peter
      "The geographical distribution of intelligence: a note on a problem,"
      Australian Journal of Psychology, 9(1957), 41-46

122   Ginsburg, Norton
      Atlas of economic development
      Chicago, University of Chicago Press, 1961

                          C-6.   Urban Population

123   Fawcett, C. B.
      "The balance of urban and rural populations,"
      Geography, 15(1929-30), 99-106

124   Jefferson, Mark
      "Distribution of the world's city folks: a study in comparative
          civilization,"
      GR, 21(1931), 446-465

125   Nice, Bruno
      "Note statistiche sulla distribuzione e la popolazione delle grande
          citte con speciale reguardo alla marettemeta ed all'altemetria,"
      BSGI, Serie 7, 11(1946), 6-15

126   Taylor, E. G. R.
      "The world-wide growth of cities,"
      Geographical Magazine, 22(1950), 412-418

127   Davis, Kingsley and Hertz, Hilda
      "The world distribution of urbanization,"
      Bulletin of the International Statistical Institute, 33(1954), 227-243

128   Gizburg, B. L.
      /"Cities of the world with a population of more than one million,"7
          (in Russian)
      Voprosy Geografii, No. 45(1959), 246-252

129   University of California, Berkeley, International Urban Research
      The world's metropolitan areas
      Berkeley and Los Angeles, University of California Press, 1959

130 Rubio, Angel
     "Población rural y urbana; problemas de definición,"
     Revista Geográfica (Pan American Institute of Geography and History),
     22, No. 48(1961), 161-165

                              C-7. Migration

131 Musoni, F.
     L'emigrazione considerata nelle sue cause più generali, specialmente in
       quanto determinate dai fatti geografici
     Udine, 1904

132 Close, Sir Charles
     "Population and migration. A statistical study with special reference
       to English-speaking peoples,"
     Geography, 14(1927), 1-24

133 Ferenczi, Imre
     International migrations. Volume I. Statistics
     New York, National Bureau of Economic Research, 1929

134 Arbos, Ph.
     "Les migrations intercontinentales aux 19. et 20. siècles,"
     AG, 39(1930), 84-88

135 Willcox, Walter F.
     International Migrations. Volume II. Interpretations
     New York, National Bureau of Economic Research, 1931

136 Grothe, Hugo
     "Die Wanderungsbewegung der Kulturvölker im Lichte geopolitischer
       Betrachtung,"
     Archiv für Wanderungswesen, 8(1936), 125-133

137 Faucher, D.
     "Les mouvements migratoires et les influences agissant sur leur
       caractère," pp. 83-93 in:
     CRCIG, Amsterdam, 1938, Vol. 2

138 Verstege, J. Ch. W.
     /"The problem of migration in demography,"_/ (in Dutch)
     TEG, 29(1938), 149-155

139 Giannini, Amededo
     "Le nuove migrazioni umane,"
     RGI, 54(1947), 92-102

140 Bergsten, Karl Erik
     "Birth-place fields and hinterlands," pp. 406-410 in:
     CRCIG, Lisbonne, 1949, Vol. 4

141 Parlato, Giovanni
     "L'emigrazione italiana nel monde (Storia, situazione presente,
       previsioni per l'avvenire, riflessi di carattere militare),"
     L'Universo, 30(1950), 725-743

142 George, Pierre
     Étude sur les migrations de population
     Paris, Centre de Documentation Universitaire, 1952

15   Migration

143 Johnsson, O. Harald
     /"Migration field and birthplace field of a town; an alternative
        formula,"/ (in Swedish)
     Svensk Geografisk Årsbok, 28(1952), 115-122

144 Lawton, Richard
     "Geographical analysis of population movements," pp. 60-64 in:
     The Indian Geographical Society Silver Jubilee Souvenir
     Madras, 1952

145 Kant, Edgar
     /"Classification and problems of migration,"/ (in Swedish)
     Svensk Geografisk Årsbok, 29(1953), 180-209

146 Wendel, Bertil
     A migration schema; theories and observations
     Lund, University, Department of Geography, Lund Studies in Geography,
        Series B, Human Geography, No. 9
     Lund, 1953

147 Girolami, Mario
     "Sovrapopolazione mondiale e migrazione di popoli,"
     L'Universo, 34(1954), 169-202

148 Schwalbach, Luis
     "O problema da emigração humana no quadro contemporaneo,"
     Boletim Paulista de Geografia, 6, No. 18(1954), 3-14

149 Sorre, Maximilien
     "Os problemas geográficas atuais das migrações,"
     Boletim Geográfico (Rio de Janeiro), 12, No. 122(1954), 269-275

150 Kulldorf, G.
     Migration probabilities
     Lund, University, Department of Geography, Lund Studies in Geography,
        Series B, Human Geography, No. 14
     Lund, 1955

151 Sorre, Maximilien
     Les migrations des peuples; essai sur la mobilité géographique
     Paris, Flammarion, 1955

152 Lövgren, Esse
     "The geographical mobility of labor; a study of migrations,"
     Geografiska Annaler, 38(1956), 344-394

153 Pokshishevskii, Vadim V.
     /"The internal migration of population as a phenomenon for geographic
        research,"/ (in Russian)
     Voprosy Geografii, No. 36(1956), 250-260

154 Porter, R.
     "Approach to migration through its mechanism,"
     Geografiska Annaler, 38(1956), 317-343

155 Bravard, Yves
     "L'âge et le sexe des émigrés: une méthode graphique de recherches,"
     RGA, 46(1958), 279-283

156 Thibault, André
     "Note sur la mobilité socio-démographique des ruraux,"
     L'Information Géographique, 22, No. 4(1958), 169-173

157 International Labour Office
     International migration, 1945-1957
     Studies and Reports, New Series, No. 54
     Geneva, 1959

          C-8. Interrelations between Population and Other Phenomena

158 Joerg, W. L. G.
     "A note on the numerical distribution of the population of the world
        according to climate,"
     AAAG, 21(1931), 127-129

159 Schleinitz, Hellmut
     "Die Entwicklung der ländlichen Bevölkerung und ihre Abhängigkeit von
        der Geschichte der Siedlung,"
     Geographische Zeitschrift, 43(1937), 323-336

160 Coulter, John Wesley
     "Le rapport entre la densité de la population et le mode d'utilisation
        du sol dans les régions coloniales," pp. 149-162 in:
     CRCIG, Amsterdam, 1938, Vol. 2

161 Zimmerman, E. W.
     "The relation between population and the manner of soil utilization in
        colonial regions," pp. 528-534 in:
     CRCIG, Amsterdam, 1938, Vol. 2

162 Cholley, André
     "Structure agraire et démographie,"
     AG, 55(1946), 81-101

163 Fleure, Herbert John
     "Population and environment," pp. 1-12 in:
     Some problems of society and environment
     Institute of British Geographers, Publication No. 12, 1947

164 Gribaudi, D.
     "Geografia agraria e popolamento rurale," pp. 187-197 in:
     Congresso Geografico Italiano, 14., Bologna, 1947. Atti
     Bologna, 1949

165 Kar, Nisith R.
     "The geographic control of population distribution over the earth,"
     Indian Geographical Journal, 22(1947), 14-22

166 United Nations, Population Commission
     "Determinants of the geographical distribution of population," Chapter
        5 in:
     Findings of studies on the relationships between population trends and
        economic and social factors
     New York, 1951

167 Jacobsen, A. P.
     "Bevölkerungsdichte und Industrialisierungsgrad,"
     Agrarwirtschaft (Hannover), 3(1954), 219-221

168   United Nations, Department of Economic and Social Affairs, Population
      Division
      Determinants and consequences of population trends; a summary of the
        findings of studies on the relationships between population changes
        and economic and social conditions
      Population Studies, No. 17
      New York, 1954

169   Van Aartsen, J. P.
      "Regional disequilibrium between population and agricultural production,"
      TESG, 45(1954), 34-40

170   Pokshishevskii, Vadim V.
      "The determinants and consequences of population trends: summary of the
        findings of studies on the relationships between population changes
        and economic and social conditions,"
      Geograficheskoe Obshchestvo SSSR, Izvestiia, 89(1957), 283-286

171   George, Pierre
      "Quelques aspects économiques des problèmes de population,"
      AG, 67(1958), 53-56

                    C-9. Definition and Measurement of Population Density

172   Tronnier, R.
      Beiträge zum Problem der Volksdichte
      Stuttgart, 1908

173   Auerbach, F.
      "Das Gesetz der Bevölkerungskonzentration,"
      PM, 59(1913), 74-76

174   Fürchtenicht-Böning, H.
      "Über die Verwendung der Grundsteuerreinerertragzahlen in
        Volksdichteuntersuchungen,"
      Geographische Zeitschrift, 19(1913), 460-462

175   Maurer, H. and Weise, L.
      "Zum Auerbachschen Gesetz der Bevölkerungskonzentration,"
      PM, 59(1913), 229-232

176   Gsteu, H.
      "Die Darstellung der Bevölkerungsverhältnisse,"
      Geographischer Anzeiger, 35(1934), 366-373

177   Sorre, Maximilien
      "Remarque sur une carte des densités de population,"
      Idées et Forces, 2(1949), 1-6

178   Czajka, Guillermo
      "Densidad y concentración de la población humana; dos conceptos contrarios
        en la geografía demográfica,"
      Tucuman, Universidad Nacional, Instituto de Estudios Geográficos, Publica-
        ciones Especiales, 2(1951), 57-66

179 Stöckl, Rudolf
     "Die Bevölkerungsdichte und verwandte Begriffe,"
     PM, 96(1952), 168-179

180 George, Pierre
     "Sur un project de calcul de la densité économique de population,"
     Association de Géographes Français, Bulletin, Nos. 237-238 (1953),
        142-145

181 Clark, Colin
     "Urban population densities,"
     Institut International de Statistique, Bulletin, 36(1958), 60-68

182 Veen, H. N. ter
     /"Population density,"/ (in Dutch)
     TESG, 49(1958), 149-152

183 Erdei, Ference
     /"Some questions of density of population and trends in agrarian
        density,"/ (in Hungarian)
     Demografia (Budapest), 2(1959), 12-31

184 Clarke, John I.
     "Persons per room, an index of population density,"
     TESG, 51(1960), 257-260

     (Also see Section D)

                  C-10. Problems of Population Pressure

185 Chisholm, George G.
     'Malthus and some recent census returns,"
     SGM, 29(1913), 453-471

186 Stolt, M.
     Über die Verwendung der Grundsteuerreinertragszahlen in Volksdichteunter-
        suchungen,"
     PM, 60(1914), 192-195

187 Rachel, H.
     "Bevölkerungsdichte und Wachstum,"
     Zeitschrift für Geopolitik, 1(1925), 418-431

188 Fischer, Alois
     "Zur Frage der Tragfähigkeit des Lebensraumes,"
     Zeitschrift für Geopolitik, 2(1925), 762-779

189 Jefferson, Mark
     "Looking back at Malthus,"
     GR, 15(1925), 177-189

190 Marbut, C. F.
     "The rise, decline, and revival of Malthusianism in relation to
        geography and character of soils,"
     AAAG, 15(1925), 1-25

191 Haushofer, A.
     "Bemerkungen zum Problem der Bevölkerungsdichte der Erde,"
     Zeitschrift für Geopolitik, 3(1926), 789-797

192 Brenier, H.
     "Les ressources alimentaires mondiales et la question de la population,"
     La Géographie, 49(1928), 468-478

193 Schilder, S.
     "Zur Frage der grössmöglichen Bevölkerung der Erde,"
     Geographische Gesellschaft in Wien, Mitteilungen, 72(1929), 127-131

194 Burky, Charles A.
     "La notion de surpeuplement,"
     Schweizer Geograph, 15(1938), 64-67

195 Demangeon, Albert
     "La question du surpeuplement,"
     AG, 47(1938), 113-127

196 Boerman, Willem E.
     /"The food-capacity of the earth and the future world population,"/
     (in Dutch)
     TEG, 31(1940), 121-132

197 Bertram, G. C. L.
     "Population trends and the world's resources,"
     GJ, 107(1946), 191-210

198 Polspoel, Lambert G.
     /"Population densities as a measure of population pressure,"/ (in
     Flemish)
     Société Belge d'Études Géographiques, Bulletin, 15(1946), 85-100

199 Baker, Oliver E.
     "The population prospect in relation to the world's agricultural re-
     sources,"
     Journal of Geography, 46(1947), 203-220

200 White, Gilbert F.
     "Toward an appraisal of world resources. New views of conservation
     problems,"
     GR, 39(1949), 625-639

201 Peattie, Roderick
     "Are you a Malthusian? A review and a bibliography of recent articles,"
     Journal of Geography, 49(1950), 365-365

202 Stamp, L. Dudley
     Land for tomorrow: the underdeveloped world
     New York, American Geographical Society, 1952

203 Hatt, Paul K., ed.
     World population and future resources; the proceedings of the Second
     Centennial Academic Conference of Northwestern University
     New York, American Book Co., 1952

204 Bonné, Alfred
     "Land resources and the growth of world population," pp. 464-477 in:
     Research Council of Israel, Special Publication No. 2
     Jerusalem, 1953

205   Cressey, George B.
      "Land for 2.4 billion neighbors,"
      EG, 29(1953), 1-9

206   Scharlau, Kurt
      Bevölkerungswachstum und Nahrungsspielraum. Geschichte, Methoden und
          Probleme der Tragfähigkeitsuntersuchungen
      Raumforschung und Landesplannung, Abhandlungen, 24
      Bremen-Horn, 1953

207   Bennett, M. K.
      The world's food: a study of the interrelations of world population,
          national diets, and food potentials
      New York, Harper & Bros., 1954

208   Russell, Sir John
      World population and world food supplies
      London, George Allen and Unwin, 1954

209   Sorre, Maximilien
      "Assessing population pressures,"
      United Nations Review, 1(1954), 12-15

210   Scharlau, Kurt
      "Bevölkerungsmaximum und Bevölkerungsoptimum,"
      Erdkunde, 9(1955), 54-59

211   Watson, James Wreford
      "Population pressure and marginal lands,"
      SGM, 72(1956), 117-121

212   Beaujeu-Garnier, Jacqueline
      "La population du monde est-elle trop nombreuse?"
      Revue Politique et Parlementaire, 60, No. 678(1958), 445-452

213   Bouthoul, Gaston
      La surpopulation dans le monde, la mutation géographique, l'ère de la
          surpopulation
      Paris, Payot, 1958

214   Broek, Jan O. M.
      "The man-land ratio," pp. 52-63 in:
      Roy G. Francis, ed.
      The population ahead
      Minneapolis, University of Minnesota Press, 1958

215   Geisert, Harold L.
      World population pressures
      Population Research Project, George Washington University
      Washington, 1958

216   George, Pierre
      "Realité de la menace du surpeuplement,"
      AG, 68(1959), 448-450

      (Also see 36, 146)

C-11.   Review Articles

217 Dussart, Frans
     "A propos de contributions récentes à la géographie du peuplement,"
     Liège. Université. Séminaire de Géographie, Travaux, 37(1933)

218 Good, Dorothy
     "Some studies of population,"
     GR, 35(1945), 122-131

219 Moore, Wilbert E.
     "Flora, fauna, land and people,"
     Population Index, 15(1949), 105-114

220 Pokshishevskii, Vadim V.
     /"Aspects of the geography of population at the Eighteenth International
        Geographical Congress,"/ (in Russian)
     Izvestiia, Akademiia Nauk SSSR, Seriia Geograficheskaia, No. 3 (1957),
        3-9

     (Also see 44, 201)

D. POPULATION MAPPING AND THE MEASUREMENT OF POPULATION DISTRIBUTION

221 Hettner, Alfred
     "Über bevölkerungsstatistische Grundkarten,"
     Geographische Zeitschrift, 6(1900), 185-193

222 Blasquez, A.
     "Los mapas demográficas,"
     Real Sociedad Geográfica, Boletín (Madrid), 35(1910), 328-337

223 Closterhalfen, K.
     "Die kartographische Darstellung der Volksdichte,"
     PM, 58(1912), 257-259

224 Schlüter, O.
     "Die Generalisierung von Gemeindekartogrammen zu Volksdichtekarten,"
     PM, 58(1912), 259-260

225 Greim, G.
     "Die kartographische Darstellung der Volksdichte,"
     PM, 59(1913), 67-68

226 Hassinger, Hugo
     "Neue Methoden der Darstellung der Volksdichte auf Karten,"
     Kartographische und Schulgeographische Zeitschrift, 6(1917)

227 Adlercreutz, B.
     "Eine Untersuchung der sphärischen absoluten Methode bei der Konstruk-
        tion von Volksmengenkarten," pp. 185-198 in:
     39 Jahresberichte der Geographischen Gesellschaft zu Greifswald 1922
     Greifswald, 1922

     Also: Terra, 40(1928), 281-292 (in Swedish)

228 Whitehouse, W. E.
        "Representation of populous centres and populated areas,"
        The Geographical Teacher, 13(1925-26), 90-100

229 Lefever, D. Welty
        "Measuring geographic concentration by means of the standard deviational
        ellipse,"
        American Journal of Sociology, 32(1926), 88-94

230 Backhoff, G. A.
        /"Project for the representation of population density for maps of
        population density constructed on the basis of the absolute dot
        method,"/ (in Russian)
        Izvestiia, Gosudarstevennoe Russkoe Geograficheskoe Obshchestva, 40(1927),
        117-121

231 Geisler, W.
        "Absolute oder relative Methode? Probleme der Bevölkerungs- und
        Wirtschaftkartographie,"
        Kartographische Mitteilungen, 1(1930), 16-19

232 Greim, G.
        "Bemerkungen zur Darstellung der Bevölkerungsdichte,"
        Geographische Gesellschaft zu Hannover, Jahrbuch, 1930, 56-79

233 Leyden, Friedrich
        "Die Darstellung der Volksdichte auf Karten,"
        Geographischer Anzeiger, 31(1930), 375-382

234 Lefebvre, Th.
        "Un mode de représentation de la densité de population," pp. 588-589 in:
        CRCIG, Paris, 1931, Vol. 3

235 Fehre, Horst
        "Neues Verfahren der kartenmässigen Darstellung der Bevölkerungs-
        entwicklung, angewandt auf die Ortschaften des Erfurter Beckens,"
        PM, 79(1933), 191-195, 252-255

236 Griffin, F. L.
        "The center of population for various continuous distributions of
        population over areas of various shapes,"
        Metron, 11(1933), 11-15

237 Fawcett, C. B.
        "Note on Prof. Sten de Geer's proposal for a population map," pp. 552-
        555 in:
        CRCIG, Warsaw, 1934, Vol. 3

238 Kelletat, H.
        "Zur Methodik der Volksdichterdarstellung,"
        Geographische Wochenschrift, 2(1934), 238-241

239 Söderlund, Alfred
        "The 'absolute' method for making out quantities on maps," pp. 545-547
        in:
        CRCIG, Warsaw, 1934, Vol. 3

240 Söderlund, Alfred
        "A proposal for a population map of the world," pp. 548-550 in:
        CRCIG, Warsaw, 1934, Vol. 3

241 Tulippe, Omer
     "Propositions relatives à la confection de cartes morphologiques du
        peuplement," pp. 401-405 in:
     CRCIG, Warsaw, 1934, Vol. 3

242 Winterbotham, H. St. J. L.
     "Population maps," pp. 343-354 in:
     CRCIG, Warsaw, 1934, Vol. 4

243 Zierhoffer, August
     "Sur une formule servant à exprimer la dispersion et la concentration
        absolue de l'habitat rural," pp. 410-415 in:
     CRCIG, Warsaw, 1934, Vol. 3

244 Fawcett, C. B.
     "Population maps,"
     GJ, 85(1935), 142-159

245 Witt, Werner
     "Zur Methode der quantitativen kartographischen Darstellung,"
     Geographischer Anzeiger, 36(1935), 533-538

246 Preuss, Wolfgang
     "Zur Darstellung von Bevölkerungsverteilung und Volksdichte,"
     Leipzig. Universität. Verein der Geographen. Mitteilungen, 14-15(1936),
        67-81

247 Wright, John K.
     "A method of mapping densities of population: with Cape Cod as an
        example,"
     GR, 26(1936), 103-110

248 Wright, John K.
     "Some measures of distribution,"
     AAAG, 27(1937), 177-211

249 Fulda, Fr. W.
     "Die Zuzugskarte,"
     Geographischer Anzeiger, 39(1938), 224-228

250 Wright, John K.
     "Problems in population mapping," pp. 1-18 in:
     American Geographical Society and Population Association in America
     Notes on statistical mapping
     New York, 1938

251 Barnes, James A. and Robinson, Arthur H.
     "A new method for the representation of dispersed rural population,"
     GR, 30(1940), 134-137

252 Grothe, Hugo
     "Die Möglichkeiten kartographischer Darstellung der Wanderungsbewegung,"
     Archiv für Wanderungswesen, 11(1940), 85-88

253 Migliorini, Elio
     "Note metodiche sui sistemi usati per rappresentare la distribuzione
        della popolazione,"
     BSGI, Serie 5, 5(1940), 262-274

254 Alexander, John W.
"An isarithmic-dot population map,"
EG, 19(1943), 431-432

255 Dumont, Maurice E.
/"Concerning two new methods for the cartographic representation of
population and habitat,"/ (in Dutch)
K.Natuurwetenschappelijk Genootschap "Dodonaea" te Gent, 29 (1947),
179-185

256 Stewart, John Q.
"Empirical mathematical rules concerning the distribution and equili-
brium of population,"
GR, 37(1947), 461-485

257 Stewart, John Q.
"Demographic gravitation: evidence and applications,"
Sociometry, 11(1948), 31-58

258 Fehre, Horst
"Zum Entwurf einer korrelativen Volksdichtekarte. Ein Beitrag zur
bevölkerungsgeographischen Kartographie,"
Berichte zur Deutschen Landeskunde, 7(1949), 102-115

259 Kagami, Kanji
/"Population map using conical symbols,"/ (in Japanese)
Geographical Review of Japan, 24(1951), 324-327

260 Mackay, J. Ross
"Some problems and techniques in isopleth mapping,"
EG, 27(1951), 1-9

261 Terán, Manuel de
La representación cartográfica de la densidad de población
Spain, Consejo Superior de Investigaciones Científicas, Instituto de
Estudios Pirenaicos, Zaragoza, No. General 46, Geografía 8
Zaragoza, 1951

262 Applebaum, William
"A technique for constructing a population and urban land use map,"
EG, 28(1952), 240-243

263 Louis, Herbert
"Über Aufgabe und Möglichkeiten einer Bevölkerungsdichtekarte der Erde;
Begleitworte zu beigegebenen Kart 1:80 mill.,"
PM, 96(1952), 284-288

264 Monkhouse, Francis J. and Wilkinson, Henry R.
"Population maps and diagrams," pp. 217-280 in:
Maps and diagrams
London, Methuen, 1952

265 Ogilvie, Alan G.
"The mapping of population, especially on scale 1/M," pp. 5-16 in:
International Geographical Union, Commission for the Study of Popula-
tion Problems, Report
Washington, 1952

266 Pannekoek, A. J.
     "Population density maps based on geographical regions," pp. 450-453 in:
     CRCIG, Washington, 1952

267 Parry, Muriel
     Cartographic representation of population data
     Master's thesis, George Washington University
     Washington, 1952

268 Oda, Takeo
     /"Some problems of population mapping,"7 (in Japanese)
     Jimbun Chiri. Human Geography, 4(1952), 5-20

269 Wilkinson, Henry R.
     "Ethnographic maps," pp. 547-555 in:
     CRCIG, Washington, 1952

270 Zelinsky, Wilbur
     "A proposal for the format of the one-millionth map of world population,"
     pp. 513-515 in:
     CRCIG, Washington, 1952

271 Byron, William G.
     Methods of mapping population distribution by dots and densitometer-
         derived isopleths
     Doctoral dissertation, Syracuse University
     Syracuse, 1954

272 Clark, Philip J. and Evans, Francis C.
     "Distance to nearest neighbor as a measure of spatial relationships in
         populations,"
     Ecology, 35(1954), 445-453

273 Hart, J. Fraser
     "Central tendency in areal distributions,"
     EG, 30(1954), 48-59

274 Hidaka, Tatsutaro and Kawai, Reiko
     /"Studies on the representation of population distribution,"7 (in
         Japanese)
     Japanese Journal of Geography, 64(1955), 121-134

275 Kant, Edgar
     "Some notes on the representation of the density of rural habitations,"
     Indian Geographical Journal, 30(1955), 1-8

276 Anderson, Theodore R.
     "Potential models and the spatial distribution of population,"
     Papers and Proceedings, Regional Science Association, 2(1956), 175-182

277 Tavener, Laurence E.
     "Population maps: problems and methods of demographic cartography,"
     Genus (Rome), 12(1956), 88-101

278 Witthauer, Kurt
     "Eine graphische Darstellung von Flachen- und Bevölkerungszahlen"
     PM, 100(1956), 225-228

279   Burgdörfer, Friedrich
      "Welt-Bevölkerungs-Atlas: Versuch einer kartographischen Darstellung
         der Verteilung der Bevölkerung der Erde im Anschluss an den ersten
         Welt-Bevölkerungs-Census,"
      Bulletin de l'Institut International de Statistique, 35(1957), 439-444

280   Duncan, Otis Dudley
      "The measurement of population distribution,"
      Population Studies, 11(1957), 27-45

281   Robinson, Arthur H. and Bryson, Reid A.
      "A method for describing quantitatively the correspondence of geographi-
         cal distributions,"
      AAAG, 47(1957), 379-391

282   Burgdörfer, Friedrich
      "Eine Welt-Bevölkerungs-Karte,"
      Bulletin de l'Institut International de Statistique, 36(1958), 248-254

283   Luna, Telesfor W.
      "Some geographic techniques used in the study of population distribution,"
      Philippine Geographical Journal, 6(1958), 33-38

284   Stewart, John Q. and Warntz, William
      "Physics of population distribution,"
      Journal of Regional Science, 1(1958), 99-123

285   Kawai, Reiko
      /"Method of making population density map by landform division and
         accumulated result,"/ (in Japanese)
      Chirigaku Hyoron. Geographical Review of Japan, 32(1959), 532-549

286   Stewart, John Q. and Warntz, William
      "Some parameters of the geographical distribution of population,"
      GR, 49(1959), 271-273

287   Das Gupta, Sivaprasad
      "The coin system in population mapping,"
      Geographical Review of India, 22(1960), 32-43

288   Horikawa, Tadashi
      /"Measures of population distribution,"/ (in Japanese)
      Jimbun Chiri. Human Geography, 12, No. 5(1960), 1-12, 88-89

289   Hunt, Arthur J. and Moisley, Henry A.
      "Population mapping in urban areas,"
      Geography, 45(1960), 79-89

290   Korčák, Jaromír
      "Extreme values in the world population map,"
      Sborník Československé Společnosti Zeměpisné, 65(1960), 234-240

290a Pillewizer, Wolfgang
      "Die Wanderkarte,"
      PM, 105(1961), 63-67

291 Yevteyev, O. A.
     "Population maps in national atlases,"
     Soviet Geography: Review & Translation, 2, No. 5(1961), 42-48
     Also: Vestnik Moskovskoe Universiteta, Seriia Geografiia, 1960, No. 4,
        20-25 (in Russian)

     (Also see Section C-9; 311, 418, 422, 423, 491, 873a, 1239, 1274, 1485,
        1488, 1673, 1707, 1757, 1778, 1779, 1828)

PART II

REGIONAL STUDIES

3240: THE TROPICS

292 Price, Archibald Grenfell
White settlers in the tropics
New York, American Geographical Society, 1939

293 Smith, T. Lynn
"Problemas e população dos tropicos,"
Boletim Geográfico, 7(1949), 728-736

294 Gourou, Pierre
The tropical world: its social and economic conditions and its future
status
New York, Longmans, Green, 1953

295 Jin-Bee, Ooi
"The distribution of present-day man in the tropics: historical and
ecological perspective," pp. 111-124 in:
Pacific Science Congress, 9th, Bangkok, Thailand, 1957, Proceedings

296 Baren, F. A. van
"Soils in relation to population in tropical regions,"
TESG, 9(1960), 230-234

3290: THE AMERICAS

a. Bibliography

297 United States Bureau of the Census and Library of Congress
General censuses and vital statistics in the Americas
Washington, 1943

298 Inter American Statistical Institute
Bibliography of selected statistical sources of the American nations
Washington, 1947

299 Doherty, Donald K.
"Bibliografia preliminar de colonização e poveamento nas Americas
Latina e Anglo-Saxônica,"
Revista Geográfica (Pan American Institute of Geography and History),
11-12(1953), 111-153

b. Population Studies

300 LeConte, René
"Colonisation et émigration allemandes en Amérique, avant 1815,"
Société de Géographie de Quebec, Bulletin, 17(1923), 80-89, 164-176

301 Sapper, Karl
"Zahl und Volksdichte der indianisches Bevölkerung in Amerika von der
Conquista bis zur Gegenwart," pp. 95-104 in:
Proceedings of the 21st International Congress of Americanists, the
Hague, 1924, Vol. 1

302 Spinden, H. J.
     "The population of ancient America,"
     GR, 18(1928), 641-660

303 Rosenblat, Angel
     "El desarrollo de la población indígena de América,"
     Sociedad de Geografía e Historia de Guatemala, Anales, 15(1939), 367-
        379, 486-503; 16(1939), 114-131

304 Schedl, Armando
     "Aspectos demográficos de América,"
     Revista Geográfica Americana, 13(1940), 302-317

305 Schmieder, Oskar
     "Raumgliederung und Bevölkerungsprobleme Amerikas, ein geographischer
        Überblick," pp. 1-100 in:
     Gegenwartsprobleme der neuen Welt
     Leipzig, Quelle und Meyer, 1943

306 Chatelain, Abel
     "Recherches et enquêtes démogéographiques: les migrations françaises
        vers le Nouveau Monde aux XIXe et XXe siècles,"
     Annales: Economies, Sociétés, Civilisations, 2(1947), 53-70

307 Gottmann, Jean
     "Le peuplement," pp. 35-62 in:
     L'Amérique
     Paris, Hachette, 1949

308 Rosenblatt, Angel
     La población indigena y el mestizaje en América. Vol. I. La población
        indigena. Vol. II. El mestizaje y las castas coloniales
     Buenos Aires, Editorial Nova Biblioteca Americanista, 1954

309 Davis, Kingsley, ed.
     A crowding hemisphere: population change in the Americas
     Annals of the American Academy of Political and Social Science, Vol. 316
     Philadelphia, 1958

310 Anonymous
     "La emigración española a América en los últimos años (1946-1957),"
     Estudios Geográficos, 21, No. 78(1960), 95-108

                          3300: NORTH AMERICA

311 Jefferson, Mark
     "The anthropography of North America,"
     American Geographical Society, Bulletin, 45(1913), 161-180

312 Mooney, James
     The aboriginal population of America north of Mexico
     Smithsonian Miscellaneous Collections, Vol. 80, No. 7
     Washington, 1928

313 Kroeber, Alfred L.
     "Map of distribution of ancient Indians on the continent of North
        America,"
     American Anthropologist, 36(1934), 1-25

314   Kroeber, Alfred L.
      Cultural and natural areas of native North America
      University of California Publications in American Archaeology and
          Ethnology, Vol. 38
      Berkeley, 1939

315   Nelson, Helge
      /"The Swedish stock; the immigrants and their descendants in North
          America,"/ (in Swedish)
      Svensk Geografisk Årsbok, 24(1948), 7-29

316   Dodge, Stanley D.
      "Notes on the theory of population distribution in relation to the
          aboriginal population of North America," pp. 234-237 in:
      Proceedings of the 29th International Congress of Americanists, New
          York, 1949

                          3380:   GREENLAND

317   Evers, Wilhelm
      "Die Bevölkerung Grönlands,"
      Geographische Rundschau, 9(1957), 71-74

      (Also see 368)

                          3400:   CANADA

                       a.   Bibliography

318   Matheson, Jean
      "Selected bibliography on colonization and land settlement in Canada,"
      Revista Geográfica (Pan American Institute of Geography and History),
          9-10(1949-50), 207-210

319   Brower, E. J., et al.
      "Canadian population statistics,"
      Population Index, 22(1956), 89-100

320   Canada, Department of Mines and Technical Surveys, Geographical Branch
      Bibliography of periodical literature on Canadian geography, 1930 to
          1955, 6 parts
      Bibliographical Series, No. 22
      Ottawa, 1959-

                     b.   National Studies

321   LeConte, René
      "L'émigration allemand au Canada,"
      Mouvement Géographique, 23(1920), 424-432

322   Dawson, C. A.
      "Population areas and physiographic regions in Canada,"
      American Journal of Sociology, 33(1927), 43-56

323 MacLean, M. C.
     "The correlation between population density and population increase in
        Canada,"
     Papers and Proceedings, Canadian Political Science Association, 5(1933),
        209-214

324 Kensit, H. E. M.
     "The center of population moves west,"
     Canadian Geographical Journal, 9(1934), 262-269

325 Ricci, Riccardo
     "Carta dell'attuale distribuzione degli Indiana in Canada,"
     BSGI, Serie 7, 1(1936), 269-274

326 Dalgiesh, R. S.
     "Emigration, with particular reference to Canada,"
     Journal of the Tyneside Geographical Society, 1(1937), 90-92

327 Whitaker, Joe Russell
     "Regional contrasts in the growth of Canadian cities,"
     SGM, 53(1937), 373-379

328 Taylor, Griffith
     "Future population in Canada; a study in technique,"
     EG, 22(1946), 67-74

329 Siegfried, André
     "Demography," pp. 43-105 in:
     Canada: an international power
     New York, Duell, Sloan and Pearce, 1949

330 Taylor, Griffith
     "Population problems, present and future," pp. 488-518 in:
     Canada: a study of cool continental environments and their effect on
        British and French settlement, 2nd ed.
     London, Methuen, 1950

331 Van Cleef, Eugene
     "Finnish settlement in Canada,"
     GR, 42(1952), 253-266

332 Veyret, Paul
     "La population du Canada,"
     RGA, 41(1953), 5-57, 161-260

        Also: Université de Grenoble, Faculté des Lettres, Publications, 7
     Paris, Presses Universitaires de France, 1953

333 Lalande, Gilles
     "Un nouvel ouvrage sur la population du Canada,"
     Revue Canadienne de Géographie, 8(1954), 3-4, 94-98

334 Lamoureux, Pierre
     "Les premieres années de l'immigration chinoise au Canada,"
     Revue Canadienne de Géographie, 9(1955), 9-28

335 Tuinman, A. S.
     "The Netherlands-Canadian migration,"
     TESG, 47(1956), 181-188

336 Sas, Anthony
     "Some aspects of Dutch immigration to Canada since 1945,"
     TESG, 48(1957), 189-190

337 Storey, Merle
     "Hungarians in Canada,"
     Canadian Geographical Journal, 55(1957), 46-53

337a McArthur, Neil and Gerland, Martin E.
     "The spread and migration of French Canadians,"
     TSGE, 52(1961), 141-147

                         c. Regional Studies

338 Collins, Beatrice Maxwell
     The distribution of population in northeastern Ontario
     Master's thesis, University of Chicago
     Chicago, 1930

339 Glendinning, Robert M.
     "The distribution of population in the Lake St. John Lowland, Quebec,"
     GR, 24(1934), 232-237

340 Lemieux, O. A., Cudmore, S. A., MacLean, M. C., Pelletier, A. J., and
     Tracey, W. R.
     "Factors in the growth of rural population in eastern Canada,"
     Papers and Proceedings, Canadian Political Science Association, 6(1934),
       196-219

341 Blanchard, Raoul
     "Habitat et peuplement," Vol. 1, pp. 176-195 and "Habitat et population,"
       Vol. 2, pp. 141-154 in:
     L'est due Canada française. "Province de Québec," 2 vols.
     Montreal, Beauchemin, 1935

342 Eggleston, Wilfrid
     "The people of Alberta,"
     Canadian Geographical Journal, 15(1937), 212-222

343 Shaw, Earl B.
     "Population distribution in Newfoundland,"
     EG, 14(1938), 239-254

344 Alty, Stella W.
     "The influence of climatic and other geographic factors upon the growth
       and distribution of population in Saskatchewan,"
     Geography, 24(1939), 10-23

345 Lewis, H. Harry
     "Population of Quebec province; its distribution and national origins,"
     EG, 16(1940), 59-68

346 Anthony, Sylvia and Charles, Enid
     "Population trends in relation to the social background on Prince
       Edward Island,"
     GR, 32(1942), 545-561

347 Duncan, M.
     The French Canadian population: its distribution and development
     Master's thesis, University of Aberdeen
     Aberdeen, 1944

348 Robinson, J. Lewis
     "Eskimo population in the Canadian eastern Arctic; distribution,
        number and trends,"
     Canadian Geographical Journal, 29(1944), 129-142

349 Blanchard, Raoul
     "Habitat et population," pp. 103-112 and "Le peuplement," pp. 324-368
        in:
     Le centre du Canada français; "Province de Quebec
     Montreal, Beauchemin, 1947

350 Brouillette, Benoit
     "L'habitat et la population au Saguenay,"
     L'Actualité Economique, 23(1947), 646-671

351 Watson, James Wreford
     "Rural depopulation in southwestern Ontario,"
     AAAG, 37(1947), 145-154

352 Blanchard, Raoul
     "Les excédents de population et l'agriculture dans la province de
        Québec,"
     L'Actualité Economique, 24(1949), 635-641

353 Brouillette, Benoit
     "Les sources de l'étude du peuplement au Canada et plus particulièrement
        dans la Province de Québec," pp. 411-420 in:
     CRCIG, Lisbonne, 1949, Vol. 4

354 Prud'homme, B.
     Etude du peuplement du Comte de Vaudreuil
     Master's thesis, Université de Montreal
     Montreal, 1949

355 Hattersley, P. E.
     "French element in the population of eastern Canada,"
     Geography, 36(1951), 89-97

356 Rumney, George B.
     "Settlements on the Canadian Shield,"
     Canadian Geographical Journal, 43(1951), 117-127

357 Hobson, Peggie M.
     "Population and settlement in Nova Scotia,"
     SGM, 70(1954), 49-63

358 Robinson, J. Lewis
     "Population in British Columbia. Trends, densities, distribution,"
        pp. 210-220 in:
     7th British Columbia Natural Resources Conference
     Victoria, 1954

359 Robinson, J. Lewis
     "Population trends and distribution in British Columbia,"
     Canadian Geographer, No. 4(1954), 27-32

360 Hamelin, Louis-Edmond
     "Emigration rurale à l'échelon paroissial,"
     Canadian Geographer, No. 5(1955), 53-61

361 Stone, Kirk H.
     "Human geographic research in the North American northern lands,"
        pp. 209-223 in:
     Arctic Research
     Arctic Institute of North America, Special Publication No. 2
     Ottawa, 1955

362 Black, William A.
     "Population distribution of the Labrador Coast, Newfoundland,"
     Canada, Department of Mines and Technical Surveys, Geographical Branch,
        Geographical Bulletin, No. 9(1956), 53-74

363 Boileau, Gilles
     "Evolution démographique de la population rurale dans 60 paroisses de
        la province de Québec, depuis le début du siècle,"
     Canadian Geographer, No. 9(1957), 49-54

364 Martin, Yves
     "L'île aux Coudres. Population et economie,"
     Cahiers de Géographie de Québec, 2(1957), 167-195

365 Summers, William F.
     A geographical analysis of population trends in Newfoundland
     Doctoral dissertation, McGill University
     Montreal, 1957

366 Bernard, E.-Mercier
     "De paroisse rurale à paroisse urbaine: Notre-Dame-des-Anges de
        Cartierville (1910-1956); essai géographique et démographique,"
     Revue Canadienne de Géographie, 12(1958), 99-115

367 Sas, Anthony
     "Dutch concentrations in rural southwestern Ontario,"
     AAAG, 48(1958), 185-194

368 Lloyd, Trevor
     "Map of the distribution of Eskimos and native Greenlanders in North
        America,"
     Canadian Geographer, No. 13(1959), 41-42

369 Blanchard, Raoul
     "La marée du peuplement," pp. 65-115 in:
     Le Canada français
     Paris, Fayard, 1960

370 Clark, Andrew H.
     "Old World origins and religious adherence in Nova Scotia,"
     GR, 50(1960), 317-344

        (Also see 422, 438, 465, 472)

3700: United States

a. Bibliography

371 United States Bureau of the Census and Library of Congress
     Catalog of United States census publications, 1790-1945
     Washington, 1950

372 Tracy, Stanley J., ed.
     A report on world population migrations, as related to the United States
       of America
     Washington, George Washington University, 1956

b. National Studies

373 Levasseur, E.
     "La population des Etats-Unis,"
     Revue de Géographie (Paris), 51(1902), 1-22

374 Blum, Richard
     Die Entwicklung der Vereinigten Staaten von Nordamerika, nach den
       amtlichen Berichten über die Volkszählungen der Vereinigten Staaten
       von 1880, 1890 und 1900 und zum Teil zurück bis 1790
     Petermanns Mitteilungen, Ergänzungsheft No. 142
     Gotha, 1903

375 Heiderich, Hans
     "Veränderungen in der Bevölkerung der Vereinigten Staaten von
       Nordamerika,"
     Geographische Zeitschrift, 12(1906), 135-145

376 Kiaer, A. N.
     /"The geographical distribution of the Norwegian-American population in
       the United States,"/ (in Norwegian)
     Norske Geografiske Selskab, Aarbok, 17(1906), 17-64

377 Jaja, G.
     "Il movimento della popolazione negli Stati Uniti nell'ultimo sessennio,"
     BSGI, Serie 4, 8(1907), 1228-1237

378 Brigham, Albert Perry
     "The distribution of population in the United States,"
     GJ, 32(1908), 380-389

379 Gannett, H.
     "The population of the United States,"
     National Geographic Magazine, 22(1911), 34-48

380 Heiderich, Hans
     "Die Einwandererfrage in den Vereinigten Staaten von Amerika,"
     Deutsche Rundschau für Geographie, 33(1911), 1-7, 59-67

381 Van Cleef, Eugene
     "The Finn in America,"
     GR, 6(1918), 185-214

382 Goldenweiser, E. A.
     "Rural population," Section 1 in:
     United States Department of Agriculture
     Atlas of American agriculture, Part IX, rural population and organiza-
     tions
     Washington, 1919

383 LeConte, René
     "Un siècle d'émigration allemande aux Etats-Unis (1819-1919),"
     Mouvement Géographique, 34(1921), 318-322, 329-331

384 Baulig, Henri
     "La population des Etats-Unis en 1920,"
     AG, 39(1924), 543-566

385 Brigham, Albert Perry
     "Distribution of population," pp. 64-81 in:
     The United States of America; studies in physical, regional, industrial,
     and human geography
     London, University of London Press, 1927

386 Baker, Oliver E.
     "Population, food supply, and American agriculture,"
     GR, 18(1928), 353-373

387 Wolfe, A. B.
     "Some population gradients in the United States,"
     GR, 18(1928), 291-301

388 Hannemann, Max
     "Negerprobleme in den Vereinigten Staaten," pp. 230-252 in:
     Petermanns Mitteilungen, Ergänzungsheft No. 209
     Gotha, 1930

389 Rossnagel, Paul
     Die Stadtbevölkerung der Vereinigten Staaten von Amerika nach Herkunft
     und Verteilung, mit besonderer Berücksichtigung des deutsches
     Elements. Ein siedlungsgeographischer Versuch
     Stuttgart, 1930

390 Bitterling, Richard
     "Binnenwanderung und Verstädterung der Neger in den Vereinigten Staaten,"
     Geographischer Anzeiger, 33(1932), 208-210

391 Green, W. D. and Harrington, V. D.
     American population before the Federal Census of 1790
     New York, 1932

392 Winid, Walenty
     "The distribution of urban settlements over 10,000 inhabitants in the
     United States in 1930,"
     SGM, 48(1932), 197-210

393 Wolfe, A. B.
     "Population censuses before 1790,"
     Journal of the American Statistical Association, 27(1932), 357-370

394 Baker, Oliver E.
     "Rural-urban migration and the national welfare,"
     AAAG, 23(1933), 59-126

395 Scates, Douglas E.
     "Locating the median of the population in the United States,"
     Metron, 11(1933), 49-65

396 Baker, Oliver E.
     "Bevölkerungsbewegung und Landwirtschaft in den Vereinigten Staaten,"
     pp. 358-383 in:
     Internationale Konferenz für Agrarwissenschaft, Bad Eilsen, Aug. 26-
     Sept. 2, 1934

397 Thornthwaite, C. Warren
     Internal migration in the United States
     Study of Population Redistribution, Bulletin 1
     Philadelphia, University of Pennsylvania, 1934

398 Belden, Allen
     "Income distribution and the relation of population density to income
     in the United States 1929,"
     GR, 25(1935), 671-674

399 Dodge, Stanley D.
     "Population regions of the United States,"
     Papers of the Michigan Academy of Science, Arts and Letters, 21 (1935),
     343-353

400 Baker, Oliver E.
     "Rural and urban distribution of the population in the United States,"
     pp. 264-279 in:
     Louis I. Dublin, ed.
     The American people: studies in population
     Annals of the American Academy of Political and Social Science, Vol. 188
     Philadelphia, 1936

401 Dureau, Agnes
     "L'immigration aux Etats-Unis,"
     AG, 45(1936), 286-302

402 Goodrich, Carter, et al.
     Migration and economic opportunity. Report: study of population dis-
     tribution
     Philadelphia, University of Pennsylvania Press, 1936

403 Sutherland, Stella Helen
     Population distribution in colonial America
     New York, Columbia University Press, 1936

404 Hannemann, Max
     "Die Verschiebungen der Negerbevölkerung in den U.S.A.,"
     Zeitschrift für Geopolitik, 14(1937), 628-638

405 O'Dell, Andrew C.
     "A note on the population of the United States of America, 1790-1930,"
     Geography, 22(1937), 205-212

406 Hartshorne, Richard
     "Racial maps of the United States,"
     GR, 28(1938), 276-288

407   United States National Resources Committee
      The problems of a changing population. Report of the Committee on
         Population Problems
      Washington, 1938

408   Vance, Rupert B.
      Research memorandum on population redistribution within the United
         States
      New York, Social Science Research Council, 1938

409   Hartshorne, Richard
      "Agricultural land in proportion to agricultural population in the
         United States,"
      GR, 29(1939), 488-492

410   Lively, C. E. and Taeuber, Conrad
      Rural migration in the United States
      Works Progress Administration, Research Monograph
      Washington, 1939

411   Friis, Herman R.
      "A series of population maps of the colonies and the United States,
         1625-1790,"
      GR, 39(1940), 463-470

      Also: American Geographical Society, Mimeographed Publication No. 3
      New York, 1940

412   Pfeifer, Gottfried
      "Amerikanische Bevölkerungsprobleme. Eine statistische Übersicht,"
      Gesellschaft für Erdkunde zu Berlin, Zeitschrift, Series 4, 9-10(1940),
         341-378

413   Broadbent, Elizabeth
      The distribution of Mexican population in the United States
      Master's thesis, University of Chicago
      Chicago, 1941

414   Hoover, Edgar M., Jr.
      "Interstate redistribution of population, 1850-1940,"
      Journal of Economic History, 1(1941), 199-205

415   Mulder, G. J. A.
      /"The population problem in the United States,"/ (in Dutch)
      Tijdschrift voor het Onderwijs in de Aardrijkskunde, 19(1941), 115-124

416   Wright, John K.
      "Certain changes in population distribution in the United States,"
      GR, 31(1941), 488-490

417   Harris, Chauncy D.
      "Growth of the larger cities in the United States, 1930-40,"
      Journal of Geography, 41(1942), 313-318

418   Alexander, John W. and Zahorchak, George A.
      "Population density maps of the United States: techniques and patterns,"
      Gr, 33(1943), 457-466

419 Berry, William J.
     "The capacity of the United States to support population,"
     GJ, 102(1943), 56-62

420 Meynen, Emil and Pfeifer, Gottfried
     "Die Ausweitung des europäischen Lebensraumes auf die neue Welt. Die
        Vereinigten Staate. Wanderungen zwischen zwei Kontinenten inbesondere
        die deutsche Uberseewanderung," pp. 351-433 in:
     Oskar Schmieder, ed.
     Gegenwartsprobleme der neuen Welt
     Leipzig, Quelle und Meyer, 1943

421 Trewartha, Glenn T.
     "The unincorporated hamlet; one element of the American settlement
        fabric,"
     AAAG, 33(1943), 32-81

422 Truesdell, Leon E.
     The Canadian born in the United States: an analysis of the statistics
        of the Canadian element in the population of the United States,
        1850-1930
     New Haven, Yale University Press, 1943

423 Mather, Eugene
     "A linear-distance map of farm population in the United States,"
     AAAG, 34(1944), 173-180

424 Kohn, Clyde F.
     "Population trends in the United States since 1940,"
     GR, 35(1945), 98-106

425 Dodge, Stanley D.
     "Periods in the population history of the United States,"
     Papers of the Michigan Academy of Science, Arts and Letters,
        32(1946), 253-260

426 Hagen, Einar
     "Swedes and Norwegians in the United States,"
     Norsk Geografisk Tidsskrift, 11(1947), 189-199

427 Van Hente, J.
     /"Dutch settlers in the United States of America, 1847-1947,"7 (in
        Dutch)
     K. Nederlandsch Aardrijkskundig Genootschap, Tijdschrift, Series 2,
        64(1947), 411-429

428 Bogue, Donald J.
     The structure of the metropolitan community
     Ann Arbor, University of Michigan, 1949

429 Brandon, Donald Golden
     Migration of Negroes in the U. S., 1910-1947
     Doctoral dissertation, Columbia University
     New York, 1949

430 Bogue, Donald J.
     "Changes in population distribution since 1940,"
     American Journal of Sociology, 56(1950), 43-57

431 Raptschinsky, B.
     /"European immigration in the United States in the Nineteenth Century,"_7
     (in Dutch)
     TESG, 41(1950), 16-23

432 Zelinsky, Wilbur
     "The population geography of the free Negro in ante-bellum America,"
     Population Studies, 3(1950), 386-401

433 Mood, Fulmer
     "Studies in the history of American settled areas and frontier lines:
         settled areas and frontier lines, 1625-1790,"
     Agricultural History, 26(1952), 16-34

434 Bogue, Donald J.
     Population growth in standard metropolitan areas, 1900-1950, with an
         explanatory analysis of urbanized areas
     Washington, Housing and Home Finance Agency, 1953

435 Bogue, Donald J. and Hagood, Margaret J.
     Subregional migration in the United States, 1935-40. Vol. II. Dif-
         ferential migration in the Corn and Cotton Belts. A pilot study of
         the selectivity of intrastate migration to cities from nonmetropolitan
         areas
     Scripps Foundation Studies in Population Distribution, No. 6
     Oxford, Ohio, Miami University, 1953

436 Beaujeu-Garnier, Jacqueline
     "Le mouvement de la population aux Etats-Unis,"
     AG, 63(1954), 33-51

437 Bogue, Donald J.
     "The geography of recent population trends in the United States,"
     AAAG, 44(1954), 124-134

438 Geddes, Arthur
     "Variability in change of population in the United States and Canada,
         1900-1951,"
     GR, 44(1954), 88-100

439 Senior, Clarence
     "Patterns of Puerto Rican dispersion in the continental United States,"
     Social Problems, 2(1954), 94-99

440 Weight, Ernst
     "Verstädterung, Stadt- und Landesbevölkerung in der USA,"
     PM, 98(1954) 218-222

441 Calef, Wesley C. and Nelson, Howard J.
     "Distribution of Negro population in the United States,"
     GR, 45(1955), 82-97

442 Siegfried, André
     "The geographical distribution of the population of the United States,"
         pp. 47-54 in:
     America at mid-century
     New York, Harcourt, Brace, 1955

443 Duncan, Otis Dudley and Reiss, Albert J., Jr.
     Social characteristics of urban and rural communities, 1950
     New York, Wiley, 1956

444 Hawley, Amos H.
     The changing shape of metropolitan America: deconcentration since 1920
     Glencoe, Free Press, 1956

445 Luna, Telesforo W.
     Changes in the distribution pattern of Negro population in the United
         States
     Master's thesis, Clark University
     Worcester, 1956

446 Schroeder, Karl
     "Bevölkerungsgeographische Probleme in Grenzraum der USA gegenüber
         Mexico,"
     Die Erde, 8(1956), 229-263

447 Baldwin, William O.
     "Nationality composition and distribution of the U. S. population,"
     Association of American Geographers, Southeastern Division, Memo-
         randum Folio, 9(1957), 1-7

448 Bogue, Donald J.
     Components of population change, 1940-1950: estimates of net migration
         and natural increase for each standard metropolitan area and state
         economic area
     Scripps Foundation Studies in Population Distribution, No. 12
     Oxford, Ohio, Miami University, 1957

449 Bogue, Donald J.; Shryock, Henry S., Jr.; and Hoermann, Siegfried A.
     Subregional migration in the United States, 1935-1940. Volume I.
         Streams of migration between subregions; a pilot study of migration
         between environments
     Scripps Foundation Studies in Population Distribution, No. 5
     Oxford, Ohio, Miami University, 1957

450 Lee, Everett S.; Miller, Ann Ratner; Brainerd, Carol P.; and Easterlin,
         Richard
     Population redistribution and economic growth: United States, 1870-
         1950
     Philadelphia, American Philosophical Society, 1957

451 Taeuber, Conrad and Taeuber, Irene B.
     The changing population of the United States
     New York, Wiley, 1958

452 Taeuber, Irene B.
     "Migration, mobility, and the assimilation of the Negro,"
     Population Bulletin, 14(1958), 127-151

453 Zelinsky, Wilbur
     "Recent publications on the distribution of population in the United
         States,"
     AAAG, 48(1958), 472-481

454 Bogue, Donald J.
     The population of the United States
     Glencoe, Free Press, 1959

455 Hart, J. Fraser
     "The changing distribution of the American Negro,"
     AAAG, 60(1960), 242-266

456 Hart, J. Fraser
     "Les migrations à l'intérieur des Etats-Unis,"
     L'Information Géographique, 24, No. 4(1960), 305-310

456a Morrill, Richard L.
     /"Population in the USA in 1960,"/ (in Swedish)
     Svensk Geografisk Årsbok, 36(1960), 149-161

457 Pokshishevskii, Vadim V.
     /"Toward the study of the geography of the clustered form of urban
        settlement in the United States,"/ (in Russian), pp. 155-169 in:
     Ekonomicheskaya Geografiia. Toponimika
     Moscow Government Pedagogical Institute, Geographical-Biological Faculty
     Moscow, 1960

457a Klove, Robert C.
     "The growing population of the United States,"
     Journal of Geography, 60(1961), 203-213

458 Zelinsky, Wilbur
     "An approach to the religious geography of the United States: patterns
        of church membership in 1952,"
     AAAG, 51(1961), 139-193

                            c. Regional Studies

                    3705: Eastern United States

459 Price, Edward Thomas, Jr.
     Mixed-blood population of eastern United States as to origins, locali-
        zations, and persistence
     Doctoral dissertation, University of California
     Berkeley, 1950

460 Price, Edward Thomas, Jr.
     "A geographic analysis of white-Negro-Indian racial mixtures in eastern
        United States,"
     AAAG, 43(1953), 138-155

461 Hauk, Sister Mary Ursula
     Changing patterns of Catholic population in the eastern United States
        (1790-1950)
     Doctoral dissertation, Clark University
     Worcester, 1958

                    3710: Northeastern states

462 Gottmann, Jean
     "Megalopolis or the urbanization of the northeastern seaboard,"
     EG, 33(1957), 189-200

3720: New England

463 Dodge, Stanley D.
     "A study of population regions in New England on a new basis,"
     AAAG, 25(1935), 197-210

464 Dodge, Stanley D.
     "The frontier of New England in the Seventeenth and Eighteenth centuries
        and its significance in American history,"
     Papers of the Michigan Academy of Science, Arts and Letters, 28(1943),
        435-439

465 Arnell, William
     "The French population of New England,"
     Geography, 34(1949), 97-101

3730: Maine

466 Packard, L. O.
     "The decrease of population along the Maine coast,"
     GR, 2(1916), 334-341

467 Fobes, Charles B.
     "Path of settlement and distribution of population of Maine,"
     EG, 20(1944), 65-69

468 Mitchell, Albert R.
     Maine population study
     Master's thesis, Clark University
     Worcester, 1960

3750: Vermont

469 Dodge, Stanley D.
     "A study of population in Vermont and New Hampshire,"
     Papers of the Michigan Academy of Science, Arts and Letters, 18(1932),
        131-136

470 Fisher-Wilson, Harold
     "Population trends in northwestern New England, 1790-1930,"
     GR, 24(1934), 272-277

3760: Massachusetts

471 Klimm, Lester B.
     The relation between certain population changes and the physical en-
        vironment in Hampden, Hampshire, and Franklin counties, Massachusetts
     Philadelphia, University of Pennsylvania, 1933

472 Rimbert, Sylvie
     "L'immigration franco-canadienne au Massachusetts,"
     Revue Canadienne de Géographie, 8(1954), 75-85

473 Laing, Jean
     "The pattern of population trends in Massachusetts,"
     EG, 31(1955), 265-271

     (Also see 247)

                         3800: New York

474 Brigham, Albert Perry
     "The population of New York state,"
     GR, 2(1916), 206-217

475 Simpson, Robert B.
     "Studies in the geography of population change, Canadaigua Lake region,
        New York,"
     Proceedings of the Rochester Academy of Science, 8(1942), 49-121

476 Novak, Robert T.
     "Distribution of Puerto Ricans on Manhattan Island,"
     GR, 46(1956), 182-186

     (Also see 683)

                         3810: New Jersey

477 Brush, John E.
     The population of New Jersey, 2nd ed.
     New Brunswick, Rutgers University Press, 1958

478 Erickson, Richard B.
     A population study of Cape May County, New Jersey
     Master's thesis, Clark University
     Worcester, 1959

479 Erickson, Richard B.
     "Measuring resort population increases,"
     Professional Geographer, 13, No. 4(1961), 16-19

                         3820: Pennsylvania

480 Batschelet, Clarence E.
     "A picture of the distribution of population in Pennsylvania,"
     GR, 17(1927), 429-433

481 Miller, E. Willard
     "Some aspects of population trends in Pennsylvania,"
     Journal of Geography, 54(1955), 64-73

482 Miller, E. Willard
     "Population and functional changes of villages in western Pennsylvania,"
     Western Pennsylvania Historical Magazine, 43(1960), 59-75

     (Also see 483)

3840:   Maryland

483   Lobeck, Armin K.
      "Physiographic influence upon the distribution of population in Maryland
        and Pennsylvania,"
      AAAG, 16(1926), 94-101

484   Warman, Henry J.
      "Population of the manor counties of Maryland,"
      EG, 25(1949), 23-40

485   Buford, Carolyn B.
      The distribution of Negroes in Maryland, 1850-1950
      Master's thesis, Catholic University of America
      Washington, 1956

3860:   Southern states

486   Hollander, A. N. J. den
      "On the relation between land utilization, systems of farming and
        density of population in the southern United States, as a conse-
        quence of white colonization with the aid of unfree, colored labor,"
        pp. 421-432 in:
      CRCIG, Amsterdam, 1938, Vol. 2

487   Vance, Rupert B.
      All these people: the nation's human resources in the South
      Chapel Hill, University of North Carolina Press, 1945

488   Mather, Eugene and Hart, J. Fraser
      "The people of the Deep South and the border states,"
      TESG, 45(1954), 1-4

489   Starsinic, Donald E.
      State of birth and the American South
      Master's thesis, University of Chicago
      Chicago, 1957

3862.A6:   Southern Appalachians

490   Hollander, A. N. J. den
      "Über die Bevölkerung der Appalachen,"
      Gesellschaft für Erdkunde zu Berlin, Zeitschrift, 7-8(1934), 241-256

491   Marschner, Francis J.
      Rural population density in the Southern Appalachians
      United States Department of Agriculture, Miscellaneous Publications, 367
      Washington, 1940

3880: Virginia

492 Gilliam, Sara K.
     Virginia's people: a study of the growth and distribution of the
       population of Virginia from 1607 to 1943
     Virginia State Planning Board, Population Study, Report 4
     Richmond, 1944

493 Wright, Dorothy Rife
     A study of population distribution in Virginia
     Master's thesis, Marshall College
     Huntington, W. Va., 1957

3890: West Virginia

494 Britton, Robert L.
     "Population distribution in West Virginia,"
     EG, 20(1944), 31-36

3900: North Carolina

495 Phillips, Coy T.
     "Population distribution and trends in North Carolina,"
     Journal of Geography, 55(1956), 182-194

496 Ballas, Donald J.
     "Notes on the population, settlement, and ecology of the Eastern
       Cherokee Indians,"
     Journal of Geography, 59(1960), 258-267

3910: South Carolina

497 Petty, Julian J.
     The growth and distribution of population in South Carolina
     South Carolina State Planning Board, State Council for Defense,
       Industrial Development Commission, No. 11
     Columbia, 1943

498 Petty, Julian J.
     "Population changes in South Carolina,"
     South Carolina Magazine, 6(1943), 56-57

499 Petty, Julian J.
     "Population," pp. 28-49 in:
     University of South Carolina
     South Carolina: economic and social conditions in 1944
     Columbia, 1945

499a Petty, Julian J.
     "South Carolina's population redistribution,"
     University of South Carolina Business and Economic Review, 7, No. 8
       (1960), 1-4

3920: Georgia

500 Booth, Alfred W.
     "Soils and population--Decatur County, Georgia,"
     Georgia State Academy of Science, Transactions, 36(1942), 113-115

501 Zelinsky, Wilbur
     "An isochronic map of Georgia settlement, 1750-1850,"
     Georgia Historical Quarterly, 35(1951), 191-195

502 Hart, J. Fraser
     "The distribution of the rural nonfarm population in Georgia,"
     Bulletin of the Georgia Academy of Science, 13(1955), 118-123

3930: Florida

503 Harper, Roland M.
     "The population of Florida. Regional composition and growth as
         influenced by soil, climate and mineral discoveries,"
     GR, 2(1916), 361-367

504 Diettrich, Sigismond deR.
     "Florida's human resources,"
     GR, 38(1948), 278-288

505 Dickson, Douglas D.
     Field survey of certain aspects of the Flat Pineland population of
         Leon County, Florida
     Master's thesis, Florida State University
     Tallahassee, 1950

506 Dyer, Donald R.
     "The place of origin of Florida's population,"
     AAAG, 42(1952), 283-294

507 Diettrich, Sigismond deR.
     "Florida's changing population 1950-1958,"
     The Oriental Geographer, 4(1960), 1-20

3960: Tennessee

508 Straw, H. Thompson
     "The population distribution and change in the Eastern Highland Rim
         Plateau of Tennessee," pp. 145-155 in:
     Proceedings of the Eighth American Scientific Congress, Vol. 9
     Washington, 1943

509 Johnson, Rayburn
     "Population trends in Tennessee from 1940-1950,"
     Tennessee Historical Quarterly, 11(1952), 254-262

510 Luebke, B. H. and Hart, J. Fraser
     "Migration from a Southern Appalachian community,"
     Land Economics, 34(1958), 44-53

3980: Mississippi

511 Vent, Herbert
"Some population trends in Mississippi,"
Journal of Geography, 53(1954), 141-143

512 King, Morton B., Jr., et al.
Mississippi's people, 1950
Sociological Study Series, No. 5
University, University of Mississippi, 1955

3990: West South Central states

513 Bollinger, Clyde J.
"A synoptic chart of population change in the Gulf Southwest,"
Texas Geographic Magazine, 6(1942), 9-12

3990-4130: West Central States

514 Wright, Joe T.
An analysis of the spatial association of rural farm population and
selected physical factors on the Great Plains
Master's thesis, State University of Iowa
Iowa City, 1959

515 Robinson, Arthur H. and Lindberg, James B.
"A correlation and regression analysis applied to rural farm population
densities in the Great Plains,"
AAAG, 51(1961), 211-221

4000: Arkansas

516 Joy, Barnard
"Population studies in three American counties,"
EG, 15(1939), 11-26

4010: Louisiana

517 Lahman, Otokar
/"Yugoslavian emigrants in the Mississippi Delta,"_/ (in Slovenian)
Geografski Glasnik, 11-12(1949-52), 135-146

518 Smith, T. Lynn and Hitt, Homer L.
The people of Louisiana
Baton Rouge, Louisiana State University Press, 1952

4020: Oklahoma

519 Bollinger, Clyde J.
"A population map of Central Oklahoma for 1920,"
GR, 20(1930), 283-287

520 Ives, Ronald L.
        "Population changes in a mountain county,"
        EG, 18(1942), 298-306

4030: Texas

521 Trexler, Harrison A.
        "Nativity of population in the Black Prairie region of Texas, 1880,"
        Texas Geographical Magazine, 6(1942), 21-23

4060: North Central States

522 Winid, Walenty
        "The distribution of urban settlements in the North Central United
            States," pp. 376-382 in:
        CRCIG, Cambridge, 1928

523 Johnson, Hildegard Binder
        "The location of German immigrants in the Middle West,"
        AAAG, 41(1951), 1-41

4080: Ohio

524 Smith, Guy-Harold
        "A population map of Ohio for 1920,"
        GR, 18(1928), 422-427

525 Smith, Guy-Harold
        "Interstate migration as illustrated by Ohio,"
        Bulletin of the Geographical Society of Philadelphia, 27(1929), 301-312

526 Van Cleef, Eugene
        "Finnish population movement in Ohio,"
        Baltic and Scandinavian Countries, 3(1937), 253-255

527 Smith, Guy-Harold
        "Population re-distribution in Ohio, 1880-1930," pp. 13-18 in: J. H.
            Sitterley, R. H. Baker, and J. I. Falconer,
        Major land-use problem areas and land utilization in Ohio, 1935
        Ohio State University, Mimeograph Bulletin No. 79
        Columbus, 1935

528 Thompson, Warren S.
        Migration within Ohio, 1935-40; a study in the re-distribution of
            population
        Oxford, Ohio, Scripps Foundation for Research in Population Problems,
        1951

529 Stephen, Charles Ross
        A study of population distribution in Ohio
        Master's thesis, Marshall College
        Huntington, W. Va., 1957

530 Thompson, John L.; Ervin, John R.; and Guy, Marjorie P.
        Ohio population; growth and distribution
        Columbus, Ohio Department of Industrial and Economic Development, 1960

4090:   Indiana

531 Buckley, Wallace T.
     "A population map of Indiana for 1940,"
     Proceedings of the Indiana Academy of Science, 51(1942), 194-200

532 Visher, Stephen S.
     "Indiana's population, 1850-1940, sources and dispersal,"
     Indiana Magazine of History, 38(1942), 51-59

533 Visher, Stephen S.
     "Population changes in Indiana 1840-1940,"
     Proceedings of the Indiana Academy of Science, 51(1942), 179-193

534 Visher, Stephen S.
     "Indiana county contrasts in population changes,"
     Proceedings of the Indiana Academy of Science, 53(1944), 139-143

535 Barton, Thomas F.
     "Cities with a population decline in southwestern Indiana, 1940-1950,"
     Proceedings of the Indiana Academy of Science, 62(1952), 250-255

536 Gentilcore, R. Louis
     "Curves of population change in Indiana, 1850-1950,"
     Proceedings of the Indiana Academy of Science, 62(1952), 272-276

537 Hart, J. Fraser
     "The rural nonfarm population of Indiana,"
     Proceedings of the Indiana Academy of Science, 65(1955), 174-179

538 Hart, J. Fraser
     "Migration and population change in Indiana,"
     Proceedings of the Indiana Academy of Science, 66(1956), 195-203

539 Lal, Amrit
     "Population trend in Indiana's villages of 1,000-2,500 population in
     1950,"
     Proceedings of the Indiana Academy of Science, 66(1956), 204-208

540 Hart, J. Fraser
     "Age pyramids for Indiana's counties and larger cities,"
     Proceedings of the Indiana Academy of Science, 67(1957), 187-193

541 Hart, J. Fraser
     "Rural population density in Indiana,"
     Proceedings of the Indiana Academy of Science, 68(1958), 218-224

542 Hart, J. Fraser
     "Changing census concepts of rural population in Indiana,"
     Proceedings of the Indiana Academy of Science," 69(1959), 249-253

4100:   Illinois

543 Beimfohr, Oliver Wendel
     "Settlement and distribution of the population resource," pp. 7-34 in:
     The industrial potential of Southern Illinois
     Carbondale, Southern Illinois University, 1954

544 Kohn, Clyde F.
     "Differential population growth of incorporated municipalities in the
        Chicago suburban region,"
     Illinois Academy of Science, Transactions, 49(1956), 85-91

545 Beveridge, Ronald Murray
     Subregional migration within Illinois, 1935-40: an analysis of selected
        data
     Doctoral dissertation, University of Illinois
     Urbana, 1958

545a Schwartz, Carroll J.
     Distribution of the foreign-born population of Illinois 1870-1950
     Master's thesis, Southern Illinois University
     Carbondale, 1959

                         4110: Michigan

546 Freeman, Otis W.
     "A geographic study of the growth and distribution of population in
        Michigan," pp. 39-53 in:
     15th Report, Michigan Academy of Science
     Lansing, 1913

547 Miller, G. H.
     "Some geographic influences in the settlement of Michigan and in the
        distribution of its population,"
     American Geographical Society, Bulletin, 45(1913), 321-348

548 Dodge, Stanley D.
     "Population regions of the southern peninsula of Michigan: a
        preliminary study,"
     Papers of the Michigan Academy of Science, Arts and Letters, 18(1933),
        345-348

549 Stilgenbauer, Floyd A. and Vozka, Henry
     "A new population map of Michigan, 1930,"
     Papers of the Michigan Academy of Science, Arts and Letters, 18(1933),
        277-288

550 Humphrey, Norman D.
     "The migration and settlement of Detroit Mexicans,"
     EG, 19(1944), 358-361

551 Maybee, R. H.
     "Population growth and distribution in lower Michigan 1810-1940,"
     Papers of the Michigan Academy of Science, Arts and Letters, 31(1947),
        253-266

552 Perejda, Andrew D.
     "Sources and dispersal of Michigan's population,"
     Michigan History, 32(1948), 355-366

553 Bruyere, Donald E.
     "The trend of rural and urban population in Michigan from 1940 to 1950,"
     Papers of the Michigan Academy of Science, Arts and Letters, 38(1953),
        Pt. 3

554   Hawley, Amos H.
      Intrastate migration in Michigan, 1935-40
      Michigan Governmental Studies, No. 25
      Ann Arbor, University of Michigan Press, 1953

                        4120: Wisconsin

555   Smith, Guy-Harold
      "The populating of Wisconsin,"
      GR, 18(1928), 402-421

556   Smith, Guy-Harold
      "Notes on the distribution of the German-born in Wisconsin in 1905,"
      Wisconsin Magazine of History, 13(1929), 107-120

557   Smith, Guy-Harold
      "The settlement and the distribution of the population in Wisconsin,"
      Wisconsin Academy of Science, Transactions, 24(1929), 53-107

558   Smith, Guy-Harold
      "Notes on the distribution of the foreign-born Scandinavian in
          Wisconsin in 1905,"
      Wisconsin Magazine of History, 14(1931), 419-431

559   Read, Mary J.
      A population study of the Driftless Hill Land during the pioneer
          period, 1832-1860
      Doctoral dissertation, University of Wisconsin
      Madison, 1941

560   Trewartha, Glenn T.
      "Population and settlements in the Upper Mississippi Hill Land during
          the period of destructive exploitation (1670-1832)," pp. 183-196 in:
      Proceedings of the Eighth American Scientific Congress, Vol. 9, History,
          Geography
      Washington, 1943

                        4140: Minnesota

561   Wilson, Leonard S.
      "Some notes on the growth of population in Minnesota,"
      GR, 30(1940), 660-664

562   Johnson, Hildegard Binder
      "The distribution of the German pioneer population in Minnesota,"
      Rural Sociology, 6(1941), 16-34

563   Wilson, Leonard S.
      "Population trends in Minnesota: 1940,"
      EG, 18(1942), 188-194

564   Johnson, Hildegard Binder
      "Factors influencing the distribution of the German pioneer population
          in Minnesota,"
      Agricultural History, 19(1945), 39-57

564a Ericson, Mary Alice, et al.
      "Some demographic characteristics of Minnesota villages in 1950,"
      Proceedings of the Minnesota Academy of Science, 27(1959), 59-67

                              4150: Iowa

565   Schilz, Gordon B.
      Rural population trends of Iowa as affected by soils
      Doctoral dissertation, Clark University
      Worcester, 1948

566   Heusinkveld, Harriet Mildred
      The historical geography of population in Marion, Mahaska, and Monroe
          counties in Iowa
      Doctoral dissertation, State University of Iowa
      Iowa City, 1958

567   Kohn, Clyde F.
      "Some spatial characteristics of Iowa's population growth,"
      Iowa Business Digest, 31(1960), 22-26

      (Also see 516)

                            4160: Missouri

568   Matingly, Paul F.
      "Population trends in Missouri,"
      Journal of Geography, 55(1956), 80-84

                             4200: Kansas

569   Hannaman, Thomas B.
      Geographic study of population and settlement changes in Colby, Kansas,
          from 1940 to 1950
      Master's thesis, University of Kansas
      Lawrence, 1951

570   Kingsbury, Patricia R.
      A geographic study of population and settlement changes in Goodland,
          Kansas
      Master's thesis, University of Kansas
      Lawrence, 1951

571   Kollmorgen, Walter M. and Jenks, George F.
      "A geographic study of population and land settlement changes in
          Sherman County, Kansas,"
      Kansas Academy of Science, Transactions, 54(1951), 449-494 and 55(1952),
          1-37

                          4210: Western States

572   Ezquerra Abadía, Ramon
      "Los Españoles in el Far West,"
      Real Sociedad Geográfica, Boletín, 79(1943), 121-150

4240: Pacific Northwest

573 Appleton, John B.
       "Migration and economic opportunity in the Pacific Northwest,"
       GR, 31(1941), 46-62

574 Martin, Howard H. and Mapes, Carl H.
       "The population pattern," pp. 3-11 in:
       The Pacific Northwest; an overall appreciation
       New York, Wiley, 1954

4280: Washington

575 Schmid, Calvin F.
       Population growth and distribution, State of Washington
       Seattle, Washington State Census Board, 1955

       (Also see 577)

4290: Oregon

576 Black, Lloyd D.
       "Middle Willamette Valley population growth,"
       Oregon Historical Quarterly, 43(1942), 40-55

577 Michels, John Lewis
       Population distribution in Oregon and Washington, 1950
       Master's thesis, University of Chicago,
       Chicago, 1954

578 Adams, Georgia Ellen
       "Two isochronic maps of settlement in Oregon,"
       Association of Pacific Coast Geographers, Yearbook, 18(1956), 36-41

       (Also see 516)

4300: Southwestern States

579 Broadbent, Elizabeth
       "Mexican population in southwestern United States,"
       Texas Geographical Magazine, 5(1941), 16-24

4320: New Mexico

580 Culbert, James I.
       "Distribution of Spanish-American population in New Mexico,"
       EG, 19(1943), 171-176

       (Also see 581)

4330: Arizona

581 Spaulding, Leslie Earl
     Population distribution in Arizona and New Mexico
     Master's thesis, University of Chicago
     Chicago, 1954

582 Simkins, Paul D.
     Regionalisms in the recent migration to Arizona
     Doctoral dissertation, University of Wisconsin
     Madison, 1961

4340: Utah

583 Langdon, W.
     "The distribution of population in the Salt Lake Oasis,"
     Journal of Geography, 27(1928), 1-14

584 Gregory, Herbert E.
     "Population of southern Utah,"
     EG, 21(1945), 29-57

4360: California

585 Mirkowich, Nicholas
     "Recent trends in population distribution in California,"
     GR, 31(1941), 300-307

586 Nelson, Howard J.
     "Die Binnenwanderung in den USA, am Beispiel Kaliforniens,"
     Die Erde, 2(1953), 109-121

587 Trotter, John Ellis
     Distribution of population in California: 1950
     Master's thesis, University of Chicago
     Chicago, 1953

588 Alexandersson, Gunnar
     / "The population development of California against its economic-
        geographic background,"_/ (in Swedish)
     Ymer, 74(1954), 1-39

589 Thompson, Warren S.
     Growth and changes in California's population
     Los Angeles, Haynes Foundation, 1955

4370: ALASKA

590 Petroff, Ivan
     Report on the population, industries and resources of Alaska
     United States Census Office, 10th Census, 1880, Census Reports,
        Volume VIII
     Washington, 1884

591   Bartz, Fritz
      "Verteilung und Aufbau der Bevölkerung," pp. 305-330 in:
      Alaska
      Stuttgart, Koehler, 1950

592   Stone, Kirk H.
      "Populating Alaska: the United States phase,"
      GR, 42(1952), 383-404

593   Stanton, W. J.
      "The purpose and source of seasonal migration to Alaska,"
      EG, 31(1955), 138-148

594   Bruyere, Donald E.
      The trend of population in southeastern Alaska
      Doctoral dissertation, University of Michigan
      Ann Arbor, 1958

595   Taeuber, Irene B.
      "The population of the forty-ninth state,"
      Population Index, 25(1959), 93-114

      (Also see 361, 368)

                        4390:   CARIBBEAN AREA

596   Abrahamson, John Deinhart
      Distribution of population in Caribbean America
      Master's thesis, University of Chicago
      Chicago, 1936

597   Proudfoot, Malcolm J.
      Population movements in the Caribbean
      Port-of-Spain, Caribbean Commission, 1950

                        4400:   LATIN AMERICA

                        a.   Bibliography

598   Pan American Institute of Geography and History
      "Bibliography of recent demographic studies and types of population
         statistics available for Latin American countries,"
      Revista Geográfica (Pan American Institute of Geography and History),
         18(1956), 124-133

                        b.   Population Studies

599   Davis, Kingsley and Casis, A.
      "Urbanization in Latin America,"
      Milbank Memorial Fund Quarterly, 24(1946), 186-207, 292-314

600   Zarur, Jorge
      "Geography and cartography for census purposes in Latin America,"
      Estadística, 6(1948), 3-24, 218-241

601 Zelinsky, Wilbur
     "The historical geography of the Negro population of Latin America,"
     Journal of Negro History, 34(1949), 153-221

602 Chang, Ching Chieh
     A geographic study of the Chinese population in Latin America
     Doctoral dissertation, University of Maryland
     College Park, 1956

603 Smith, T. Lynn
     "Un análisis comparativo de la migración rural-urbana en Latino-
     américa,"
     Estadística, 16(1958), 436-453

604 Mörner, Magnus
     /"Immigration and the rise of modern Latin America,"/ (in Swedish)
     Ymer, 80(1960), 260-274

                         4405: MIDDLE AMERICA

605 Kulenkampf-Schenck, E.
     Die Volksdichte von Mittelamerika unter Berücksichtigung der
        klimatischen und wirtschaftlichen Verhältnisse
     Bonn. Universität. Romanisches Auslandsinstitut. Veröffentlich-
        ungen, IV
     Bonn, 1923

606 Leon, Albert P. and Aldama, Alvaro C.
     "Problemas de población en la America del Caribe y Central,"
     Sociedad Mexicana de Geografía y Estadística, Boletín,61(1946), 3-10

607 United Nations, Department of Economic and Social Affairs, Population
        Division
     Future population estimates by sex and age. Report I. The population
        of Central America (including Mexico), 1950-1980
     Population Studies, No. 16
     New York, 1954

608 United Nations, Department of Economic and Social Affairs, Population
        Division
     Los recursos humanos de Centroamerica, Panamá y México en 1950-1980, y
        sus relaciones con algunos aspectos del desarrollo económico
     New York, 1960

                          4410: MEXICO

                          a. National

609 Wittich, Ernst
     "Die Volkszählung in der Republik Mexico 1910,"
     PM, 57(1911), 191-194

610 Cushing, Sumner W.
     "The distribution of population in Mexico,"
     GR, 11(1921), 227-242

611   Sapper, Karl
      "Die Volkszählung in der Republik Mexico 1921,"
      PM, 73(1927), 153-158

611a Sapper, Karl
      "Zahl, Rasse und Dichte der mexikanischen Bevölkerung," pp. 307-321 in:
      Twenty-Second International Congress of Americanists, 1926 Vol. 2
      Roma, 1928

612   Landa y Pina, Andres
      "El servicio de migración en Mexico,"
      Sociedad Mexicana de Geografía y Estadística, Boletín, 42(1930), 499-560

613   Wittich, Ernst
      "Die Volkszählung in der Republik Mexico im Mai 1930,"
      PM, 77(1931), 249-254

614   Deasy, George F. and Gerhard, Peter
      "Densidad de la población de habla indígena en la República Mexicana,"
      Memorias del Instituto Nacional Indigenista, 1
      México, 1950

615   Flores Talavera, Rodolfo
      "México y su población,"
      Sociedad Mexicana de Geografía y Estadística, Boletín, 78(1954), 343-
      367

616   Marino Flores, Anselmo and Uribe Macip, Venus
      "Generalidades sobre la población rural y urbana de México,"
      Anales del Instituto Nacional de Antropología e Historia, México, 10,
      No. 39 (1956), 29-65

617   Doerr, Arthur and Freile, Luis
      "Population distribution in Mexico--1950,"
      Journal of Geography, 55(1956), 235-242

618   Whetten, Nathan L. and Burnight, Robert G.
      "Internal migration in Mexico,"
      Rural Sociology, 21(1956), 140-151

619   Vivó, Jorge A.
      "Zonas culturales y demografía," pp. 148-161 in:
      Geografía de México
      México, Fonde de Cultura Económica, 1958

620   Enjalbert, Henri
      "La pression démographique au Mexique,"
      Les Cahiers d'Outre-Mer, 13, No. 52(1960), 451-460

621   Loyo Gilberto
      La población de México; estado actual y tendencias, 1950-1980
      México, Investigación Económica, 1960

      (Also see 413, 550, 579)

b. Regional

622 Tamayo, Jorge L.
     "Población," pp. 184-210 in:
     Geografía moderna de México
     México, Librería Patria, 1960

623 Sauer, Carl O.
     "Aboriginal population of northwestern Mexico,"
     Ibero-Americana, 10(1935), 1-33

624 Foglio Miramontes, Fernando
     "Población," pp. 129-189 in:
     Geografía económica agricola del Estado de Michoacan, Tomo II
     México, Secretaria de Agricultura y Fomento, 1936

625 Eddy, Florence Reata
     Distribution of population in the states of Mexico, Morelos, and the
          Federal District of Mexico
     Master's thesis, University of Chicago
     Chicago, 1938

626 México, Secretaria de la Economía Nacional, Departmento de Estudios
          Económicos, Sector de Geografía Económica
     "Distribución geográfica de la población," pp. 40-55 in:
     Geografía económica del Estado de Hidalgo
     México, 1939

627 Butijn, J. A. A.
     /"The population of Yucatan,"7 (in Dutch)
     TEG, 32(1941), 193-199

628 Deasy, George F. and Gerhard, Peter
     "Settlements in Baja California, 1768-1930,"
     GR, 34(1944), 574-586

629 Almada, Francisco R.
     "Población en general" and "Cuadros demográficos," pp. 79-87 in:
     Geografía del Estado de Chihuahua
     Chihuahua, 1945

630 Cook, Sherburne F. and Simpson, Leslie B.
     The population of central Mexico in the Sixteenth Century
     Ibero-Americana, Vol. 31
     Berkeley, University of California Press, 1948

631 Cook, Sherburne F.
     The historical demography and ecology of the Teotlalpan
     Ibero-Americana, Vol. 33
     Berkeley, University of California Press, 1949

632 Cook, Sherburne F.
     Soil erosion and population in central Mexico
     Ibero-Americana, Vol. 34
     Berkeley, University of California Press, 1949

633 Termer, Franz
     "La densidad de población en los Imperios Mayas como problema
        arqueológico y geográfico,"
     Sociedad Mexicana de Geografía y Estadística, Boletín, 70(1950), 211-
     239

634 Barreda Fernández, María H.
     Geografía demográfico económica del Estado de Colima
     México, 1951

635 Aschmann, Homer
     The central desert of Baja California: demography and ecology
     Berkeley, University of California Press, 1959

636 Chevalier, François and Huguet, Louis
     "Peuplement et mise en valeur du Tropique Mexicain," pp. 395-438 in:
     Miscellanea Paul Rivet
     México, 1959

637 Vivó Escoto, Jorge A.
     "Estudio de geografía económica y demográfica de Chiapas,"
     Sociedad Mexicana de Geografía y Estadística, Boletín, 87(1959), 7-262

638 Borah, Woodrow and Cook, Sherburne F.
     The population of central Mexico in 1548
     Ibero-Americana, Vol. 43
     Berkeley, University of California Press, 1960

639 Cook, Sherburne F. and Borah, Woodrow
     The Indian population of Central Mexico, 1531-1610
     Ibero-Americana, Vol. 44
     Berkeley, University of California Press, 1960

                              4800: CENTRAL AMERICA

640 Sax, Karl
     "Population problems of Central America,"
     Ceiba (Tegucigalpa), 4(1954), 143-164

                              4810: GUATEMALA

641 Sapper Karl
     "Die Volksdichtigkeit der Republik Guatemala,"
     Globus, 71(1897), 188-191

642 Termer, Franz
     "Zur Geographie der Republik Guatemala. II. Teil. Beiträge zur
        Kultur- und Wirtschaftsgeographie von Mittel- und Süd-Guatemala,"
     Geographischen Gesellschaft in Hamburg, Mitteilungen, 47(1941), 7-262

643 McBryde, Felix Webster
     "Demography," pp. 9-16 in:
     Cultural and historical geography of southwest Guatemala
     Smithsonian Institution, Institute of Social Anthropology, Publ. No. 4
     Washington, 1945

644 Monteforte Toledo, Mario
     "Demografía," pp. 39-110 in:
     Guatemala; monografía sociológica
     México, Universidad Nacional Autónoma de México, 1959

645 Slutsky, Herbert
     An ecological study of total mortality among Guatemalan pre-school
        children, with special emphasis on protein malnutrition and
        kwashiorkor
     Doctoral dissertation, University of Illinois
     Urbana, 1959

                         4820: BRITISH HONDURAS

     See 668

                         4830: HONDURAS

646 Tosco, Manuel and Mondragon, Rubén
     Análisis dinámico y económico-social de la población de Honduras
     Honduras, Servico Informativo del Banco Central de Honduras y del Banco
        Nacional de Fomento
     Tegucigalpa, Taleres Tipo, 1952

                         4840: EL SALVADOR

647 Castro, Rodolfo Barón
     La población de El Salvador: estudio acerca de su desenvolvimiento
        desde la época prehispánica hasta nuestros días
     Madrid, Instituto Gonzalo Fernández de Oviedo, 1942

648 Vogt, William
     La población de El Salvador y sus recursos naturales
     Washington, Pan American Union, 1946

649 Pacheco, Mario and Martinez, Alfredo
     "Population of El Salvador and its natural resources," pp. 125-133 in:
     Proceedings of the Inter-American Conference on Conservation of
        Renewable Natural Resources, Denver, Colorado, September 7-20, 1948
     United States Department of State, Publication 3382, International
        Organization and Conference Series II, American Republics 4
     Washington, 1949

650 Larde, Jorge
     "La población de El Salvador; su origen y distribución geográfica,"
     Anales del Museo Nacional "David Guzmán" (San Salvador), 4(1953), 73-92

651 El Salvador, Dirección General de Estadística y Censos
     Atlas censal de El Salvador
     San Salvador, n.d. (Based on 1950 materials)

652 Gierloff-Emden, Hans-Günter
     "Die Bevölkerungsdichte und -verteilung von El Salvador,"
     Geographische Berichte, 3(1958), 121-136

4850: NICARAGUA

653 Perpiña Grau, R.
     Síntesis corológica de la población de Nicaragua
     Managua, Escuela Nacional de Economía y Administración, 1956

654 Perpiña Grau, R.
     Corología de la población de Nicaragua
     Spain, Consejo Superior de Investigaciónes Científicas, Instituto
       "Balmes" de Sociología
     Madrid, 1959

4860: COSTA RICA

655 Waibel, Leo
     "White settlement in Costa Rica,"
     GR, 29(1939), 529-560

656 Monge Alfaro, C.
     Geografía social y humana de Costa Rica
     San José, 1942

657 Vogt, William
     The population of Costa Rica and its natural resources
     Washington, Pan American Union, 1946

658 Morrison, Paul Cross
     "Population pattern, central district of Turrialba Canton, Costa Rica,"
     Papers of the Michigan Academy of Science, Arts and Letters, 37(1951),
       219-225

659 Costa Rica, Dirección General de Estadística y Censos
     Atlas estadística de Costa Rica
     San José, 1952

660 Quiros Amador, Tulia
     "Población," pp. 58-97 in:
     Geografía de Costa Rica
     San José, Instituto Geográfico de Costa Rica, 1954

661 Jiménez Castro, Wilburg
     Migraciónes internas en Costa Rica
     Pan American Union, Consejo Interamericano Economico y Social
     Washington, 1956

662 Nunley, Robert Edward
     The distribution of population in Costa Rica
     Doctoral dissertation, University of Michigan
     Ann Arbor, 1959

     Also: National Research Council, Publication 743
     Washington, 1960

4870: PANAMA

663   Rubio, Angel
      "La dispersión demográfica en Panamá,"
      Acta Americana, 4(1946), 1-9

664   Rubio, Angel
      "Distribuzione della popolazione nel Panama, nel 1950,"
      BSGI, Serie 8, 5(1952)

665   Rubio, Angel
      "Le attuali condizioni demografiche ed economische del Pananiá,"
      BSGI, Serie 8, 6(1953), 1-10

      (Also see 726)

4900: WEST INDIES

666 Chevalier, Louis
      "Les mouvements de la population dans les dépendances Caraibes,"
      Population, 4(1949), 356-361

667 Augelli, John P.
      "The country-to-town movement in the West Indies," pp. 719-723 in:
      CRCIG, Washington, 1952

668 Kuczynski, Robert R.
      Demographic survey of the British colonial empire. Volume III. West
        Indian and American territories
      London, Royal Institute of International Affairs, 1953

669 Geisert, Harold L.
      The Caribbean: population and resources
      George Washington University, Population Research Project
      Washington, 1960

4910: GREATER ANTILLES

670 McBryde, F. Webster
      Census atlas maps of Latin America. Part II. Greater Antilles
      United States Bureau of the Census, Census Atlas Project
      Washington, 1956

4920: CUBA

671 Chaves, Antonio F.
      "A dot map of the distribution of population in Cuba,"
      Acta Americana, 5(1947), 261-266

672 Marrero, Levi
      "Población," pp. 142-163 in:
      Geografía de Cuba
      Habana, 1950

67 Puerto Rico

672a Dyer, Donald R.
"Urbanism in Cuba,"
GR, 47(1957), 224-233

4930: HISPANIOLA

673 Dyer, Donald R.
"Distribution of population on Hispaniola,"
EG, 30(1954), 337-346

4940: HAITI

674 Lubin, Maurice A.
"En marge du recensement en Haiti,"
Société Haïtienne d'Histoire, de Géographie et de Géologic, Revue,
21(1950), 105-116

4960: JAMAICA

675 Cumper, G. E.
"Population movements in Jamaica, 1830-1950,"
Social and Economic Studies (Mona, Jamaica), 5(1956), 261-280

676 Roberts, George W.
The population of Jamaica: an analysis of its structure and growth
Cambridge, Cambridge University Press, 1957

677 Lowenthal, David
"Production and population in Jamaica,"
GR, 48(1958), 568-571

4970: PUERTO RICO

678 Bothwell, Lyman D.
"The geographic factor in the distribution, trends, and peaks of the
population of Puerto Rico, 1900-1930,"
Papers of the Michigan Academy of Science, Arts and Letters, 22(1936),
321-327

679 Bartlett, Frederic P. and Howell, Brandon
The population problem in Puerto Rico
Puerto Rico Planning, Urbanizing, and Zoning Board, Technical Paper
No. 2
Santurce, 1944

680 Chaves, Antonio F.
"Aspectos geográficos del poblamiento de Puerto Rico,"
Revista Geográfica (Pan American Institute of Geography and History),
5-8(1949), 57-68

681   Chaves, Antonio F.
      La distribución de la población en Puerto Rico
      San Juan, Universidad de Puerto Rico, 1949

682   Hunker, Henry L.
      "The problem of Puerto Rican migrations to the United States,"
      Ohio Journal of Science, 51(1951), 342-346

683   Hollander, A. N. J. den
      /"Emigration from Puerto Rico to New York,"/ (in Dutch)
      K. Nederlandsch Aardrijkskundig Genootschap, Tijdschrift, 69(1952),
      432-475

      (Also see 439)

                          4980:   BAHAMA ISLANDS

684   Sharer, Cyrus
      The population growth of the Bahama Islands
      Doctoral dissertation, University of Michigan
      Ann Arbor, 1955

                      5010:   VIRGIN ISLANDS (U. S.)

685   Shaw, Earl B.
      "Population adjustments in our Virgin Islands,"
      EG, 11(1935), 267-279

                       5060:   FRENCH WEST INDIES

686   Revert, Eugène
      "Le peuplement," pp. 197-245 in:
      La Martinique; étude géographique
      Paris, Editions Latines, 1949

687   France, Institut National de la Statistique et des Etudes Economiques
      Démographie des Antilles françaises. Martinique et Guadeloupe
      Paris, 1955

688   Lasserre, Guy
      "Présentation de cartes de densité de la population en Guadeloupe,"
      Association de Géographes Français, Bulletin, Nos. 280-281(1959), 33-48

                            5140:   BARBADOS

689   Lowenthal, David
      "The population of Barbados,"
      Social and Economic Studies (Jamaica), 6(1957), 445-501

5150: TRINIDAD

690   Augelli, John P. and Taylor, Harry W.
      "Race and population patterns in Trinidad,"
      AAAG, 50(1960), 123-138

5160: TOBAGO

691   Niddrie, David L.
      Land use and population in Tobago; an environmental study
      World Land Use Survey, Monograph 3
      Bude, Cornwall, Geographical Publications, 1961

5170: NETHERLANDS WEST INDIES

692   Keur, John Y. and Keur, Dorothy L.
      "Population patterns," pp. 154-160 in:
      Windward children: a study in human ecology of the three Dutch Wind-
          ward Islands in the Caribbean
      Assen, Prakke & Prakke, 1960

5200: SOUTH AMERICA

693   Jefferson, Mark
      "The distribution of people in South America,"
      Bulletin of the Geographical Society of Philadelphia," 5(1907), 182-192

694   LeConte, René
      "L'émigration allemande en Amérique du Sud,"
      Mouvement Géographique, 23(1920), 485-489, 521-526, 532-536

695   Ricard, Robert
      "L'émigration des Juifs marocains en Amérique du Sud,"
      Revue de Géographie Marocaine, 7(1928), 237-240

696   Guyol, Nathaniel B.
      The distribution of population in South America
      Master's thesis, University of Chicago
      Chicago, 1936

697   James, Preston E.
      "The distribution of people in South America," pp. 217-240 in:
      Charles C. Colby, ed.
      Geographic aspects of international relations, lectures of the Harris
          Foundation, 1937
      Chicago, University of Chicago Press, 1938

698   United Nations, Department of Economic and Social Affairs, Population
          Division
      Future population estimates by sex and age. Report II. The population
          of South America, 1950-1980
      Population Studies, No. 21
      New York, 1955

699 Witthauer, Kurt
     "Bevölkerungsverteilung und -entwicklung in Südamerika,"
     PM, 100(1956), 122-136, 153-160

700 James, Preston E.
     Latin America, 3rd ed.
     New York, Odyssey Press, 1959

701 Lavell, Carr B.
     Population growth and the development of South America
     George Washington University, Population Research Project
     Washington, 1959

702 Yamazaki, Teiichi
     /"Distribution of population and development of cities in South
      America,"/ (in Japanese)
     Jimbun Chiri. Human Geography, 11(1959), 41-53

703 White, C. Langdon
     "Whither South America: population and natural resources,"
     Journal of Geography, 60(1961), 103-112

5240: THE GUIANAS

704 Quelle, Otto
     "Die Bevölkerungsentwicklung von Europäisch-Guayana: eine anthropo-
      geographische Untersuchung,"
     Die Erde, Nos. 3-4(1951-52), 366-378

705 Lowenthal, David
     "Population contrasts in the Guianas,"
     GR, 50(1960), 41-58

5250: BRITISH GUIANA

706 Roberts, George W.
     "Some observations on the population of British Guiana,"
     Population Studies, 2(1948), 185-218

707 Taeuber, Irene B.
     "British Guiana: some demographic aspects of economic development,"
     Population Index, 18(1952), 3-19

5260: SURINAM

708 Kuyp, E. van der
     Report on the demographic problems of Surinam for the conference on
      demographic problems of the area served by the Caribbean Commission,
      Port of Spain, Trinidad, July-Aug., 1957
     Paramaribo, Radhakishun and Co., 1959

5270: FRENCH GUIANA

709 Chevalier, Louis and Vizot, A.
     "Le problème démographique de la Guyane française et les perspectives
       d'immigration,"
     Population, 2(1947), 796-800

710 Lowenthal, David
     "Colonial experiments in French Guiana, 1760-1800,"
     Hispanic American Historical Review, 32(1952), 22-43

711 Papy, Louis
     "La Guyane française,"
     Cahiers d'Outre-Mer, No. 31(1955), 209-232

712 Hauger, Jean
     "La population de la Guyane française,"
     AG, 66(1957), 509-518

5280: VENEZUELA

713 Vogt, William
     The population of Venezuela and its natural resources
     Washington, Pan American Union, 1946

714 Vila, Marco-Aurelio
     "Población," etc., pp. 187-226 in:
     Aspectos geográficos del Zulia
     Caracas, Imprenta Nacional, 1952

715 Vila, Marco-Aurelio
     "Población," etc., pp. 166-216 in:
     Aspectos geográficos del Estado Anzoategui
     Caracas, Corporación Venezolana de Fomento, 1953

716 Dupuoy, W.
     "The Indian in the map of Venezuela,"
     Boletín Indigenista, Dec., 1954, 309-319

717 Sterling, Henry S.
     "La población," pp. 56-67 in:
     Problemas económicas y sociales de los Andes Venezolanos
     Caracas, Consejo de Bienestar Rural, 1955

718 Alexander, Charles S.
     "Modern population patterns," pp. 140-143 in:
     The geography of Margarita and adjacent islands, Venezuela
     University of California Publications in Geography, Vol. 12, No. 2
     Berkeley and Los Angeles, 1958

719 Vila, Marco-Aurelio
     "Población," etc., pp. 150-189 in:
     Aspectos geográficos de Nueva Esparta
     Caracas, Corporación Venezolana de Fomento, 1958

5290: COLOMBIA

720 Ossa, V. Peregrino
     "Immigración en Colombia,"
     Sociedad Geográfica de Colombia, Boletín, 6(1939), 149-156

721 Parsons, James J.
     "The settlement of the Sinu Valley of Colombia,"
     GR, 42(1952), 67-86

722 Guhl, Ernesto
     "Algunos aspectos de la geografía y demografía de Colombia,"
     Revista Geográfica (Pan American Institute of Geography and History),
        15(1954), 81-104

723 Parsons, James J.
     "English-speaking settlement of the western Caribbean,"
     Yearbook of the Association of Pacific Coast Geographers, 16(1954), 3-16

724 Fals-Borda, Orlando
     El hombre y la tierra en Boyaca
     Bogotá, Ediciones Documentos Colombianos, 1957

725 Robledo, Emilio
     "Migraciones oceánicas en el pobliamento de Colombia,"
     Sociedad Geográfica de Colombia, Boletín, 15(1957), 96-112

726 West, Robert C.
     "Population and settlement," pp. 82-125 in:
     The Pacific lowlands of Colombia; a negroid area of the American tropics
     Baton Rouge, Louisiana State University Press, 1957

727 Dambaugh, Luella N.
     "Colombia's population resource,"
     Journal of Geography, 58(1959), 174-180

5300: ECUADOR

728 Paz y Niño, Luis Telmo
     "La distribución geográfica de la población del Ecuador," pp. 91-123 in:
     Realidades Ecuatorianas, Publicaciones de la Universidad Central
     Quito, 1938

729 Quelle, Otto
     "Der Strukturwandel der Bevölkerung von Ecuador 1535-1935,"
     Ibero-Americanisches Archiv, 14(1940), 29-43

730 Teran, Francisco
     "Población," pp. 241-301 in:
     Geografía del Ecuador, 4th ed.
     Quito, Talleres Gráficos de Educación, 1956

731 Saunders, John Van Dyke
     La población del Ecuador; un analisis del Censo de 1950
     Quito, Editorial Casa de la Cultura Ecuatoriana, 1959

732 Saunders, John Van Dyke
     The people of Ecuador; a demographic analysis
     Latin American Monographs, No. 14
     Gainesville, University of Florida Press, 1961

     (Also see 726)

                              5310: PERU

733 Sievers, W.
     "Zur Kenntnis der Bevölkerung der Sierra von Nordperu,"
     Deutsche Rundschau für Geographie, 34(1912), 478-487

734 Ferrero, Rómulo
     Tierra y población en el Perú
     Lima, Banco Agricola del Perú, 1938

735 Arca Parró, Alberto
     "La distribución geográfica de la población y la economía peruana,"
     Revista de Economía y Finanzas, 7(Sept. and Nov., 1939), 145-148, 290-
        296

736 Rio, Mario del
     La immigración y su desarrollo en el Peru
     Lima, Imprenta Torres Aguirre, 1939

737 Graña, Francisco
     La población del Perú a través de la historia, 3rd ed.
     Lima, Imprenta Torres Aguirre, 1940

738 Arca Parró, Alberto
     "Census of Peru, 1940,"
     GR, 32(1942), 1-20

739 Arca Parró, Alberto
     "El medio geográfico y la población del Perú,"
     Estadística Peruana, 1, No. 2(1945), 8-32 and No. 3(1945), 7-36

740 Rowe, John Howland
     "The distribution of Indians and Indian languages in Peru,"
     GR, 37(1947), 203-215

741 Ubilluz, Edmundo
     "Los dos grandes alineamientos de los centros poblados de la vertiente
        peruana del Pacífico,"
     Universidad de San Marcos. Instituto Superior de Geografía. Revista,
        1(1954), 74-79

742 Ford, Thomas R.
     "The land and the people," pp. 5-20 in:
     Man and land in Peru
     Gainesville, University of Florida Press, 1955

743 Orbegoso Rodriguez, Efraín
     "Notas sobre la población y las ciudades del departamento de La Liber-
        tad,"
     Universidad de San Marcos. Instituto Superior de Geografía. Revista,
        5(1958), 71-80

744 Ubilluz, Edmundo
     "Distribución geográfica de la población del Peru en 1957,"
     Sociedad Geográfica de Lima, Boletín, 75(1958), 42-52

744a Pendleton, Jesse L.
     Structural changes of the Peruvian population, 1940-1955
     Master's thesis, Clark University
     Worcester, 1961

                            5320: BOLIVIA

745 Bowman, Isaiah
     "The distribution of population in Bolivia,"
     Bulletin of the Geographical Society of Philadelphia, 7(1909), 28-46

746 Nordenskiöld, Erland
     "Die Bevölkerungsbewegung unter den Indianern in Bolivien,"
     PM, 63(1917), 108-112

747 Camacho, José Mario
     "Población de Bolivia,"
     Sociedad Geográfica de La Paz, Boletín, 31, No. 57(1925)

748 Pando Gutierrez, Jorge
     Bolivia y el mundo. Geografía económica. Tomo I. Población,
       geografía, transportes
     La Paz, 1947

749 Leonard, Olen E.
     "Growth and distribution of population," pp. 35-42 in:
     Bolivia; land, people and institutions
     Washington, Scarecrow Press, 1952

                            5330: CHILE

750 Rubens, Robert
     "Chile nach der Volkszählung von 1895,"
     Geographische Zeitschrift, 3(1897), 468-472

751 Steffen, Hans
     "Die Bevölkerung der Republik Chile nach der Zählung von 1907,"
     Geographische Zeitschrift, 15(1909), 701-704

752 Martin, Carl and Martin, Christoph
     "Bevölkerung," pp. 348-432 in:
     Landeskunde von Chile
     Hamburg, Friederichsen, 1923

753 Kaufmann, Gabriele
     Ansiedlung und Volksdichte in Chile
     Doctoral dissertation, Heidelberg University
     Heidelberg, 1926

754 Knoche, Walter
     "Chile und die deutsche Auswanderung,"
     Zeitschrift der Geopolitik, 5(1928), 425-432

755 Knoche, Walter
     "Das numerische Verhältniss der Geschlechter in Chile,"
     Zeitschrift der Geopolitik, 5(1928), 502-510

756 Rojas, Omar
     "Chile y su población a través de los censos,"
     Revista Geográfica de Chile, 2(1949), 37-50

757 Butland, Gilbert J.
     "The people," pp. 12-28 in:
     Chile; an outline of its geography, economics and politics
     London, Royal Institute of International Affairs, 1951

758 Börgel, Reynaldo
     "La población en el valle de Nilahue,"
     Informaciones Geográficas (Santiago), 3(1953), 35-39

759 Flôres Silva, Euzébio
     "Comentarios sobre unos mapas de densidade de población de Chile,"
     Revista Geográfica (Pan American Institute of Geography and History),
        16(1955), 89-191

760 Cabello, O.
     "The demography of Chile,"
     Population Studies, 9(1956), 237-250

761 Meza Villalobos, Lilia Ana
     "Población salitrera, segun los censos desde 1907 a 1952,"
     Revista Geográfica de Chile. Terra Australis, Nos. 15-16(1958), 37-40,
        No. 17(1959), 37-54

762 Rojas, Omar
     "Los indígenas de Chile a través de los censos de población,"
     Revista Geográfica de Chile. Terra Australis, No. 18(1960), 170-184

5340: RIO DE LA PLATA NATIONS

763 Deffontaines, Pierre
     "Participation des Pyrénées au peuplement des pays de la Plata,"
        pp. 269-277 in:
     Actes du 1er Congrès International d'Etudes Pyrénées
     Zaragoza, 1952

5350: ARGENTINA

764 Delachaux, Enrique A. S.
     La población de la República Argentina. Su repartición, densidad, y
        ley de crecimiento
     Buenos Aires, Imprenta "Didot" de Félix Lajouane & Co., 1905

765 Schmidt, Wilhelm and Grotewold, Christian
"Bevölkerung," pp. 78-97 in:
Argentinien in geographisches, geschichtliches und wirtschaftliches
Beziehung
Hannover, Hahnsche, 1912

766 Denis, Pierre
"La population," pp. 265-281 in:
La République Argentine
Paris, Colin, 1920

767 Ardissone, Romualdo
"Población aglomerada y dispersa de la Argentina propuesta para el
próximo censo,"
Gaea (Buenos Aires), 2(1927), 456-468

768 Kühn, Franz
"Población," pp. 125-154 in:
Geografía de la Argentina
Barcelona, Editorial Labor, 1930

769 Kühn, Franz
"Demographische Morphologie . . ." pp. 76-91 in:
Grundriss der Kulturgeographie von Argentinien
Hamburg, Friedrichsen, de Gruyter, 1933

770 Ardissone, Romualdo
"La instalación human en las provincias de Buenos Aires y San Juan,"
Revista Geográfica Americana, 10(1938), 177-196

771 Argentina, Ministerio de Hacienda, Dirección General de Estadística de la
Nación
La población y el movimiento demográfico de la República Argentina en
los años 1939 y 1938 y sintesis de años anteriores
Buenos Aires, 1940

772 Daus, Federico A. and García Gache, Roberto
"Distribución de la población argentina por regiones geográficas,"
Revista de Economía Argentina, 44(1945), 294-296

773 Delucia, Sebastian J.
Estudio sobre la distribución geográfica de la población en la
República Argentina
Ministerio de Salud Publica de la Nación, Dirección General de
Estadística y Racionalización. Instituto de la Población, Publicación
No. 7-E-1
Buenos Aires, 1949

774 Daus, Federico A. and García Gache, Roberto
"Distribución geográfica de la población argentina y sus representación
cartográfica," pp. 226-246 in:
Semana de Geografía, 15., Mendoza, 1951
San Juan, 1951

775 García Aller, Arturo H.
"El hombre y el suelo en tres provincias andinas. Estudio del arraigo
rural en la población argentina,"
Anales del Instituto Etnico Nacional, 4(1951), 53-68

775a Gaignard, Romain
     "La montée démographique argentine: le recensement du 30 Septembre
        1960,"
     Cahiers d'Outre-Mer, 14(1961), 85-97

                              5370:   URUGUAY

776 Saint-Jours,
     "L'immigration dans l'Uruguay,"
     Société de Géographie Commerciale de Bordeaux, Bulletin, 31(1908),
        101-103

777 Narancio, Eduardo M. and Capurro Calamet, Federico
     Historia y análisis estadístico de la población del Uruguay
     Facultad de Derecho y Ciencias Sociales, Biblioteca de Publicaciones
        Oficiales, Sec. 3, No. 17
     Montivideo, Peña y Cía., 1939

778 Mädje, Wolfgang
     Uruguay, Volkwerdung und landwirtschaftliche Erschliessung in einem
        überseeischen Einwanderungsland
     Berlin, E. S. Mittler & Sohn, 1941

                              5380:   PARAGUAY

779 Riccardi, Riccardo
     "Carta della densità di popolazione nel Paraguay,"
     BSGI, Serie 6, 12(1935), 391-393

780 Arditi, Nessim
     An essay on the problem of population in Paraguay
     Master's thesis, Southern Illinois University
     Carbondale, 1952

                              5400:   BRAZIL

                            a. Bibliography

781 Mortara, Giorgio
     "Contribuicões do Instituto Brasileiro de Geografia e Estatística
        para os estudos demográficos, 1936-1951,"
     Revista Brasileira de Estatística, 13(1952), 97-106

782 Brazil, Conselho Nacional de Estatistica
     Bibliográfia geográfico-estatística brasileira. Vol. I. 1936/1950
     Rio de Janeiro, 1956

                             b. National

783 Rambaud, Jacques
     "L'émigration italienne au Brésil, d'après les rapports italiens
        récents,"
     AG, 16(1907), 270-274

784 Bürger, Otto
     "Die Bevölkerung," pp. 9-24 in:
     Brasilien: eine Landes- und Wirtschaftskunde für Handel, Industrie und
        Einwanderung
     Leipzig, Dieterich, 1926

785 Freise, F. W.
     "Brasiliens Bevölkerungskapazität,"
     PM, 82(1936), 143-147

786 Domaniewski, Zbigniew
     "Japanische Einwanderung in Brasilien,"
     Zeitschrift für Geopolitik, 14(1937), 25-30

787 Deffontaines, Pierre
     "The origin and growth of the Brazilian network of towns,"
     GR, 28(1938), 377-399

788 Deffontaines, Pierre
     "La population blanche au Brésil," pp. 33-38 in:
     CRCIG, Amsterdam, 1938, Vol. 2

789 Hauser, Henri
     "Notes sur la population noire du Brésil,"
     AG, 47(1938), 509-514

790 Gauld, Charles A.
     "Brazil takes a census,"
     Journal of Geography, 40(1941), 138-144

791 Smith, T. Lynn
     "The growth and redistribution of population in Brazil,"
     Proceedings of the Louisiana Academy of Sciences, 8(1943), 103-114

792 Mortara, Giorgio
     "A população do Brasil,"
     Revista Brasileira de Geografia, 7(1945), 631-648

793 Hehl Neiva, Artur
     "Aspectos geográficos da imigração e colonização do Brasil,"
     Revista Brasileira de Geografia, 9(1947), 249-270

794 Castro, Josue de
     Géographie de la faim. La faim au Brésil
     Paris, Editions Ouvrières, Economie et Humanisme, 1949

795 Borreto, Castro
     "A população brasileira. Formação e evolução,"
     Boletim Geográfico, 11(1953), 32-43

796 Smith, T. Lynn
     Brazil: people and institutions
     Baton Rouge, Louisiana State University Press, 1954

797 Aagesen, Aage
     /"The Japanese population in Brazil,"7 (in Danish)
     Kulturgeografi, 7(1955), 1-8

798   Mortara, Giorgio
      "Distribuição territorial dos japonêses no Brasil,"
      Revista Brasileira de Estatística, 17(1956), 1-4

799   Pfeifer, Gottfried
      "Städtische und ländliche Bevölkerung in Brasilien und die
        Binnenwanderungsbewegungen," pp. 392-402 in:
      Emil Meynen, ed.
      Geographisches Taschenbuch, 1956/57
      Wiesbaden, Franz Steiner, 1956

800   Magnanini, Ruth Lopes da Cruz
      "Densidade de população do Brasil, em 1950,"
      Boletim Geográfico, 15(1957), 69-70

801   Torres, João Batista de Vasconcelos
      Movimentos migratórios das populações rurais brasileiras
      Rio de Janeiro, Freitas Bastos, 1957

802   Accioly Borges, T. Pompeu
      "Migrações internas no Brasil,"
      Boletim Geográfico, 16(1958), 358-376

803   Camargo, José Francisco de
      "Migrações internas e desenvolvimento econômico no Brasil,"
      Boletim Paulista de Geografia, No. 30(1958), 5-12

804   Carvalho, Alceu Vincente W. de
      A população brasileira (estudo e interpretação)
      Rio de Janeiro, Conselho Nacional de Estatística, 1960

                              c. Regional

805   Schurz, W. L.
      "The distribution of population in the Amazon Valley,"
      GR, 15(1925), 206-225

806   Quelle, Otto
      "Die Bevölkerungsbewegungen in Nordostbrasilien: eine anthropo-
        geographische Studie,"
      Geographische Zeitschrift, 35(1929), 408-415

      Also: pp. 10-17 in:
      Festschrift für Alfred Philippson
      Leipzig and Berlin, 1930

807   Deffontaines, Pierre
      "Recherches sur les types de peuplement dans l'état de Saint-Paul
        (Brésil),"
      Association de Géographes Français, Bulletin, 87(1935), 66-71

808   Monbeig, Pierre
      "Colonisation, peuplement, et plantation de cacao dans la sud de l'État
        de Bahia,"
      AG, 46(1937), 278-299

809 Monbeig, Pierre
     "La population de l'Etat de São Paulo, Brésil,"
     AG, 46(1937), 91-94

810 James, Preston E.
     "The changing patterns of population in Sao Paulo State, Brazil,"
     GR, 28(1938), 353-362

811 Ribeiro, Orlando
     "L'immigration dans l'Etat de Saint Paul, Brésil,"
     AG, 48(1939), 520-523

812 Galvani, Luigi
     "Esbôço demográfico do Estado de S. Paulo," pp. 653-679 in:
     Congreso Brasileiro de Geografia, Anais, Vol. 3
     Firianópolis, 1940

813 Monbeig, Pierre
     "A população do Estado de São-Paulo," pp. 103-109 in:
     Ensaios de geografia humana brasileira
     São Paulo, Martins, 1940

814 Fróis Abreu, S.
     "Feições morfológicas e demográficas do Litoral do Espírito Santo,"
     Revista Brasileira de Geografia, 5(1943), 215-234

815 Monbeig, Pierre
     "Comentário em tôrno do mapa da evolução da população do Estado de São
         Paulo entre 1934 e 1940, por município,"
     Associação dos Geógrafos Brasileiros, Boletim, 3(1943), 42-48

816 Monbeig, Pierre
     "Observações relativas à distribuição das densidades de população no
         estado do Ceará,"
     Associação dos Geógrafos Brasileiros, Boletim, 4(1944), 79-84

     Also: pp. 471-512 in:
     Congreso Brasileiro de Geografia, 10., Rio de Janeiro, 1944, Anais,
         Vol. 3
     Rio de Janeiro, 1944

817 Bouchaud Lopes da Cruz, Ruth
     "Distribuição da população no estado do Espírito Santo em 1940,"
     Revista Brasileira de Geografia, 12(1950), 393-412

818 Cavalcanti Bernardes, Lysia M.
     "Distribuição da população no estado do Paraná em 1940,"
     Revista Brasileira de Geografia, 12(1950), 565-582

819 Waibel, Leo
     "European colonization in southern Brazil,"
     GR, 40(1950), 529-547

820 Gonçalves Egler, Eugênia
     "Distribuição da população no Estado do Maranhão em 1940,"
     Revista Brasileira de Geografia, 13(1951), 71-83

821 Gonçalves Egler, Eugênia
     "Distribuição da população no Estado de Minas Gerais em 1940,"
     Revista Brasileira de Geografia, 13(1951), 123-152

822 Strauch, Ney
     "Distribuição da população rural de uma parte do sertão nordestino,"
     Revista Brasileira de Geografia, 13(1951), 480-489

823 Bernardes, Nilo
     "A colonização Européia no Sul do Brasil,"
     Boletim Geográfico, 10(1952), 89-102

824 Carvalho, Eloísa de
     "Densidade da população rural no sudeste do Planalto Central em 1940,"
     Revista Brasileira de Geografia, 14(1952), 203-208

825 Coelho de Sousa, Elza
     "Distribuição da população do Estado do São Paulo, em 1940,"
     Revista Brasileira de Geografia, 14(1952), 317-338

826 Gonçalves Egler, Eugênia
     "Distribuição da população no Estado do Piauí,"
     Revista Brasileira de Geografia, 14(1952), 486-495

827 Guerra, Antônio Teixeira
     A população do território federal do Amapá e a importância das
       atividades econômicas na sua distribuição
     Macapa, Imprensa Oficia, 1952

828 Coelho de Souza Keller, Elza
     "Crescimento da população do Estado do Rio de Janeiro. Comparações
       entre os recenseamentos de 1920 e 1940,"
     Revista Brasileira de Geografia, 15(1953), 165-169

829 Coelho de Souza Keller, Elza
     "Distribuição da população no Estado de Mato Grosso em 1940,"
     Revista Brasileira de Geografia, 15(1953), 123-131, 303-311

830 Silva Lessa, Maria Luisa da
     "Crescimento da população do Estado do Rio Grande do Norte (comparação
       entre os recenseamentos de 1920 e 1940,"
     Revista Brasileira de Geografia, 15(1953), 312-317

831 Silva Lessa, Maria Luisa da
     "Crescimento da população no Estado do Rio Grande do Norte.
       Comparações entre os recenseamentos de 1940 e 1950,"
     Revista Brasileira de Geografia, 15(1953), 132-137

832 Coelho de Souza Keller, Elza
     "Notas sôbre a evolução da população no Estado de São Paulo," pp. 209-
       236 in:
     Aspectos geográficos da Terra Bondeirante
     Rio de Janeiro, Conselho Nacional de Geografia, 1954

833 Filho, O. B.
     "Ecologia e aspectos demográficos do Estado de São Paulo,"
     Boletim Paulista de Geografia, No. 16(1954), 30-44

834 Guerra, Antônio Teixeira
     "Crescimento demográfico . . ." pp. 181-199 in:
     Estudio geográfico do Território do Amapá
     Rio de Janeiro, Conselho Nacional de Geografia, 1954

835 Lessa Curtis, Maria Luiza
     "Distribuição da população no Estado do Ceará em 1950,"
     Revista Brasileira de Geografia, 17(1955), 111-124

836 Strauch, Ney
     "A população e meios de vida," pp. 45-76 in:
     A bacia do Rio Doce; estudio geográfico
     Rio de Janeiro, Instituto Brasileiro de Geografia e Estatística, 1955

837 Guerra, Antônio Teixeira
     "Povoamento e população . . ." pp. 62-78 in:
     Estudio geográfico do Território do Acre
     Rio de Janeiro, Conselho Nacional de Geografia, 1955

838 Waibel, Leo
     Die europäische Kolonisation Südbrasiliens
     Bonn. Universität. Geographisches Institut. Colloquium Geographicum.
     Band 4
     Bonn, Dümmler, 1955

839 Mattos Strauch, Lourdes Manhaés
     "Distribuição da população na Ilha do Governador,"
     Revista Brasileira de Geografia, 17(1955), 65-87, 301-325

840 Santos, Milton
     "A população da Bahia,"
     Boletim Geográfico, 16, No. 146(1958), 622-625

5670: EASTERN HEMISPHERE

841 Beloch, J.
     Die Bevölkerung der griechisch-römischen Welt
     Leipzig, Duncker & Humbolt, 1886

842 Usher, Abbott Payson
     "The history of population and settlement in Eurasia,"
     GR, 20(1930), 110-132

843 Mulder, E. J.
     /Some demographic aspects of Europe and Asia,"_/ (in Dutch)
     K. Nederlandsch Aardrijkskundig Genootschap, Tijdschrift, 65(1948),
     66-88

5700: EUROPE

a. Bibliography

844 United States Bureau of the Census and Library of Congress
     National censuses and vital statistics in Europe: 1918-1939. An
     annotated bibliography
     Washington, 1948

845 United States Bureau of the Census and Library of Congress
     National censuses and vital statistics in Europe: 1940-1948. Supplement
     Washington, 1948

                              b. Population Studies

846 Le Monnier, Fr. R. v.
     "Die Bevölkerung Europas auf Grund die Zählungsepoche 1888-1891,"
     Deutsche Rundschau für Geographie und Statistik, 16(1893), 481-485

847 Lancaster, A.
     "La population d'Europe,"
     Le Mouvement Géographique, 17(1900), 54-58

848 Pasanisi, Fr. M.
     "La popolazione dell'Europa,"
     BSGI, Serie 4, 1(1900), 813-836, 929-956

849 Hasting, J.
     Die Dichte der städtischen Siedlungen in Europa
     Doctoral dissertation, University of Jena
     Berlin, 1909

849a Weise, Ludwig
     Darstellung der Bevölkerungsverteilung in Europa
     Doctoral dissertation, University of Giessen
     Giessen, 1913

850 Sarabon, V.
     "Die Verschiebung der Bevölkerung von Europa im 19. Jahrhundert,"
     Geographische Gesellschaft in Wien, Mitteilungen, 60(1917), 53-64

851 Tamss, Friedrich
     Die Bevölkerung der Erde. Bd. 14: Europa ohne Russland
     Ergänzungsheft Nr. 212 zu Petermanns Geographischen Mitteilungen
     Gotha, Haack, 1931

852 Bogardus, J. G.
     "The population of Europe," pp. 48-61 in:
     Europe: a geographical survey
     New York, Harper, 1934

853 Haliczer, Josef
     "Cartes quantitatives de la population de l'Europe vers 1720, 1820 et
        1930. Situation du centre de gravité du peuplement," pp. 556-570 in:
     CRCIG, Varsovie, 1934, Vol. 3

854 Haliczer, Josef
     "The population of Europe, 1720, 1820, 1930,"
     Geography, 19(1934), 261-273

855 Haliczer, Josef
     "Agglomeration und Verteilung der Bevölkerung in Europa auf Grund einer
        neuer Karte im Masse 1:4,000,000," pp. 167-180 in:
     CRCIG, Amsterdam, 1938, Vol. 2

856 Kulischer, Eugene M.
     The displacement of population in Europe
     Montreal, International Labour Office, 1943

857 Kirk, Dudley
     Europe's population in the interwar years
     League of Nations, 1946

858 Schechtman, Joseph B.
     European population transfers, 1939-1945
     New York, Oxford University Press, 1946

859 Kulischer, Eugene M.
     Europe on the move: war and population changes, 1917-1947
     New York, Columbia University Press, 1948

860 Pinon, René
     "Le déplacement de population en Europe,"
     Revue de Géographie Humaine et d'Ethnologie, 1(1948), 21-32

861 Kiesewetter, Bruno
     "Die europäische Völkerwanderung während des Zweiten Weltkrieges und
        in der Nachkriegzeit,"
     Geographische Rundschau, 3(1951), 55-60

862 Frumkin, Grzegorz
     Population changes in Europe since 1939
     New York, A. Kelley, 1951

863 Sauvy, Alfred
     "La répartition géographique de la population européenne. Peuplement
        rationnel ou historique?"
     Centre Européen Universitaire, 1(1952), 61-80

864 Van Valkenburg, Samuel and Held, Colbert C.
     "Population: problems and distribution," pp. 186-207 in:
     Europe, 2nd ed.
     New York, Wiley, 1952

865 Houston, J. M.
     "The geographical interpretation of population data," pp. 218-241 in:
     A social geography of Europe
     London, Duckworth, 1953

866 Horstmann, Kurt
     "Der Binnenwanderung in den Ländern Europas,"
     Raumforschung und Raumordnung, 13(1955), 193-202

867 Sorre, Maximilien
     "La mosaïque ethnique européenne,"
     Geographia (Paris), Nos. 50 and 51(1955), 16-28

868 Gottmann, Jean
     "Expansion urbaine et mouvements de population,"
     Research Group for European Migration Problems, Bulletin, 5(1957),
        53-60

869 Ogilvie, Alan G.
     "Population," pp. 230-251 in:
     Europe and its borderlands
     Edinburgh, Nelson, 1957

870   Velikonja, Joseph
      "Postwar population movements in Europe,"
      AAAG, 48(1958), 458-472

871   Cicchitti-Suriani, Arnaldo
      "I Musulmani in Europa (1959),"
      L'Universo, 40(1960), 679-708

      (Also see 431, 2504)

                          5720: WESTERN EUROPE

872   Beaujeu-Garnier, Jacqueline
      "L'occupation humaine," "Le développement humain," and "L'expansion
         humaine," pp. 180-242 in:
      Jacqueline Beaujeu-Garnier and A. Guilcher
      L'Europe du Nord et du Nord-Ouest. Tome premier. Généralités physiques
         et humaines
      Paris, Presses Universitaires de France, 1958

873   L'Institut Catholique de Recherches Socio-Ecclésiales, La Haye
      Etude cartographique de la structure économique et démographique de
         l'Europe Occidentale
      Assen, Van Gorcum & Co., 1959

873a Kormoss, I. B. F.
      Les communautés européennes; essai d'une carte de densité de la
         population dressée à l'échelle de 1:1.000.000e pour la Communauté
         Européenne de l'Energie Atomique (Euratom)
      Les Cahiers de Bruges, Recherches Européennes
      Bruges, Collège d'Europe, 1959

                          5740: GREAT BRITAIN

                          a. National

874   Bellet, Daniel
      "La population de la Grand-Bretagne,"
      Revue de Géographie, 33(1893), 18-24, 95-101, 191-196

875   Lavagne, Paul
      "Répartition de la population en Angleterre au cours du XIXe siècle,"
      Revue de Géographie, 49(1901), 548-601

876   Robert, Elie
      "La densité de la population en Bretagne calculée par zones d'égal
         éloignement de la mer,"
      AG, 13(1904), 296-309

877   Fawcett, C. B.
      "British conurbations in 1921,"
      Sociological Review, 14(1922), 111-122

878   Hosgood, B.
      "Post-war migration from Britain,"
      SGM, 40(1924), 282-293

879 Dickinson, Robert E.
       "Some new features of the growth and distribution of population in
          England and Wales,"
       GR, 22(1932), 279-295

880 Fawcett, C. B.
       "The distribution of urban population in Great Britain in 1931,"
       GJ, 129(1932), 100-116

881 Fussell, G. A.
       "English countryside and population in the Eighteenth Century,"
       EG, 12(1936), 294-310, 411-430

882 Sölch, Johannes
       "Der 'Zug nach dem Süden' in Grossbritannien,"
       Geographischen Gesellschaft in Wien, Mitteilungen, 80(1937), 179-193

883 Arden-Close, Charles
       "Centres of population of England and Wales and some other central
          points,"
       Geography, 29(1944), 38-40

884 Smailes, Arthur E.
       "The urban mesh in England and Wales,"
       Institute of British Geographers, Transactions, No. 11(1946), 87-101

885 Stevens, Arthur J.
       "The distribution of rural population in Great Britain,"
       Institute of British Geographers, Transactions, No. 11(1946), 23-53

886 Smith, Clifford T.
       "The movement of population in England and Wales in 1851 and 1861,"
       GJ, 117(1951), 200-210

887 Gilbert, Edmund W.
       "English conurbations in the 1951 Census,"
       GJ, 118(1952), 64-88

888 Vince, Stanley W. E.
       "Reflections of the structure and distribution of rural population
          in England and Wales, 1921-31,"
       Institute of British Geographers, Publications, No. 18(1952), 53-76

889 Willatts, Edward C. and Newsom, Marion G. C.
       "The geographical pattern of population changes in England and Wales,
          1921-1951,"
       GJ, 119(1953), 431-454

890 Osborne, Richard H.
       "Internal migration in England and Wales, 1951,"
       Advancement of Science, 12(1956), 424-434

891 Brzenk, Eleanor T.
       The distribution of Polish immigrants in Great Britain
       Doctoral dissertation, Northwestern University
       Evanston, 1957

892 Thomas, J. Gareth
       "Distribution of Welsh-born population in England, 1951,"
       Geography, 42(1957), 250-253

893 Kosiński, Leszek
     /"Poles in Great Britain,"/ (in Polish)
     Czasopismo Geograficzne, 29(1958), 441-442

894 Lawton, Richard
     "Irish immigration to England and Wales in the mid-nineteenth century,"
     Irish Geography, 4(1959), 35-54

895 Clarke, John I.
     "Rural and urban sex-ratios in England and Wales,"
     TESG, 51(1960), 29-38

896 Osborne, R. H.
     "The 'drift south' in Britain continues,"
     TESG, 51(1960), 286-289

896a Osborne, Richard H.
     "Population changes in England and Wales, 1951-1961,"
     East Midland geographer, 2, No. 15(1961), 41-50

     (Also see 184)

                              b.   Regional

                          5750:   England

897 Fleure, Herbert J. and Whitehouse, W. E.
     "Early distribution and valleyward movement of population in south
        Britain,"
     Archaeologia Cambrensis, 16(1916), 101-140

898 Hutchinson, Grace E.
     "Population and parishes in the Ravensbourne and Darent Basins,"
     Geographical Teacher, 11, No. 50(1921), 63-72

899 King, H.
     "The distribution of population in south-west Lanchashire, its social
        significance,"
     Journal of the Manchester Geographical Society, 39(1923-24), 137-144

900 Redmill, C. E.
     "The growth of population in the East Warwickshire Coalfield,"
     Geography, 16(1931), 125-140

901 Dunlop, Margaret
     "The demography of south-east Lancastria," pp. 145-152 in:
     CRCIG, Amsterdam, 1938, Vol. 2

902 Smailes, Arthur E.
     "Population changes in the colliery districts of Northumberland and
        Durham,"
     GJ, 91(1938), 220-232

903 Couzens, F. C.
     "Distribution of population of the Mid-Derwent Basin since the
        Industrial Revolution,"
     Geography, 26(1941), 31-38

904 Smith, Wilfrid
     The distribution of population and the location of industry on
          Merseyside
     London, University Press, 1942

905 Darby, Henry C.
     "The movement of population to and from Cambridgeshire between 1851
          and 1861,"
     GJ, 101(1943), 118-125

906 Pounds, Norman J. G.
     "Population movement in Cornwall and the rise of mining in the 18th
          Century,"
     Geography, 28(1943), 37-46

907 Bainbridge, T. H.
     "Cumberland population movements 1871-81,"
     GJ, 108(1946), 80-84

908 Constant, A.
     "The geographical background of inter-village population movements in
          Northamptonshire and Huntingdonshire, 1754-1943,"
     Geography, 33(1948), 78-88

909 Dury, George H.
     "The population of Guernsey; an essay in historical geography,"
     Geography, 33(1948), 61-69

910 Grytzell, K. C.
     /"Movements of population within the London district, 1801-1911,"7
          (in Swedish)
     Svensk Geografisk Årsbok, 24(1948), 133-170

911 Bainbridge, T. H.
     "Population changes over the West Cumberland coalfield,"
     EG, 25(1949), 128-133

912 Wise, Michael J.
     "Some notes on the growth of population in the Cannock Chase coal-
          field,"
     Geography, 36(1951), 235-248

913 Osborne, Richard H.
     "Population concentrations and conurban tendencies in the Middle Trent
          counties,"
     East Midland Geographer, 2(1954), 30-37

914 Powell, Arthur G.
     "The 1951 Census: an analysis of population changes in Derbyshire,"
     East Midland Geographer, 2(1954), 13-23

915 Osborne, Richard H.
     "Inter-county migration in south-eastern Great Britain,"
     Geography, 40(1955), 47-48

916 Powell, Arthur G.
     "The 1951 Census. (2) An analysis of population changes in Leicester-
          shire,"
     East Midland Geographer, 3(1955), 3-16

917 Powell, Arthur G.
     "The 1951 Census: (3) An analysis of population changes in Nottingham-
         shire,"
     East Midland Geographer, 4(1955), 29-42

918 McIntosh, N. A.
     "Changing population distributions in the Cart Basin in eighteenth and
         early nineteenth centuries,"
     Institute of British Geographers, Transactions and Papers, 22(1956),
         139-157

919 Hooson, David J. M.
     "The recent growth of population and industry in Hertfordshire,"
     Institute of British Geographers, Transactions, 1958, 197-208

920 Lawton, Richard
     "Population movements in the West Midlands, 1841-61,"
     GJ, 124(1958), 164-176

921 House, John W.
     North Eastern England; population movements and the landscape since the
         early 19th Century
     University of Durham, King's College, Department of Geography, Research
         Series, No. 1
     Newcastle upon Tyne, 1959

922 Morley, C. D.
     "Population of Northampton and the Ise Valley, 1801-1951,"
     East Midland Geographer, 11(1959), 20-30

923 Mills, Dennis R.
     "The Poor Laws and the distribution of population c. 1600-1800, with
         special reference to Lincolnshire,"
     Institute of British Geographers, Publications, 26(1959), 185-195

                              5760: Wales

924 Trueman, A. E.
     "Population changes in the eastern part of the South Wales coalfield,"
     GJ, 53(1919), 410-419

925 Carter, Harold
     "Population changes in Wales, 1931-1951,"
     Geography, 41(1956), 126-129

926 Carter, Harold and Thomas, J. Gareth
     "Population and language," pp. 230-263 in:
     E. G. Bowen, ed.
     Wales; a physical, historical and regional geography
     London, Methuen, 1957

     (Also see 892)

5770: Scotland

927 Cossar, James
     "The distribution of the towns and villages of Scotland,"
     SGM, 26(1910), 183-191, 298-319

928 Chisholm, G. G.
     "Density of population, Scotland 1911,"
     SGM, 27(1911), 466-470

929 Richardson, Ralph
     "Italian emigration to Scotland,"
     SGM, 29(1913), 580-585

930 Dennery, E.
     "L'émigration ecossaise depuis la guerre,"
     AG, 35(1926), 126-143

931 Crowe, Percy R.
     "The population of the Scottish lowlands,"
     SGM, 43(1927), 147-167

932 O'Dell, Andrew C.
     "The population of Scotland 1755-1931, a general survey,"
     SGM, 48(1932), 282-290

933 Ross, W. C. A.
     "Highland emigration,"
     SGM, 50(1934), 155-166

934 Mathieson, J.
     "The tragedy of the Scottish Highlands,"
     SGM, 54(1938), 257-263

935 Snodgrass, Katherine P.
     "The density of agricultural population in Scotland with English and
         European comparisons,"
     GJ, 97(1941), 236-246

936 Snodgrass, Katherine P.
     "Recent population changes in Scotland,"
     SGM, 60(1944), 33-38

937 Hance, William Adams
     The Outer Hebrides in relation to highland depopulation
     Doctoral dissertation, Columbia University
     New York, 1949

938 Learmouth, Andrew T. A.
     "The population of Skye,"
     SGM, 66(1950), 77-103

939 Walton, Kermeth
     "The distribution of population in Aberdeenshire, 1696,"
     SGM, 66(1950), 17-76

940 O'Dell, Andrew C.
     "Population and natural resources,"
     SGM, 68(1952), 49-56

941 Barclay, R. S. and Darling, F. Fraser
     "Population," pp. 69-152 in:
     West Highland survey; an essay in human ecology
     Oxford, Oxford University Press, 1955

942 Dewdney, John C.
     "Change in the population distribution in the County of Fife, 1755-
        1951,"
     SGM, 71(1955), 27-42

943 Osborne, Richard H.
     "Scottish migration statistics: a note,"
     SGM, 72(1956), 153-159

944 Osborne, Richard H.
     "The movements of people in Scotland, 1851-1951,"
     Scottish Studies, 2(1958), 1-46

945 Rae, Gordon and Brown, Charles E.
     "Population," pp. 81-86 in:
     A geography of Scotland; general and regional
     London, Bell, 1959

946 Gailey, Robert A.
     "Settlement and population in Kintyre, 1750-1800,"
     SGM, 76(1960), 99-107

946a Proudfoot, V. Bruce and Vaughan, T. D.
     "Changes in settlement and population in Northern Ireland, 1835-1860,"
     Ulster Folklife, 5(1959), 20-26

5790: Northern Ireland

947 Vaughan, T. D.
     "Population changes in Northern Ireland,"
     Geography, 45(1960), 214-217

5780: EIRE

948 Thomas, E. Gwyn
     "Some demographic problems of the Irish Free State,"
     Geography 20(1935), 28-37

949 Freeman, Thomas W.
     "Migration movements and the distribution of population in Eire,"
     Journal of the Statistical and Social Inquiry Society of Ireland, 1939

950 Freeman, Thomas W.
     "The changing distribution of population in Donegal, with special
        reference to the congested areas,"
     Journal of the Statistical and Social Inquiry Society of Ireland, 1940

951 Freeman, Thomas W.
     "The changing distribution of population in Kerry and West Cork,"
     Journal of the Statistical and Social Inquiry Society of Ireland, 1942

952 Freeman, Thomas W.
     "The changing distribution of population in County Mayo,"
     Journal of the Statistical and Social Inquiry Society of Ireland, 1943

953 Freeman, Thomas W.
     "The congested districts of western Ireland,"
     GR, 33(1943), 1-14

954 Connell, K. H.
     The population of Ireland, 1750-1845
     Oxford, Clarendon Press, 1950

955 Blume, Helmut
     "Some geographical aspects of the Palatine settlement in Ireland,"
     Irish Geography, 2(1952), 172-179

956 Flatrés, Pierre
     "L'évolution de la population irlandaise,"
     Annales de Bretagne, 69(1953), 133-137

957 Davies, Gordon L.
     "Population changes in the Republic of Ireland, 1951-6,"
     Geography, 41(1956), 263-265

958 Leister, Ingeborg
     "Ursachen und Auswirkungen der Entvölkerung von Eire zwischen 1841 und
        1951,"
     Erdkunde, 10(1956), 54-68

959 Bouman, F. J.
     /"The Irish population problem,"/ (in Dutch)
     TESG, 48(1957), 14-20

960 Freeman, Thomas W.
     "Population and emigration," pp. 13-50 in:
     Pre-famine Ireland; a study in historical geography
     Manchester, Manchester University Press, 1957

961 Nygard, Knud
     /"The depopulation of Eire since 1845,"/ (in Danish)
     Kulturgeografi, No. 57(1958), 39-46

962 Gailey, Robert A.
     "Settlement and population in the Aran Islands,"
     Irish Geography, 4(1959), 65-78

963 Cousens, S. H.
     "The regional pattern of emigration during the Great Irish Famine,
        1846-51,"
     Institute of British Geographers, Publications, 28(1960), 119-134

964 Freeman, Thomas W.
     "Population," pp. 118-145 in:
     Ireland; a general and regional geography
     London, Methuen, 1960

     (Also see 894, 2506)

5830:   FRANCE

a.   National

965   Noirit, J.
      "Population de la France,"
      Société de Géographie Commerciale de Bordeaux, Bulletin, 15(1893), 86-87,
         97-107, 129-153

966   Milhaud, Albert
      "La densité de la population française en 1801, 1846, 1896,"
      AG, 7(1898), 172-177

967   Barré, Henri
      "La répartition des centres de dépopulation et d'infécondité dans la
         France métropolitaine,"
      Société de Géographie et d'Etudes Coloniales de Marseilles, Bulletin,
         31(1907), 5-31

968   Neukirch, Karl
      "Frankreichs Bevölkerung im Jahre 1906,"
      Geographische Zeitschrift, 13(1907), 584-592

969   Maurette, F.
      "La population de la France au début du 20e siècle,"
      AG, 18(1909), 125-140

970   Zimmermann, Maurice
      "La population de la France en 1921,"
      AG, 31(1922), 37-51

971   Demangeon, Albert and Matrechot, M.
      "Les variations de la population de la France de 1881 à 1921,"
      AG, 35(1926), 499-510

972   Gargas, S.
      /"Polish immigration in France,"/ (in Dutch)
      TEG, 17(1926), 134-137

973   Mauco, Georges
      "Les étrangers dans les campagnes françaises. Propriétaires, fermiers
         et métauers établis en France,"
      AG, 35(1926), 97-125

974   Sorre, Maximilien
      "L'immigration étrangère en France, spécialement dans la region du
         Nord,"
      Société de Géographie de Lille, Bulletin, 69(1927), 111-117

975   Zimmermann, Maurice
      "La population de France d'après le recensement du 7 mars 1926,"
      AG, 36(1927), 328-335

976   Larnaude, Marcel
      "L'émigration temporaire des indigènes algériens dans la métropole,"
      Revue de Géographie Marocaine, 7(1928), 45-51

977 Du Bus, Charles
     Démocartographie de la France. I. Des origines à nos jours
     Paris, Alcan, 1931

978 Weber, E.
     "Die Bevölkerungsbewegung in Frankreich 1801-1926, ihre Ursachen und
         Folgen,"
     PM, 77(1931), 237-243

979 Cholley, André
     "La population de la France en 1931,"
     AG, 41(1932), 638-640

980 Granger, Ernest
     "Les hommes," pp. 165-227 in:
     La France; son visage, son peuple, ses ressources
     Paris, Fayard, 1932

981 Mauco, Georges
     "Remarques sur le mouvement de la population en France depuis le
         début du 19e siècle,"
     AG, 44(1935), 371-384

982 Hartke, Wolfgang
     "Die Ergebnisse der französischen Volkszählung 1936,"
     Zeitschrift für Erdkunde, 5(1937), 490-494

983 Soulas, Jean
     "Conurbations françaises,"
     AG, 48(1939), 466-471

984 Fish, W. B.
     "Population trends in France,"
     Geography, 25(1940), 107-120

985 Chatelain, Abel
     "Démogéographie du grand tronc ferré Sudest: Paris-Lyon-Méditerranée,
     Etudes Rhodaniennes, Nos. 1-4(1947), 35-82

986 Nussbaum, Fritz
     "Bevölkerungsprobleme Frankreichs,"
     Geographica Helvetica, 3(1948), 110-113

987 Gachon, Lucien
     "Les démographies comparées de trois regions hercyniennes: l'Ouest,
         le Massif Central, les Vosges," pp. 307-327 in:
     Université de Renne, Cinquantième Anniversaire du Laboratoire de
         Géographie (1902-1952), Volume Jubilaire
     Rennes, 1952

988 Sluka, A. E.
     /"Principal features of the geography of population migrations in
         France,"/ (in Russian)
     Voprosy Geografii, 29(1952), 225-246

989 Chabot, Georges
     Les migrations intérieures de population provoquées par les mariages
     Clermont-Ferrand, Arbos, 1953

990 Pitié, --
     "Un fait géographique méconnu: le surpeuplement rural,"
     Poitiers, Université, Faculté des Lettres, Institut de Géographie,
        Groupe Poitedin d'Etudes Géographiques, Bulletin, 6(1953), 1-10

991 Nougier, Louis-René
     "Essai sur le peuplement préhistorique de la France,"
     Population, 9(1954), 241-274

992 Chatelain, Abel
     "La répartition de la richesse des populations en France,"
     Revue de Géographie de Lyon, 30(1955), 291-308

993 Gachon, Lucien
     "La disparité démographique de la France en Europe,"
     Revue de Geographie de Lyon, 31(1956), 209-213

994 Perrin, Nadine
     "La répartition géographique de la population française et
        l'aménagement du territoire,"
     Population, 11(1956), 701-724

995 Balseinte, Raymond
     "Note sur la population française vivant dans les communes dont le
        chef-lieu est situé entre 900 et 2000 mètres d'altitude,"
     RGA, 45(1957), 155-170

996 Balseinte, Raymond
     "Valeurs approchées de l'indice de vitalité démographiques des
        départements français et des principales agglomerations urbaines
        pour l'année 1954,"
     RGA, 47(1959), 61-79

997 Chatelain, Abel
     "La géographie des salaires en France et son incidence sur les
        migrations de population,"
     Revue de Géographie de Lyon, 35(1960), 381-393

     (Also see 306, 1525)

                              b. Regional

                      1. Western France and Brittany

998 Robert, Elie
     "Essai sur la densité et répartition de la population dans la
        presqu'île de Crozon,"
     Annales de Bretagne, 19(1903-04), 99-108

999 Sion, Jules
     "La population actuelle," pp. 432-466 in:
     Les paysans de la Normandie orientale; étude géographique
     Paris, Colin, 1909

1000 Potet, E.
      "L'émigration Vendéenne dans le Bassin Aquitaine,"
      AG, 21(1912), 265-268

1001 Châtaigneau, Yves
      "L'émigration Vendéenne,"
      AG, 26(1917), 423-438

1002 Musset, René
      "La population," pp. 438-464 in:
      Le Bas-Maine: étude géographique
      Paris, Colin, 1917

1003 Fish, W. B.
      Les mouvements de population en Basse-Normandie, 1821-1936
      Doctoral dissertation, University of Paris
      Alencon, Alençonnaise, 1940

1004 Meynier, André
      "Les déplacements de population vers la Bretagne en 1939-40,"
      Annales de Bretagne, 55(1948), 129-155

1005 Le Lannou, Maurice
      "La population bretonne," pp. 373-402 in:
      Géographie de la Bretagne. Tome II. Economie et population
      Rennes, Plihon, 1952

1006 Chatelain, Abel
      "Evolution des densités de population en Anjou, 1806-1936,"
      Revue de Géographie de Lyon, 31(1956), 43-60

1007 Suret-Canale, J.
      "L'évolution démographique récente du Bas-Maine,"
      Association de Géographes Français, Bulletin, Nos. 261-262 (1956),
          195-201

                        2. Northern France

1008 Demangeon, Albert
      "La population," pp. 399-418 in:
      La Picardie et les régions voisines
      Paris, Colin, 1905

1009 Blanchard, Raoul
      La densité de population du département du Nord au XIXe siècle
      Annexe au Bulletin de Société de Géographie de Lille, Vol. 45
      Lille, 1906

1010 Hartke, Wolfgang
      "Die Ausländer in Nord-Frankreich,"
      PM, 79(1933), 6-8

1011 Haubold, Siegfried
      "Das Bevölkerungsbild Nordfrankreichs,"
      Zeitschrift für Erdkunde, 11(1943), 31-38

1012 Sevrin, Robert
      "Les échanges de population à la frontière entre la France et le
      Tournaisie,"
      AG, 58(1949), 237-244

                        3. North-Central France

1013 Mocquery, Charles
      "Le mouvement de la population de la Côte-d'Or de 1852 à 1897,"
      Société Bourguignonne de Géographie et d'Histoire, Mémoires, 16(1900),
      1-30

1014 Levainville, J.
      "La population," pp. 260-282 in:
      Le Morvan; étude de géographie humaine
      Paris, Colin, 1909

1015 Mauve, E.
      "Variations de la population dans le département de l'Allier 1836 à
      1926,"
      AG, 36(1927), 361-363

1016 Korzybski, St.
      "Les fluctuations numériques de la population rurale du Bassin
      Parisien au cours des XIXème et XXème siècles. Recherches sur
      la délimitation des homogènes," pp. 53-60 in:
      CRCIG, Varsovie, 1934, Vol. 4

1017 Brunet, M. P.
      "Essai sur le peuplement de la Brie,"
      Association de Géographes Français, Bulletin, Nos. 237-238(1953),
      161-169

1018 Grosbois, R.
      "La densité de la population dans les pays de brandes du département
      de la Vienne en 1846 et en 1946,"
      Norois, 2(1955), 209-222

                        4. Eastern France

1019 Kellen, T.
      "Die Bevölkerungsverhältnisse in Elsass-Lotheringen,"
      Globus, 67(1895), 237-241

1020 Neukirch, Karl
      Studien über die Darstellbarkeit der Volksdichte mit besonderer
      Rücksichtnahme auf den elsässischen Wasgau
      Doctoral dissertation, University of Freiburg
      Braunschweig, Scholz, 1897

1021 Andriot, E.
      "Répartition de la population dans l'arrondissement de Lunéville
      d'après le relief, la nature du sol, le culture, les industries,"
      Société de Géographie de l'Est, Bulletin, 20(1898), 409-437

1022   Schmid, Friedrich
       "Die geographische und wirtschaftliche Bedeutung des Waldes und seine
       Rückwirkung auf die Volksdichte unter besonderer Berücksichtigung
       der Verhältnisse im Oberelsass,"
       Gesellschaft für Erdkunde und Kolonialwesen zu Strassburg,
       Mitteilungen, 3(1912), 1-81

1023   Crusius, E.
       Die Veränderungen der Volksdichte in den lothringischen Kreisen Forbach
       und Saargemünd 1801-1910
       Doctoral dissertation, University of Strassburg
       Metz, 1913

1024   Vidal de la Blache, P.
       "Evolution de la population en Alsace-Lorraine et dans les départe-
       ments limitrophes,"
       AG, 25(1916), 97-115, 161-180

1025   Baulig, Henri
       "La population de l'Alsace et de la Lorraine en 1921,"
       AG, 32(1923), 12-25

1026   Schmitt, Alphonse
       La population du département de la Meuse depuis le début du XIXe
       siècle.   Etude de géographie humaine
       Annales de L'Est, 42-43
       Nancy, 1929

1027   Chenet, Ct.
       Le sol et les populations de la Lorraine et de Ardennes
       Paris, Champion, 1949

1028   Juillard, Etienne
       "La rupture de l'équilibre démographique," pp. 297-330 in:
       La vie rurale dans la plaine de Basse-Alsace; essai de géographie
       sociale
       Strassbourg, Roux, 1953

1029   Juillard, Etienne
       Géographie d'une population.   Le département du Bas-Rhin
       Institut des Hautes Etudes Alsaciennes, Publications, No. 11
       Strassbourg, 1954

                          5.   Southwestern France

1030   Capot-Rey, B.
       "La dépopulation dans le Lot-et-Garonne (canton de Porte-Sainte-
       Maries),"
       AG, 28(1919), 64-70

1031   Richard, Marcelle
       "La dépopulation dans l'arrondissement de Dax,"
       Revue de Géographie Commerciale (Société de Géographie Commerciale de
       Bordeaux), 51(1927), 1-10

1032   Van Aartsen, J. P.
       /"Depopulation in the southwest of France,"/ (in Dutch)
       TEG, 23(1932), 90-92

1033 Kendall, Henry M.
      "Notes on the population of France, with special reference to the
        population of the Aquitain Basin,"
      Papers of the Michigan Academy of Science, Arts and Letters, 22(1937),
        373-384

1034 Pinède, Christiane
      "Les migrations temporaires en Quercy,"
      Revue Géographique des Pyrénées et du Sud-Ouest, 27(1956), 122-134

1035 Toujas-Pinède, Christiane
      "Une émigration de survivance: les Vendéens en Aquitaine,"
      Revue Géographique des Pyrénées et du Sud-Ouest, 31(1960), 399-423

1036 Pinède, Christiane
      "L'immigration bretonne en Aquitaine,"
      Revue Géographique des Pyrénées de du Sud-Ouest, 31(1960), 5-43

                          6. Massif Central

1037 Savey-Casard, --
      "Le peuplement dans les Monts du Lyonnais," pp. 18-33 in:
      Société de Géographie de Lyon et Région Lyonnaise, B. Session 1927-
        1928
      Lyon, 1928

1038 Epinat, J.
      "Le mouvement de la population dans l'arrondissement de Montbrisson
        de 1821 à 1926,"
      RGA, 17(1929), 659-746

1039 Vaganay, H.
      "Le mouvement de la population dans le bassin du Gier au XIXe et au
        XXe siècle,"
      Les Etudes Rhodaniennes, 5(1929), 41-62

1040 Marres, Paul
      "L'émigration caussenarde,"
      Société Languedocienne de Géographie, Bulletin, n.s. 1, fasc. 1(1930),
        41-51

1041 Marres, Paul
      "Les phénomènes démographiques," pp. 387-409 in:
      Les Grands Causses: étude de géographie physique et humaine. Tome II.
        Le labeur humain
      Tours, Arrault, 1935

1041a Perrin, M.
      La population dans la région de Saint-Etienne. Etude de géographie
        humaine
      Tours, Arrault, 1937

1042 Gachon, Lucien
      "La population," pp. 243-282 in:
      Les Limagnes du sud et leurs bordures montagneuses; étude de géographie
        physique et humain
      Tours, Arrault, 1938

1043   Arbos, Ph.
       "La population, l'habitat," pp. 83-105 in:
       L'Auvergne
       Paris, Colin, 1945

1044   Guiot, Paul
       Thurins: démogéographie d'une commune rurale de l'ouest Lyonnais
       Cahiers de la Fondation Nationale des Sciences Politiques, 10
       Paris, Colin, 1949

1045   Estienne, Pierre
       "Les problèmes du surpeuplement rural; l'exemple de la Combraille,"
       RGA, 38(1950), 301-334

1046   Gachon, Lucien
       "Récentes déprises et reprises humaines sur les massifs anciens du
          Centre de la France. L'exemple du Livraois,"
       RGA, 40(1952), 265-290

1047   Estienne, Pierre
       "Les populations de la Combraille,"
       RGA, 43(1955), 757-791

1048   Chatelain, Abel
       "La formation de la population lyonnaise. Les courants de migrations
          au milieu de XXe siècle d'après le fichier électoral,"
       Revue de Géographie de Lyon, 3(1956), 199-208

1049   Estienne, Pierre
       "Un demi-siècle de dépeuplement dans le Massif Central,"
       RGA, 44(1956), 463-472

1050   Bozon, Pierre
       "La population de la Cévenne vivaroise,"
       RGA, 46(1958), 683-715

1051   Estienne, Pierre
       "L'émigration contemporaine dans la montagne auvergnante et vellave,"
       RGA, 46(1958), 463-493

1052   Caralp, Raymonde
       "Une problème de population dans le Massif-Central: les agglomera-
          tions ferroviaires,"
       Revue de Géographie de Lyon, 34(1959), 235-254

1053   Carron, M.-A.
       "Evolution démographiques récente de trois cantons de la 'Montagne'
          limousine,"
       Association de l'Association de Géographes Française, Bulletin,
          Nos. 294-295(1960), 169-185

7. Pyrenees and Midi

1054   Sorre, Maximilien
       "La répartition des populations dans le Bas-Languedoc,"
       Société Languedocienne de Géographie, Bulletin, 29(1906), 237-278,
          364-387

1055 Barré, Henri
      "La répartition des originaires des Bouches-du-Rhône dans les autres
      départementes,"
      Société de Géographie et d'Etudes Coloniales de Marseilles, 32(1908),
      297-302

1056 Callon, G.
      "Le mouvement de la population dans le département des Bouches-du-
      Rhône au cours de la periode 1821-1920 et depuis la fin de cette
      période,"
      Société de Géographie et d'Etudes Coloniales de Marseilles, 51(1930),
      1-35

1057 Delaruelle, F.
      "La population sur les plateaux lauraguais et toulousains,"
      Revue Géographique des Pyrénées et du Sud-Ouest, 1(1930), 98-120

1058 Boyer, Armand
      "Migrations saisonnières dans le canton de Burzet (Ardeèche),"
      RGA, 20(1932), 341-360

1059 Cavailles, H.
      "De l'Afrique du Nord aux Pyrénées,"
      Revue Géographique des Pyrénées et du Sud-Ouest, 3(1932), 379-381

1060 Marres, Paul
      "La population du Bas-Languedoc et du Roussillon,"
      Société Languedocienne de Géographie, Bulletin, 2e série, 3(1932),
      42-47

1061 Goron, L.
      "Les migrations saisonnières dans les départements pyrénées au début
      de XIXe siècle,"
      Revue Géographique de Pyrénnés et du Sud-Ouest, 4(1933), 230-272

1062 Chabillier, C.
      "La population du Gard, étude démographique,"
      Société Languedocienne de Géographie, Bulletin, 2e série, 5, fasc.
      4(1934)

1063 Sion, Jules
      "La population," pp. 158-173 in:
      La France méditerranéenne
      Paris, Colin, 1934

1064 Gallon, G.
      "Le mouvement de la population dans le département de l'Hérault au
      cours de la période 1821-1920 et depuis la fin de cette période,"
      Société de Géographie de Toulouse, Bulletin, 54(1935), 29-31

1065 George, Pierre
      "Le peuplement," pp. 283-301 in:
      La région de Bas Rhône; étude de géographie régionale
      Paris, Baillière, 1935

1066 Appolis, Emile
      "La densité de la population dans le diocèse de Lodève à la fin de
      l'ancien régime,"
      Société Languedocienne de Géographie, Bulletin, 2e série, 8(1937),
      132-139

1067 George, Pierre
      "Etude du peuplement et de l'habitat rural. Essai de représentation
      cartographique de la répartition de la population dans une région
      française, la région Montpellieraine," pp. 85-90 in:
      CRCIG, Amsterdam, 1938, Vol. 2

      Also: Association de Géographes Français, Bulletin, No. 111(1938),
      36-41

1068 Chatelain, Abel
      "Influence de l'apport étranger sur les densités de population du
      Midi Méditerraneen,"
      Etudes Rhodaniennes, 21(1946), 5-32

1069 George, Pierre
      "Structure agraire et problème démographique dans la Vallée d'Aspe
      (Basses-Pyrénées)," pp. 91-100 in:
      Dépeuplement et peuplement rationnel
      Institut National d'Etudes Démographiques, Travaux et Documents, No. 8
      Paris, 1949

1070 Lesenne, Gisèlle
      "Le dépeuplement des vallées d'Argelès, d'Azun et de Cauterets: ses
      causes et ses conséquences,"
      Revue Géographique des Pyrénées et du Sud-Ouest, 27(1956), 135-160

                        8. Southeastern France

1071 Barré, Henri
      "La répartition de la population sur le sol de la Provence,"
      Société de Géographie de Marseille, Bulletin, 26(1902), 260-272

1072 Legaret, Georges
      "Répartition et mode de groupement des populations dans le Jura
      Central et Méridional,"
      Société de Géographie de Lyon, Bulletin, 19(1904), 253-271, 20(1905),
      42-54, 115-128, 215-231, 301-313, 21(1906), 31-49

1073 Moisson, Paul
      "Mouvement de la population du département des Hautes-Alpes au XIXe
      siècle,"
      La Géographie, 20(1909), 111-116

1074 Thomas, Louis J.
      "L'émigration temporaire dans le Bas-Languedoc et le Roussillon au
      commencement du XIXe siècle,"
      Société Languedocienne de Géographie, Bulletin, 33(1910), 301-308

1075 Robert, Jean
      "La densité de population des Alpes françaises d'après le dénombre-
      ment de 1911,"
      RGA, 8(1920), 5-124

1076 Letonnelier, Gaston
      "L'émigration des Savoyards,"
      RGA, 8(1920), 541-584

1077   Blanchard, Raoul
       "Migrations alpines,"
       AG, 31(1922), 308-312

1078   Mouralis, Denis
       "L'émigration alpine en France,"
       RGA, 11(1923), 223-240

1079   Blanchard, Raoul
       "Le peuplement," pp. 83-94 in:
       Les alpes françaises
       Paris, Colin, 1925

1080   Provence, Marcel
       "La dépopulation rurale de la Provence,"
       Société de Géographie et Etudes Coloniales de Marseille, Bulletin,
          14(1925), 36-41

1081   Gex, François
       "La population de la Savoie, de 1921 à 1926,"
       RGA, 16(1928), 221-250

1082   Letonnelier, Gaston
       "Les étrangers dans le département de l'Isère,"
       RGA, 16(1928), 697-743

1083   Allix, André
       "La population," pp. 739-818 in:
       L'Oisans; étude géographique
       Paris, Colin, 1929

1084   Allix, André
       "Anciennes émigrations dauphinoises,"
       RGA, 20(1932), 121-126

1085   Hartke, Wolfgang
       "Die Ausländer in Südost-Frankreich,"
       PM, 80(1934), 52-53

1086   Souchon, Louis
       "Dépeuplement et économie d'une région de la Haute-Provence: le pays
          de l'Asse,"
       Société de Géographie et d'Etudes Coloniales de Marseille, Bulletin,
          58(1937), 33-63

1087   Mejean, P.
       "Phénomènes démographiques dans le Diois,"
       RGA, 26(1938), 195-206

1088   Masson, Paul
       "La répartition de la population en Provence et son évolution,"
       France, Ministère de l'Education Nationale, Bulletin de la Section
          de Géographie, 53(1939), 67-92

1089   Chatelain, Abel
       "Peuplement et population du Valromey,"
       Etudes Rhodaniennes, 16(1940-41), 119-139

1090 Chatelain, Abel
      "Les densités de population dans le Jura méridional,"
      Etudes Rhodaniennes, 17(1942), 41-60

1091 Onde, Henri
      "Les mouvements de la population en Maurienne et en Tarentaise,"
      RGA, 30(1942), 365-411

1092 Exertier, Odette
      "La population rurale du Val du Bourget au cours des 200 dernières
          années,"
      RGA, 32(1944), 487-497

1093 Guichonnet, P.
      "L'émigration saisonnière en Faucigny pendant la première moitié du
          XIXe siècle, 1783-1860,"
      RGA, 33(1945), 465-534

1094 Veyret-Verner, Germaine and Vincent, Paulette
      "Etude démographique du Haut-Dauphiné septentrional au XIXe siécle,"
      RGA, 34(1946), 333-354

1095 Bravard, M.
      "L'émigration récente en France de quelques hautes communes du
          Briançonnais,"
      RGA, 35(1947), 747-758

1096 Cachon, Lucien and Estienne, Pierre
      "L'étude de la dépopulation en montagne et de ses enseignements
          récents,"
      RGA, 35(1947), 367-378

1097 Chatelain, Abel
      "Un type de migration temporaire actuelle: la migration viagère,"
      Annales; Economies, Sociétés, Civilisations, 2(1947), 411-416

1098 Pfister, Maurice
      "Quelques pyramides d'âge en Dauphiné,"
      RGA, 35(1947), 111-118

1099 Chatelain, Abel
      'Méthodes d'enquêtes démographiques dans la région lyonnaise,"
      Etudes Rhodaniennes, 23(1948), 121-125

1100 Guichonnet, P.
      "L'émigration alpine vers les pays de langue allemande,"
      RGA, 36(1948), 533-576

1101 Chatelain, Abel
      "Les migrations temporaires anciennes à Lyon et dans les pays
          environnantes,"
      Etudes Rhodaniennes, 24(1949), 37-50

1102 Veyret-Verner, Germaine
      "Le problème de l'équilibre démographique en montagne,"
      RGA, 37(1949), 331-342

1103 Roux, E.
      "L'émigration récente en France des communes du Haut Embrunais,"
      RGA, 38(1950), 679-688

1104 Serre, Maxime
      "Problèmes démographiques d'hier et d'aujourdhui. Notes sur
      l'immigration italienne à Toulon et sans le Var,"
      RGA, 40(1952), 643-667

1105 Veyret-Verner, Germaine
      "L'évolution de la population du département de l'Isère (1936-1954).
      Enseignements pour un aménagement éventuel du territoire,"
      RGA, 43(1954), 655-662

1106 Acher, Gilbert
      "L'évolution du peuplement dans le département des Alpes-Maritimes,"
      RGA, 44(1956), 497-522

1107 Blanchard, Raoul
      "Les problèmes du peuplement," pp. 519-588 in:
      Les Alpes occidentales. Tome septième. Essai d'une synthèse
      Paris, Arthaud, 1956

1108 Bravard, Yves
      "L'arrêt du dépeuplement des Alpes du Sud,"
      RGA, 44(1956), 355-369

1109 Estrangin, Louis
      "La population agricole du département des Alpes-Maritimes,"
      Bulletin de Géographie d'Aix-Marseille, N.s., 67(1956), 41-56

1110 Bravard, Yves
      "La continuation de l'exode montagnarde: vers la fin de Puget-
      Rostang (Alpes-Maritimes),"
      RGA, 44(1958), 167-179

1111 Bernard, E. M.
      "Structures démographiques comparées du départements de l'Isère, de
      l'agglomération grenoblaise et de la France,"
      RGA, 45(1957), 407-411

1112 Bravard, Yves
      "Sondages à propos de l'émigration dans les Alpes du Nord,"
      RGA, 45(1957), 91-113

1113 Chatelain, Abel
      "Des migrations viagères aux migrations définitives au milieu du
      XXe siècle, d'après le fichier électoral,"
      Revue de Géographie de Lyon, 32(1957), 187-200

1114 Veyret-Verner, Germaine
      "Quelques principes de démographie alpine et d'économie alpine,"
      RGA, 46(1958), 21-46

1115 Corbel, J.
      "La région du Pôle et ses habitants,"
      Revue de Géographie de Lyon, 34(1959), 241-262

1116   Perrot, Jean
       "Essai d'analyse démographique par zone homogènes dans le cadre du
          département de l'Isère,"
       RGA, 47(1959), 51-59

1117   Bravard, Yves
       "Le dépeuplement des hautes vallées des Alpes-Maritimes. Ses
          caractères et ses conséquences démographiques, économiques et
          sociales,"
       RGA, 49(1961), 5-128

                            9. Corsica

1118   Anfossi, G.
       "Recherches sur la distribution de la population en Corse,"
       Recueil des Travaux de l'Institut de Géographie Alpine, Université de
          Grenoble, 6(1918), 71-135

1119   Lefèbvre, Paul
       "La population de la Corse,"
       RGA, 45(1957), 557-577

                        5990: LOW COUNTRIES

1120   Leyden, Friedrich
       Die Volksdichte in Belgien, Luxemburg und den Niederlanden in ihrer
          Verteilung nach den einzelnen Gemeinden und in ihren Beziehungen zur
          Wohndichte und zur Häuserdichte in den drei Staaten
       Ergänzungsheft Nr. 204 zu Petermanns Geographischen Mitteilungen
       Gotha, 1929

1121   Michotte, P. L. and Vent, P. C. de
       "Population in relation to resources in Belgium and Holland,"
       SGM, 54(1938), 96-108

                        5997: NETHERLANDS

1122   Kuyper, J.
       /"The density of population in the Netherlands,"7 (in Dutch)
       K. Nederlandsch Aardrijkskundig Genootschap, Tijdschrift, 15(1898,
          149-153

1123   Kuyper, J.
       /"A sketch of the Netherlands population,"7 (in Dutch)
       K. Nederlandsch Aardrijkskundig Genootschap, Tijdschrift, 16(1899),
          619-636

1124   Ramaer, J. C.
       /"Centers of population in the Netherlands past and present,"7 (in
          Dutch)
       K. Nederlandsch Aardrijkskundig Genootschap, Tijdschrift, 38(1921),
          1-38, 174-215

107   Netherlands

1125   Van Lohuizen, Ir. Th. K.
       /"Concentration and decentralization. Population change in the
       provinces of Holland and Utrecht and their urban influences,"/
       (in Dutch)
       TEG, 15(1925), 344-350

1126   Van Hinte, E.
       /"The world population problem in the light of certain measures
       applied in the Netherlands,"/ (in Dutch)
       TEG, 20(1929), 301-308

1127   Bogardus, J. F.
       "The population of the Netherlands,"
       EG, 8(1932), 43-52

1128   Vent, P. C. de
       "Les Pays-Bas sont-ils surpeuplés?" pp. 588-595 in:
       CRCIG, Varsovie, 1934, Vol. 3

1129   Holwerda, A. O.
       /"The growth of population in the Netherlands and, in particular, in
       Amsterdam, 's-Gravenhage, and Rotterdam,"/ (in Dutch)
       TEG, 26(1935), 25-30

1130   Broek, A. J. P. van den
       "La population des Pay-Bas,"
       K. Nederlandsch Aardrijkskundig Genootschap, Tijdschrift, N.s. 4(1938),
       537-696

       Also: pp. 51-64 in:
       CRCIG, Amsterdam, 1938, Vol. 2

1131   Vooys, Adriaan C. de
       /"Some notes on the population problem in Zeeland,"/ (in Dutch)
       K. Nederlandsch Aardrijkskundig Genootschap, Tijdschrift, 58(1941),
       883-891

1132   Hofstee, E. W.
       /"The census of agriculture and population; some remarks on the
       statistics of our agricultural population,"/ (in Dutch)
       TEG, 33(1942), 29-40

1133   Steigenga, Willem
       /"Some observations on population increase in the Netherlands country-
       side,"/ (in Dutch)
       TEG, 34(1943), 113-122

1134   Roemen, H. C. W.
       /"Emigration from Limbourg to overseas countries from 1851 to 1877,"/
       (in Dutch)
       TEG, 37(1946), 372-376

1135   Roemen, H. C. W.
       /"Population structures in the municipalities of Limburg, their
       statistical observation and their significance as demographic
       data,"/ (in Dutch)
       TEG, 37(1946), 175-184

1136   Keuning, H. J.
       /"The effacement of frontiers. Labor migration across the Netherlands-
          Belgian frontier,"/ (in Dutch)
       TESG, 39(1948), 441-447

1137   Steigenga, Willem
       /"An analysis of population movements between the two World Wars.
          Provisional results,"/ (in Dutch)
       TESG, 39(1948), 408-425

1138   Angenot, L. H. J.
       /"Population increase and geographical expansion,"/ (in Dutch)
       De Economist, 97(1949), 84-104

1139   Hofstee, E. W.
       /"The function of international migration,"/ (in Dutch)
       TESG, 40(1949), 10-22

1140   Netherlands, Rijksdienst voor het Nationale Plan
       /The distribution of population in the Netherlands, I. Statement of
          the problem/ (in Dutch)
       Publicatie, No. 3
       's Gravenhage, 1949

1141   Perks, W. A. G.
       /"Modifications in migrational currents,"/ (in Dutch)
       TESG, 42(1951), 118-227

1142   Groenman, Sjoerd
       "L'asséchement du Zuyderzée et le problème de la population aux Pays-
          Bas,"
       Population, 7(1952), 661-674

1143   Vooys, Adriaan C. de
       /"The distribution of the population in the Dutch countryside in
          1622-1795,"/ (in Dutch)
       K. Nederlandsch Aardrijkskundig Genootschap, Tijdschrift, 70(1953),
          316-330

1144   Steigenga, Willem
       /"The problem of regional population prediction,"/ (in Dutch)
       TESG, 23(1954), 80-88

1145   Hamming, Edward
       "People--Holland's most important export,"
       Journal of Geography, 58(1959), 380-385

1146   Jong, P. de
       /"Population development in the western part of the Netherlands since
          1950,"/ (in Dutch)
       TESG, 51(1960), 638-643

       Also see 335-336, 427

6010: BELGIUM

1147 Blanchard, Raoul
      "Le problème de la surpopulation," pp. 475-519 in:
      La Flandre; étude géographique
      Paris, Colin, 1906

1148 Boutry, Léon
      "La population de l'Ardenne,"
      AG, 29(1920), 119-210

1149 Lefévre, Marguerite A.
      "Carte régionale du peuplement de la Belgique,"
      La Géographie, 36(1921), 1-94

1150 Lefévre, Marguerite A.
      "La densité des maisons rurales en Belgique,"
      AG, 32(1923), 398

1151 Michotte, P. L.
      "La Belgique est-elle surpeuplée?" pp. 572-587 in:
      CRCIG, Varsovie, 1934, Vol. 3

1152 Kendall, Henry M.
      "A survey of population changes in Belgium,"
      AAAG, 28(1938), 145-164

1153 Kendall, Henry M.
      "A map of the distribution of population in Belgium. Part 1. The
         Province of Luxembourg,"
      Papers of the Michigan Academy of Science, Arts and Letters, 24(1939),
         25-28

1154 Mertens, C.
      La répartition de la population sur le territoire belge. Etude de
         démographie sociale
      Bruxelles, Larcier, 1946

1155 Strenger, Jean
      "L'évolution démographique à l'époque contemporaine,"
      Société Royale Belge de Géographie, Bulletin, 72(1948), 89-120

1156 Milone, Ferdinando
      "Il carbone e l'emigrazione italiana in Belgio,"
      BSGI, Serie 8, 2(1949), 103-123

1157 Monkhouse, Francis J.
      "Population and settlement," pp. 196-232 in:
      The Belgian Kempenland
      Liverpool, Liverpool University Press, 1949

1158 Tulippe, Omer
      "Le vieillissement de la population belge; étude régionale,"
      Société Belge d'Etudes Géographiques, Bulletin, 21(1952), 233-257

1159 Nicolai, Henri
      "Observations sur la population rurale de la Belgique,"
      Société Royale Belge de Géographie, Bulletin, 76(1952), 59-78

1160 Alexandre, S. and Alexandre, J.
      "Les migrations définitives et alternantes dans les régions voisines
      de la région industrielle liégoise,"
      Cercle des Géographes Liégeois, Travaux, No. 95(1955), 311-317

1161 Michel Andrée
      "L'immigration algerienne en Moselle,"
      AG, 65(1956), 341-361

1162 Alexandre, J.
      Etudes sur la population des régions industrielles liégeoise et
        hutoise
      Cercle des Géographes Liégeois, Travaux, No. 121
      Liège, 1957

      Also: Centre d'Etudes et de Documentation Social de la Province de
        Liège, Bulletin Mensuel, Jan.-Feb., 1957, 3-21

1163 Smet, Lucien de
      "La Belgique: population et démographie," pp. 20-35 in:
      Federation Belge des Géographes Professeurs de l'Enseignement Moyen,
        Normal et Technique
      Semaine Internationale de Géographie, Bruxelles, 1958
      Ghent, 1959

1164 Uhlig, Harald
      "Belgien: Entwicklung, Struktur und räumliche Gliederung seiner
        Bevölkerung," pp. 373-389 in:
      Geographisches Taschenbuch; Jahrweiser zur Deutschen Landeskunde,
        1958-59 (Stuttgart)
      Wiesbaden, Steiner, 1959

      (Also see 1136)

                          6020: LUXEMBOURG

1165 Edwards, Kenneth C.
      "The relation between urban and rural settlement in the Grand Duchy
        of Luxemburg," pp. 153-159 in:
      CRCIG, Amsterdam, 1938, Vol. 2

                          6040: SWITZERLAND

1166 Studer, Th.
      "Ueber die Bevölkerung der Schweiz,"
      Geographische Gesellschaft, Bern, Jahresbericht, 13(1891), 3-13

1167 Zemmrich, Johannes
      "Verbreitung und Bewegung der Deutschen in der französischen schweiz,"
      Forschungen zur Deutschen Landes- und Volkskunde, 8(1894), 361-405

1168 Zahler, H.
      "Die Bevölkerung der Schweiz,"
      Zeitschrift für Schulgeographie, Wien, 24(1903), 272-282

111   Switzerland

1169   Zivier, Heinrich
       "Die Verteilung der Bevölkerung im Oberrheingebiet nach ihrer Dichte.
       Ein Beitrag zur Anthropogeographie des Kantons Graubünden,"
       Geographische Gesellschaft, Bern, Jahresbericht, 18(1903), 129-167

1170   Montbas, Hughes de
       Le peuplement des Alpes Suisses. Sa répartition et ses limites
          d'altitude
       Société Fribourgeoise des Sciences Naturelles, Mémoires: Géologie et
          Géographie, 8, fasc. 3
       Freiburg, Fragnière, 1919

1171   Nussbaum, Fritz
       "Die Volksdichte des Kantons Bern, nebst Bemerkungen über die
          Darstellung der Volksdichte in der Schweiz,"
       Geographische Gesellschaft, Bern, Jahresbericht, 25(1919-22), 117-153

1172   Leemann, Walter
       "Uber Bevölkerungsbewegung und Abwanderung im Val Tavetsch,"
       Schweizer Geograph, 7(1930), 70-72, 81-85

1173   Früh, J.
       "Die Bevölkerung," pp. 664-751 in:
       Geographie der Schweiz, Vol. 2
       St. Gallen, Zollikofer, 1932

1174   Nussbaum, Fritz
       "Die Bevölkerungsbewegung in der Schweiz nach den Ergebnissen der
          letzten Volkszählung dargestellt,"
       Schweizer Geograph, 9(1932), 1-15, 33-44

1175   Kundig, Werner
       "Der hypsometrische Aufbau des Areals und der Bevölkerungsdichte der
          Schweiz,"
       Schweizer Geograph, 12(1935), 113-128

1176   Gschwend, Max
       "Wanderungsprobleme im Verzasca-Tal (Tessin),"
       Schweizer Geograph, 22(1945), 81-96

1177   Laubscher, Otto
       Die Entwicklung der Bevölkerung im Berner Jura inbesondere seit 1850
       Weinfelden, Neuenschwander, 1945

1178   Vogel, Hermann E.
       "L'émigration suisse hors d'Europe, 1919 à 1939,"
       Geographica Helvetica, 3(1948), 1-103

1179   Siegfried, André
       "The Swiss people," pp. 33-67 in:
       Switzerland; a democratic way of life
       London, Jonathan Cape, 1950

1180   Mayer, Kurt B.
       The population of Switzerland
       New York, Columbia University Press, 1952

1181 Tricart, Jean
      "Contribution à l'étude géographique de la population de la Suisse,"
      L'Information Géographique, 16(1952), 137-143

1182 Rousseau, R.
      "Les Suisses dans le canton de St. Julien-en-Genevois: étude sta-
          tistique,"
      Association de Géographes Français, Bulletin, Jan.-Feb., 1953, 38-51

1183 Winkler, Ernst
      "Zur Wirtschafts- und Bevölkerungsstruktur der Schweiz," pp. 349-355
          in:
      Geographisches Taschenbuch, 1954/55
      Wiesbaden, Steiner, 1955

1184 Kündig, Werner
      "Fläche, Bevölkerung und Dichte der schweizerischen Gemeinden; eine
          statistische Charakteristik,"
      Geographica Helvetica, 12(1957), 41-43

1185 Lobsiger, Georges
      "L'accroissement de la population du canton de Genève; causes et
          conséquences,"
      Le Globe, 99(1959), 27-64

                          6080: GERMANY

                          a. National

1186 Auerbach, Bertrand
      "La répartition géographique de la population sur le sol allemande,"
      AG, 5(1895), 59-71

1187 Wegemann, G.
      "Der Bevölkerungsschwerpunkt des Deutschen Reiches,"
      PM, 49(1903), 210-212

1188 Schlüter, Otto
      "Beiträge zur Bevölkerungs- und Siedlungsgeographie Deutschlands,"
      PM, 56(1910), 7-10, 64-67

1189 Clozier, René
      "Le développement démographique et la production agricole de
          l'Allemagne,"
      La Géographie, 45(1926), 176-178

1190 Gees, H.
      Das Verhältniss von Bevölkerung und Nahrungsspielraum in Deutschland
          vor dem Kriege und in der Gegenwart
      Doctoral dissertation, University of Berlin
      Berlin, 1930

1191 Witt, Werner
      "Innerdeutsche Bevölkerungswanderungen in den Jahren 1910-1925,"
      Erde und Wirtschaft, 5(1931), 115-120

1192 Sölch, Johannes
      "Raum und Zahl: Die Zukunftsfrage des deutschen Volkes,"
      Geographische Zeitschrift, 29(1933), 40-42

1193 Olbricht, Konrad
      "Die Gross- und Mittelstädte des deutschen Raumes zu Beginn des
      Dreissigjähren Krieges,"
      Zeitschrift für Erdkunde, 6(1938), 482-490

1194 Riccardi, Mario
      "Alcuni dati sulle variazioni della poplazione delle principali città
      delle Germania tra il 1939 e il 1946,"
      BSGI, Serie 8, 2(1949), 317-321

1195 Myers, Paul F. and Mauldin, W. Parker
      Population of the Federal Republic of Germany and West Berlin
      United States Bureau of the Census, International Population Sta-
      tistics Reports, Series P-90, No. 1
      Washington, 1952

1196 Dickinson, Robert E.
      "The distribution of population," pp. 106-122 in:
      Germany: a general and regional geography
      New York, Dutton, 1953

1197 Harris, Chauncy D. and Wülker, Gabriele
      "The refugee problem of Germany,"
      EG, 29(1953), 10-25

1198 Nellner, Werner
      "Verteilung der Vertriebenen und Bevölkerungsausgleich im Bundes-
      gebiet,"
      Raumforschung und Raumordnung, 13, No. 2(1955), 77-84

1199 Mellor, Roy E. H.
      "The German refugee problem: ten years retrospect,"
      SGM, 73(1957), 1-18

1200 Meynen, Emil
      "Bevölkerungsdichte der Bundesrepublik Deutschland nach naturräum-
      lichen Einheiten," pp. 312-333 in:
      Geographisches Taschenbuch, 1956/57
      Wiesbaden, Steiner, 1957

1201 Chtutser, N. P.
      /"Concerning changes in the population geography of Germany during
      the period 1939-1955 (on the basis of an analysis of population
      density),"/ (in Russian)
      Geograficheskoe Obshchestvo, S.S.S.R., Izvestiia, 90(1958), 373-381

      (Also see 109, 300, 321, 420, 694, 754, 1019, 1020, 1022, 1023, 1024,
      1768, 2273, 2274, 2288, 2403.)

b. Regional

6090: Eastern Germany

1202 Klinger, Ludwig
      "Verteilung und Zunahme der Bevölkerung im Thüringerwald nach
      Höhenstufen,"
      Geographsiche Gesellschaft zu Jena, Mitteilungen, 9(1890), 112-149

1203 Kaesemacher, C.
      "Die Volksdichte der Thüringisches Triasmulde,"
      Forschungen zur Deutschen Landes- und Volkskunde, 6(1892), 167-226

1204 Buschick, Richard A. G.
      Die Abhängigkeit der verschiedenen Bevölkerungsdichtigkeiten der
      Königreichs Sachsen von den geographischen Bedingungen
      Verein für Erdkunde zu Leipzig, Veröffentlichen
      Leipzig, 1895

1205 Früchtenicht, Hugo
      "Die Volksdichte im Herzogtum Anhalt nach der Volkszählung vom
      2. Dezember 1895,"
      Verein für Erdkunde zu Halle a. S., Mitteilungen, 1897, 64-74

1206 Goetze, Fritz
      Bevölkerungsdichtigkeit und Bevölkerungsverschiebung im erzgebirg-
      ischen Industriegebiet dargestellt nach den Volkszählungen von
      1858 und 1900
      Doctoral dissertation, University of Kiel
      Hannover, Schrader, 1905

1207 Elsheimer, Ernst
      Volksdichte und Siedelungen im Meissnerlande
      Doctoral dissertation, University of Marburg
      Kiel, Lüdtke & Martens, 1907

1208 Fränzel, Ernst
      "Der Einfluss der Sommerfrischen auf Volksdichte und Verkehr im
      nordwestlichen Teile des Thüringer Waldes,"
      Geographische Gesellschaft zu Jena, Mitteilungen, 26(1908), 1-31

1209 Priester, Hermann
      "Bevölkerungsbewegung Mecklenburgs im 19. Jahrhundert,"
      Geographische Gesellschaft zu Rostock, Mitteilungen, 7(1910), 39-43

1210 Vogel, R.
      "Die Bevölkerungsverschiebung in der Halle-Leipziger Tieflandsbucht
      1871-1905,"
      Verein für Erdkunde, Dresden, Mitteilungen, N.s., 1(1926), 10-93

1211 Udem, E.
      "Die Siedlungsdichte in Mecklenberg-Schwerin,"
      Geographischen Gesellschaft in Rostock, Mitteilungen, 22-23(1930-32),
      81-120

1212 Körner, Fritz
      "Die Beziehungen der Bevölkerungsnahme 1870-1910 zur Verkehrslage
      in den Ortschaften des Kreises Roda-Jena,"
      Geographische Gesellschaft in Jena, Mitteilungen, 39(1931), 26-36

1213 Künzel, W.
      "Die Methode der räumlichen Gruppenbildung am Beispiel einer neuen
      Volksdichtekarte von Sachsen,"
      Leipzig, Universität, Verein der Geographen, Mitteilungen, 10-11
      (1932), 37-42

1214 Würzburger, H.
      Die Volksdichte des Regierungsbezirkes Magdeburg nach der Zählung
      1925 und ihre Entwicklung seit 1867
      Doctoral dissertation, University of Halle
      Leipzig, Fock, 1932

1215 Flohn, Hermann
      "Die Volksdichte typischer ostdeutscher Landschaften in ihren
      Beziehungen zu Besitzverteilung, Bodengüte und Volkstum,"
      Geographischer Anzeiger, 36(1935), 245-249

1215a Dreschler, A.
      Die Bevölkerungsdichte von Ost-Thüringen
      Doctoral dissertation, University of Jena
      Zeulenroda, 1936

1216 Stollt, Oskar
      "Betrachtungen zu einer Karte der Bevölkerungsverteilung in
      Thüringen,"
      Geographischer Anzeiger, 43(1942), 413-420

1217 Brüning, Kurt
      "Bevölkerungszahl und Ernahrungskraft des Landes Niedersachsen.
      Eine wirtschaftsgeographisch-ernährungsphyiologische Methode
      zur Beurteilung der Tragfähigkeit eines Landes,"
      Neues Archiv für Niedersachsen, No. 7/9(1953), 314-331

1218 Zastrow, Elsa
      "Bevölkerungsentwicklung und Lebenshaltung 1950-1955 in der
      Sowjetzone Deutschlands,"
      Geographische Rundschau (Zürich), 8(1956), 475-479

1219 Körner, Fritz
      "Die Bevölkerungsverteilung in Thüringen am Ausgang des 16. Jahr-
      hunderts,"
      Wissenschaftliche Veröffentlichungen des Deutschen Instituts für
      Länderkunde, N.F., 15-16(1958), 178-315

                    6300: Western and Northern Germany

1220 Wolff, Eduard Heinrich
      Die Verbreitung der Bevölkerung im Harz
      Doctoral dissertation, University of Halle
      Halle, 1893

1221 Damköhler, Eduard
      "Die Bevölkerung des Harzgebietes,"
      Verein für Erdkunde zu Halle a.S., 1894, 35-44

1222 Ambrosius, Ernst
      "Die Volksdichte am deutschen Niederrhein,"
      Forschungen zur Deutschen Landes- und Volkskunde, 12(1900), 153-267

1123 Bergmann, Karl
"Die Volksdichte der grossherzoglich hessischen Provinz Starkenburg auf
Grund der Volkszählung vom 2. Dezember 1895,"
Forschungen zur Deutschen Landes- und Volkskunde, 12(1900), 293-364

1224 Krausmüller, Georg
"Die Volksdichte der Grossherzoglich Hessischen Provinz Oberhessen auf
Grund der Volkszählung vom 2. Dezember 1895,"
Geographische Mitteilungen aus Hessen, 1-2(1900), 5-102

1225 Thiele, Otto
"Die Volksverdichtung im Regierungsbezirk Aurich,"
Forschungen zu Deutschen Landes- und Volkskunde, 13(1901), 361-426

1226 Krause, Robert
Volksdichte und Siedlungsverhältnisse der Insel Rügen
Doctoral dissertation, University of Leipzig
Greisswald, Abel, 1903

Also: Geographische Gesellschaft zu Greisswald, Jahresberichte,
8(1904), 37-110

1227 Wagner, Eduard
"Die Bevölkerungsdichte in Südhannover und deren Ursachen,"
Forschungen zu Deutschen Landes- und Volkskunde, 14(1903), 517-675

1228 Zörb, Karl
"Die Volksdichte der Grossherzoglich Hessischen Provinz Rheinhessen
auf Grund der Volkszählung vom 1. Dezember 1900,"
Geographische Mitteilungen aus Hessen, 3(1903), 116-166

1229 Schmidt, Johannes
"Die Volksdichte im Kreise Melsungen und die sie hauptsächlich
bedingenden Faktoren,"
Verein für Naturkunde, Kassel, Abhandlungen und Bericht, 51(1907), 48-125

1230 Stracke, Albert
Die Bevölkerungsverhältnisse des Fürstentums Waldeck auf agrargeschicht-
licher Grundlage
Doctoral dissertation, University of Berlin
Marburg, Koch, 1907

1231 Fricke, A.
Die Bevölkerungsentwicklung in den Regierungsbezirken Cassel und
Wiesbaden zwischen 1885 und 1905, mit besonderer Berücksichtigung
der Wanderungen und ihrer wirtschaftlichen Grundlagen
Doctoral dissertation, University of Giessen
Giessen, 1910

1232 Closterhalfen, K.
"Die polnische Bevölkerung in Rheinland und Westfalen,"
Die Erde, 10(1911), 114-120

1233 Sievers, Max
Die Bevölkerungs- und Siedelungsverhältnisse der Lünenberger Südheide,
mit besonderer Berücksichtigung der letzten 40 Jahre
Doctoral dissertation, University of Marburg
Marburg, 1911

1234 Krückemeyer, Ernst
      Die Volksdichte im Weserberglande (westlich der Weser) um die Jahrhunder-
      tende
      Doctoral dissertation, University of Giessen
      Giessen, Kindt, 1912

1235 Smend, Oswald
      Die Volksdichte zwischen Wiehengebirge und Osning
      Doctoral dissertation, University of Münster
      Münster, 1912

1236 Gäde, K.
      Zur Kenntnis der Volksdichte des nordöstlichen Holstein und des Kreises
      Eckernförde
      Doctoral dissertation, University of Kiel
      Kiel, 1913

1237 Böhmer, U.
      Die Volksdichte des Knüllgebietes. Ein Beitrag zur Anthropogeographie
      Hessens
      Doctoral dissertation, University of Rostock
      Rostock, 1919

1238 Fickert, Herman
      Die Bevölkerungsdichtigkeit der Rheinprovinz im Umfange von 1914
      Doctoral dissertation, University of Halle
      Halle, 1919

1239 Fickert, Herman
      "Eine neue Volksdichtekarte der Rheinprovinz nach der Gemarkungsmethode,"
      PM, 66(1920), 159-161

1239a Greim, Georg
      "Die Verteilung der Bevölkerung in Hessen 1919,"
      PM, 71(1925), 12-14

1240 Assmann, L.
      Die Volksdichte in den kulturgeographischen Einheinten der deutschen
      Mittelgebirgsschwelle
      Doctoral dissertation, University of Berlin
      Berlin, 1930

1241 Knirim, E.
      Die Verschiebungen der Volksdichte im engeren westfälischen Ruhrgebiet
      von 1818 bis 1925 und ihre geographischen Grundlagen
      Doctoral dissertation, University of Münster
      Münster, 1930

1242 Witt, Werner
      "Darstellung der Volksdichte in Nord- und Mitteldeutschland 1925,"
      PM 77(1931), 281-285

1243 Hess, G.
      Die Bevölkerung der Provinz Oberhessen und deren berufliche Gliederung,
      dargestellt in ihrer Entwicklung während der letzten 150 Jahre
      Giessen, Universität, Anstalt für Hessische Landesforschung, Arbeiten, 10
      Giessen, 1932

1244 Willems, F.
      Die geographische und wirtschaftlichen Grundlagen der Volksdichte und
      Volksdichteverschiebungen im Regierungsbezirk Aachen von 1825-1925
      Aachen, La Ruelle, 1934

1245 Böhler, J.
      "Die Bevölkerungsverhältnisse in der Pfalz und Rheinhessen mit Rand-
      gebieten," pp. 231-238 in:
      Festschrift Hundertjahrfeier des Vereins für Geographie und Statistik
      zu Frankfurt
      Frankfurt, 1936

1246 Holthaus, F.
      Bevölkerungsentwicklung und Bevölkerungsbewegung Oldenburgs 1886-1935
      Doctoral dissertation, University of Köln
      Köln, 1937

1247 Krebs, Norbert
      "Bevölkerungsverlagerungen in Nord- und Mitteldeutschland 1920 bis
      1930,"
      Deutsche Geographische Blätter, 42(1938), 15-23

1248 Kupferschmidt, F.
      "Zur Bevölkerungsentwicklung in Mitteldeutschland,"
      Leipzig, Deutsches Institut für Länderkunde, Wissenschaftliche
      Veröffentlichungen, N.s., 5(1938), 3-28

1249 Stollt, Oskar
      Verteilung und Entwicklung der Bevölkerung in Schleswig-Holstein
      Doctoral dissertation, University of Greisswald
      Götersloh, 1938

1250 Uekötter, H.
      Die Bevölkerungsbewegung in Westfalen und Lippe 1818-1933
      Münster, Geographische Kommission für Westfalen, Arbeiten, 5
      Münster, 1941

1251 Klöpper, Rudolf
      "Die Bevölkerungsentwicklung in den Ostfriesischen Marschen,"
      Deutsche Geographische Blätter, 45(1949), 37-77

1252 Hahn, Helmut
      Der Einfluss der Konfessionen auf die Bevölkerungs- und Sozial-
      geographie des Hunsrücks
      Bonner Geographische Abhandlungen, No. 4
      Bonn, 1950

1253 Kollnig, Karl R.
      Wanderungen im Bevölkerungsbild des pfälzischen Oberrheingebietes
      Heidelberger Veröffentlichungen zur Landesgeschichte und Landeskunde,
      Heidelberg, C. Winter, 1952

1254 Kuhlmann, Martin
      Bevölkerungsgeographie des Landes Lippe
      Forschungen zur Deutschen Landeskunde, Band 76
      Remagen, Verlag der Bundenanstalt für Landeskunde, 1954

1255 Schwind, Martin
      "Bevölkerungsdichte und Bevölkerungsverteilung in Schleswig, 1800-
      1950,"
      Berichte zur Deutschen Landeskunde, 13(1954), 32-43

1256 Reekers, S.
      Westfalens Bevölkerung 1818-1955. Die Bevölkerungsentwicklung der
      Gemeinden und Kreise im Zahlenbild
      Münster i.W., Achendorffsche Verlagsbuch, 1956

                        6410:   Southern Germany

1257 Neumann, Ludwig
      "Die Volksdichte im Grossherzogtum Baden. Eine anthropogeographische
      Untersuchung,"
      Forschungen zur Deutschen Landes- und Volkskunde, 7(1893), H. 1

1258 Neumann, Ludwig
      Die Veränderungen der Volksdichte im Südlichen Schwarzwalde 1852-1895
      Freiburg, Moler, 1896

1259 Uhlig, Carl
      Die Veränderungen der Volksdichte im nördlichen Baden von 1852 bis 1895
      Doctoral dissertation, University of Freiburg
      Stuttgart, Engelhorn, 1898

1260 Kiefer, Albert
      Die Veränderungen der Volksdichtigkeit im Königreich Bayern von 1840
      bis 1895
      Doctoral dissertation, University of Erlangen
      Leipzig, Günther & Müller, 1902

1261 Bleisteiner, Georg
      Bevölkerungsdichte in Nord- und Mittelschwaben
      Doctoral dissertation, University of Erlangen
      Augsburg, Rackl & Lochner, 1908

1262 Reinhardt, Wilhelm
      "Volksdichte und Siedlungsverhältnisse des württembergischen Ober-
      schwabens,"
      Forschungen zur Deutschen Landes- und Volkskunde, 17(1908), 417-435

1263 Krebs, Norbert
      "Die Verteilung der Bevölkerung Süddeutschlands auf geographische
      Einheiten,"
      Gesellschaft fur Erdkunde zu Berlin, Zeitschrift, 1923, 180-187

1264 Metz, Friedrich
      "Das Oberrheinland als Ein- und Auswanderungsgebiet," pp. 222-237 in:
      Verhandlungen, Deutscher Geographischer Tag, Karlsruhe 1927
      Berlin, 1928

1265 Gradmann, Robert
      "Bevölkerungszahl und Volksdichte," pp. 196-203 in:
      Süddeutschland
      Stuttgart, Engelhorn, 1931

1266 Wolter, Elizabeth
      Die Bevölkerungsverteilung in den einzelnen Landschaften Württembergs
        von 1834-1925. Ein Beitrag zur Bevölkerungs- und Wirtschaftsgeo-
        graphie
      Stuttgarter Geographische Studien, 41-42
      Stuttgart, Fleischbauer und Spohn, 1934

1267 Büttner, Karl
      Die Auswanderung aus Württemberg. Ein Beitrag zur Bevölkerungs-
        geographie Württembergs
      Stuttgarter Geographische Studien, 64-65
      Stuttgart, Fleischbauer und Spohn, 1938

                    6099: FORMER GERMAN TERRITORY

1268 Träger, E.
      Die Volksdichtigkeit Niederschlesiens
      Doctoral dissertation, University of Kiel
      Kiel, 1888

1269 Friedrich, Ernst Georg
      Die Dichte der Bevölkerung im Regierungsbezirk Danzig
      Doctoral dissertation, University of Königsberg
      Königsberg, 1895

1270 Stoltenburg, Hans
      "Die Verteilung der Bevölkerung im Regierungsbezirk Köslin,"
      Geographische Gesellschaft zu Greisswald, Jahresbericht, 6(1896), 94-
        137

1271 Hahn, Friedrich
      "Die Entstehung der Bevölkerung Ostpreussens. Begleitworte zur
        Nationalitätkarte von Ostpreussen,"
      Die Erde, 6(1907), 2-6

1272 Groll, M.
      "Die Verteilung der Bevölkerung in der Provinz Schlesien,"
      Gesellschaft für Erdkunde zu Berlin, Zeitschrift, Series 4, 8(1909),
        379-386

1273 Poerschke, Werner
      Die Volksdichte im Kreise Dirschau
      Doctoral dissertation, University of Königsberg
      Königsberg, 1910

1274 Steinroeck, H.
      Die Volksdichte des Kreises Goldap. Ein Beitrag zur Methodik der
        Volksdichtedarstellung
      Doctoral dissertation, University of Königsberg
      Königsberg, 1910

1275 Dumont, Max
      Die Volksdichte und die Siedelungen des Kreises Allenstein und die
        hauptsächlich bedingenden geographischen Faktoren
      Doctoral dissertation, University of Königsberg
      Königsberg, 1911

1276 Mortensen, Hans
      "Die völkischen Verhältnisse der Ostseerandbebiete zwischen Weichsel
      und Kennischen Meerbusen,"
      Geographische Zeitschrift, 30(1924), 177-187

1277 Ganss, J.
      Die völkischen Verhältnisse des Memellandes
      Königsberg, Universität, Geographisches Institut, Veröffentlichungen
      Berlin, 1925

1278 Wittschell, L.
      "Die völkschen verhältnisse in Masuren und im südlichen Ermland,"
      PM, 71(1925), 241-244

1279 Horn, Werner
      Die Bevölkerungsverteilung in Ostpreussen und ihre Veränderungen
      Königsberg, Universität, Geographisches Institut, Veröffentlichungen,
      N.F. 2
      Königsberg, 1931

1280 Mortensen, Hans
      "Auswertung von Statistiken für geographische Zwecke, belegt am
      Beispiel der Bevölkerung Ostpreussens,"
      PM, 78(1932), 234-240

1281 Meiser, H.
      Die Bevölkerungsverhältnisse der südlichen Grenzmark
      Leipzig, Universität, Geographisches Institut, Veröffentlichungen
      Leipzig, 1934

1282 Lämmerhirt, F.
      Die Verteilung der Bevölkerung in Mittelschlesien
      Doctoral dissertation, University of Leipzig
      Dresden, 1935

1283 Mollenhauer, J.
      Wirtschafts- und bevölkerungsgeographische Verhältnisse der nördlichen
      Grenzmark
      Doctoral dissertation, University of Greisswald
      Greisswald, 1935

1284 Müggenburg, H.
      "Die Bevölkerungsverteilung im Regierungsbezirk Köslin,"
      Leipzig, Museum für Länderkunde, Wissenschaftliche Veröffentlichungen,
      N.F., 3(1935), 13-34
1285 Olbricht, Konrad
      Die Bevölkerungsentwicklung der Gross- und Mittelstädte der Ostmark
      Zur Wirtschaftsgeographie des Deutschen Ostens, 10
      Berlin, 1936

1286 Schleinitz, Helmut
      Besiedlung und Bevölkerung der südlichen Grenzmark. Beiträge zur
      Siedlungs- und Bevölkerungsgeographie des Deutschen Ostens
      Grenzmärkisches Heimatblatt, Sonderheft
      Grimmen i. Pom., 1936

1287 Neumann, Rudolf
      "Die Bevölkerungsentwicklung Pommerns nach 1945,"
      Geographische Rundschau (Braunschweig), 9(1957), 327-366

1288   Quante, Peter
       "Die Bevölkerungsentwicklung der preussischen Ostprovinzen im 19.
          und 20. Jahrhundert,"
       Zeitschrift für Ostforschung, 8(1959), 481-499

1289   Winklewski, Jan
       /"The population of eastern Pomerania in the years 1772-1910,"/ (in
          Polish)
       Zeszyty Geograficzne, 2(1960), 131-132

       (Also see 1402)

                            6480:   AUSTRIA-HUNGARY

1290   Grissinger, Karl
       "Die Verteilung der städtischen Bevölkerung Oesterreich-Ungarns nach
          der Höhenlage der Orte,"
       Geographische Gesellschaft in Wien, Mitteilungen, 37(1893), 150-175

1291   Rebhann, Andreas
       "Das Wachstum der Bevölkerung in Osterreich-Ungarn,"
       Geographische Zeitschrift, 7(1901), 287-290

                                6490:   AUSTRIA

1292   Müllner, Johann
       "Die Verteilung der Bevölkerung Tirols nach den Höhenverhältnissen
          der bewohnten Fläche,"
       Wien, Universität, Verein der Geographen, Berichte, 16(1890), 31-43

1293   Wallner, H.
       "Die jährlich Verschiebung der Bevölkerung und Siedlungsgrenze durch
          die Almwirtschaft im Lungau,"
       Geographische Gesellschaft in Wien, Mitteilungen, 54(1911), 358-403

1294   Krebs, Norbert
       "Die bewohnten und unbewohnten Areale der Ost-Alpen,"
       Geographische Zeitschrift, 18(1912), 443-454

1295   Krebs, Norbert
       "Die Verteilung der Kulturen und die Volksdichte in den österreich-
          ischen Alpen,"
       Geographische Gesellschaft in Wien, Mitteilungen, 55(1912), 243-303

1296   Marek, Richard
       "Geographische Ergebnisse der Volkszählung in Osterreich vom 31.
          Dezember 1910,"
       Geographische Zeitschrift, 18(1912), 682-696

1297   Von Pfaundler, Richard
       "Die Ergebnisse der Volkszählung vom 31. Dezember 1910 in den deutsch-
          österreichischen Alpenländern,"
       Die Erde, 11(1912), 96-109

1298 Leiter, M.
      "Besiedlung und Bevölkerungsdichte," pp. 98-114 in:
      Zur Geographie der Wiener Beckens, Heiderich-Festschrift
      Wien, 1923

1299 Engelmann, Richard
      "Die Verteilung der Bevölkerung in Osterreich nach der Höhe,"
      Geographische Gesellschaft in Wien, Mitteilungen, 67(1924), 87-118

1300 Engelmann, Richard
      "Eine Besiedlungskarte von Osterreich,"
      Geographische Gesellschaft in Wien, Mitteilungen, 77(1934), 244-249

1301 Marek, Richard
      "Einige geographische Ergebnisse der neuen Volkszählung in Osterreich
          (März 1934),"
      Geographische Zeitschrift, 42(1936), 98-105

1302 Kallbrunner, Annemarie
      "Zum Einfluss der Wirtschaft auf die Bevölkerungsbewegung,"
      Geographische Gesellschaft in Wien, Mitteilungen, 81(1938), 16-18

1303 Kallbrunner, Annemarie
      "Die Bevölkerungsbewegungen im südwestlichen Niederösterreich 1869-
          1934,"
      Geographische Gesellschaft in Wien, Mitteilungen, 81(1938), 130-137

1304 Paschinger, Herbert
      "Die Veränderung der Hausdichte und Bevölkerungsdichte in den einzelnen
          Ortsgemeinden Kärntens 1900-1934,"
      Deutsches Archiv für Landes- und Volksforschung, 2(1938), 654-667

1305 Fliri, Franz
      Bevölkerungsgeographische Untersuchungen im Unterinntal: Baumkirchen,
          Fritzens, Gnadenwald und Terfens
      Innsbruck, Universitätsverlag Wagner, 1948

1306 Troger, Ernest
      Bevölkerungsgeographie des Zillertales
      Innsbruck, Universitätsverlag Wagner, 1954

1307 Lässer, Adolf
      St. Leonhard im Pitztal; bevölkerungsgeographische Untersuchung unter
          besonderer Berüksichtigung der Wanderbewegung
      Innsbruck, Universitätsverlag Wagner, 1956

1308 Hanstuwka, H. et al.
      "Grundzüge der Veränderungen in der Verteilung der österreichischen
          Bevölkerung seit dem Jahre 1869," pp. 568-597 in:
      International Union for the Scientific Study of Population
      Internationaler Bevölkerungskongress. Wien 1959
      Wien, Winkler, 1959

1309 Leitner, Wilhelm
      "Die Verteilung der Bevölkerung nach natürlichen Landschaften in der
          Steiermark,"
      Geographische Gesellschaft in Wien, Mitteilungen, 101(1959), 72-85

1309a Arnberger, Erik
       "Grundlagen und Methoden zur kartographischen Darstellung der
         Bevölkerungsentwicklung der letzten hundert Jahre in Österreich,"
       Österreichischen Geographischen Gesellschaft, Mitteilungen, 102(1960),
         271-313

                              6500: HUNGARY

1310 Hátsek, Ignácz
       /"Relative density of population in Hungary according to the results
         of the enumeration of 1890-91,"/ (in Hungarian)
       Földrajzi Közlemények, 20(1892), 92-96

1311 Langhans, Paul
       "Die Verbreitung der Deutschen in der Länder der Ungarischen Krone
         1890,"
       PM, 42(1896), 280-282

1312 Thirring, Gusztáv
       "Die Bevölkerungsverhältnisse der ungarischen Städte im Jahre 1777,"
       Földrajzi Közlemények, 26(1898), 42-50

1313 Thirring, Gusztáv
       "Die Auswanderung aus Ungarn,"
       Földrajzi Közlemények, 30(1902), 17-45

1314 Thirring, Gusztáv
       /The emigration from Hungary and Hungarians in other lands/ (in
         Hungarian)
       Budapest, Kilián, 1904

1315 Zombory, Ida
       "Die Volksdichtigkeit Ungarns im Gebiete jenseits der Donau auf Grund
         der Daten der Volkszählung im Jahre 1900,"
       Földrajzi Közlemények, 33(1905), 7-10

1316 Wallis, B. C.
       "Distribution of nationalities in Hungary,"
       GJ, 47(1916), 177-188

1317 Wallis, B. C.
       "Central Hungary: Magyars and Germans,"
       GR, 6(1918), 421-435

1318 Wallis, B. C.
       "The Rumanians in Hungary,"
       GR, 6(1918), 156-171

1319 Wallis, B. C.
       "The Slavs of northern Hungary,"
       GR, 6(1918), 341-353

1320 Benyon, E. D.
       "Isolated racial groups of Hungary,"
       GR, 17(1927), 586-604

1321 Isbert, Otto Albrecht
      "Bevölkerungsrückgang und Auswanderung im Bakonyer Wald,"
      Deutsch-Ungarische Heimatsblätter, 3(1931), 206-219

1322 Thirring, Gusztáv
      "Die Bevölkerung Ungarns geographisch betrachtet,"
      Földrajzi Közlemények, 63(1935), 264-278

1323 Benyon, E. D.
      "Migrations of Hungarian peasants,"
      GR, 27(1937), 214-228

1324 Bulla, Béla
      "Zur Frage der Bevölkerungs- und Staatengeographie des ungarischen
        Beckens,"
      Földrajzi Közlemények, 66(1938), 62-76

1325 George, Pierre
      "Transformation économique et répartition de la population en Hongrie,"
      Association de Géographes Français, Bulletin, No. 212-213(1950), 147-
      156

1326 George, Pierre
      "La population de la République Hongroise; état et perspectives,"
      Population, 6(1951), 625-634

1327 Acsádi, György
      /"Internal migration of population in Hungary,"/ (in Hungarian)
      Statisztikai Szemle (Budapest), 34(1956), 451-462

1328 Siegel, Jacob S.
      The population of Hungary
      U. S. Department of Commerce, Bureau of the Census, International
        Population Statistics Reports, Series P-90, No. 9
      Washington, 1958

1329 Tajti, V.
      /"Geographical researches on the population of the territory between
        the Danube and the Tisza,"/ (in Hungarian)
      Földrajzi Ertesítö, 7(1958), 167-198

1330 Wallner, Erno
      /"Characteristics of the population geography and the habitat in the
        Paks region,"/ (in Hungarian)
      Földrajzi Ertesítö, 7(1958), 419-479

1331 Csihás, Janos
      /"The demography of Hungary, with particular reference to the former
        distribution of population,"/ (in Swedish)
      Svensk Geografisk Årsbok, 35(1959), 22-38

      (Also see 114, 337)

6510: CZECHOSLOVAKIA

1332 Lepař, Zd.
      /"Die Bewegung der Bevölkerung in den Ländern der böhmische Krone
        nach dem Census von 1900,"/ (in Czech)
      Česká Společnost Zeměvědna, Sborník, 9(1903), No. 1

1333 Rauchberg, Heinrich
      "Die nationale Bevölkerungsbilanz Böhmens,"
      Gesellschaft für Erdkunde zu Berlin, Zeitschrift, 10(1911), 40-45

1334 Zemmrich, Johannes
      "Die Ergebnisse der Volkuzählung vom 31. Dezember 1910 in den
        österreichischen Sudetenländern,"
      Gesellschaft für Erdkunde zu Berlin, Zeitschrift, 11(1912), 153-165

1335 Hassinger, Hugo
      "Die Bevölkerung und die Volkskultur," pp. 91-125 in:
      Die Tschechoslowakei; ein geographisches, politisches und wirtschaft-
      liches Handbuch
      Wien and Leipzig, Rikola, 1925

1336 Pohl, Josef
      Densité de la population dans la République Tschéchoslovaque
      Praha, Universita Karlova, Travaux Géographiques Tchéques, No. 12
      Praha, 1926

1337 Cumin, Gustavo
      "Cenni sulla distribuzione della popolazione nella Republica
        cecoslovaca,"
      BSGI, Serie 6, 4(1927), 677-688

1338 Brandt, Bernhard
      Eine neue Bevölkerungskarte der Sudetenländer
      Sonderaufdruck aus dem Sudendeutschen Jahrbuch, 1929
      Kassel-Wilhelmshöhe, Stauda, 1929

1339 Sobotik, Robert
      Westschlesien (Tschechoslowakei). Eine anthropogeographische Studie,
        mit einem Atlas. Erster Teil: Raum und Bevölkerung
      Praha, Deutsche Universität, Geographisches Institut, Arbeiten, No. 11
      Praha, 1930

1340 Nekovar, Fr.
      /"Density, increase, and decrease of the population of the Czecho-
        slovak Republic according to the Census of December 1, 1930,"/ (in
        Czech)
      Československá Společnost Zeměpisná, Sborník, 37(1931), 144-150

1341 Moscheles, J.
      "Berufliche Gliederung und Verstädterung der Bevölkerung in den
        historischen und karpathischen Ländern der Tschechoslowakischen
        Republik,"
      Geographische Gesellschaft in Wien, Mitteilungen, 75(1932), 85-91

1342   Pohl, Josef
       /"Depopulation of the Bohemian countryside from 1850 to 1930/ (in
       Czech)
       Praha, Author, 1932

1343   Pohl, Josef
       /"The development of population in Bohemia during the period 1850-
       1900,"/ (in Czech)
       Československá Společnost Zeměpisná, Sborník, 38(1932), 156-163

1344   Käubler, Rudolf
       "Wirtschaftsgebiete, Volksdichte und Wanderungsbewegung in Böhmen,"
       Geographische Wochenschrift, 3(1935), 847-852

1345   Ludwig, Walter
       Bevölkerung und Wirtschaft Schlesiens innerhalb der Tschechoslowa-
       kischen Republik
       Wiener Geographische Studien, 5
       Wien, 1936

1346   Wolters, Elizabeth
       "Zur Bevölkerungsbewegung der einzelnen Völker und Volksgruppen in
       der Tschechoslowakei,"
       Deutsches Archiv für Landes- und Volksforschung, 1(1937), 332-343

1347   Pohl, Josef
       "La dépopulation des campagnes en Tchéchoslovaquie après la guerre
       mondiale," pp. 76-82 in:
       CRCIG, Amsterdam, 1938, Vol. 2

1348   Olbricht, Konrad
       "Die Bevölkerungsentwicklung der grösseren Städte im Sudetengau,"
       Geographischer Anzeiger, 42(1941), 173-178

1349   George, Pierre
       "La population de la Tchécoslovaquie,"
       Population, 14(1947), 281-292

1350   Shute, John
       "Czechoslovakia's territorial and population changes,"
       EG, 24(1948), 35-44

1351   Smetana, Ján
       /"L'évolution démographique de la région de l'Orava en 1822 à 1940,"/
       (in Czech)
       Geographica Slovaca, 1(1949), 141-170

1352   Wynne, Waller, Jr.
       The population of Czechoslovakia
       U. S. Bureau of the Census, International Population Statistics
       Reports, Series P-90, No. 3
       Washington, 1953

1353   Hammerschmidt, Annelies
       "Wandlungen der Bevölkerungsverteilung in Nordwestböhmen seit dem
       zweiten Weltkrieg,"
       Berichte zur Deutschen Landeskunde, 12(1954), 233-238

1354 Vrána, Otakar
/"Density of population in the Liberic Region,"/ (in Czech)
Československá Společnost Zeměpisná, Sborník, 59(1954), 129-139

1355 Wanklyn, Harriet
"Population and settlement," pp. 378-406 in:
Czechoslovakia
London, George Philip, 1954

1356 Tverdohlebov, I. T.
/"The geography of the population of Slovakia,"/ (in Russian)
Geograficheskoe Obshchestvo, S.S.S.R., Krymskii Otdel (Simferopol),
Izvestiia, No. 4(1957), 85-88

1357 Matousek, Vladimir
/"On the question of rural underpopulation,"/ (in Czech)
Československá Společnost Zeměpisná, Sborník, 63(1958), 323-328

1358 Votrubic, Ctibor
/"Der Anteil des natürlichen Bevölkerungszuwachsen und der Migration
am Wachstum der Städte der ČSR in den Jahren 1954-1958,"/ (in
Czech)
Geografický Časopis, 11(1959), 111-136

1359 Zdeněk, Pavlík
/"Recent data on migration in Czechoslovakia,"/ (in Czech)
Československá Společnost Zeměpisná, Sborník, 64(1959), 324-337

1360 Blažek, Miroslav
"Esquisse des problèmes de géographie de la population en Tchéco-
slovaquie,"
AG, 69(1960), 477-483

1361 Votrubic, Ctibor
/"Migration to larger towns in central and northern Bohemia during
the years 1954-1958,"/ (in Czech)
Československá Společnost Zeměpisná, Sborník, 65(1960), 21-28

1362 Vávra, Zdeněk
/"The growing old of the population in Czech countries and its
geographical importance,"/ (in Czech)
Československá Společnost Zeměpisná, Sborník, 66(1961), 56-71

6520: POLAND

a. National

1363 Zechlin, Erich
Die Bevölkerungs- und Grossbesitzverteilung im Zartum Polen
Berlin, Georg Reimer, 1916

1364 Praesent, Hans
"Die Bevölkerungsdichte in Kongres-Polen,"
Gesellschaft für Erdkunde zu Berlin, Zeitschrift, Series 4, 17(1918),
161-174

1365 Poland, Comité des Publications Encyclopédiques sur la Pologne
      Atlas de l'encyclopédie polonaise. Fasc. II. Territoire et population
      Fribourg, Saint-Paul, 1920

1366 Romer, Eugenjusz
      "The population of Poland according to the census of 1921,"
      GR, 13(1923), 398-412

1367 Smolénski, Jerzy
      Die relativen Uberschüsse und Defizite der polnischen Bevölkerung in
        der Republik Polen
      Kraków, Universytet Jagiellónski, Instytut Geograficny, Prace, 6
      Kraków, 1926

1368 Gargas, S.
      /"Polish emigration since the World War,"/ (in Dutch)
      TEG, 18(1927), 283-287, 321-332, 335-363, 394-402

1369 Pierajkiewicz, Jan
      /"The second census of Poland,"/ (in Polish)
      Przegląd Geograficzny, 11(1931), 109-118

1370 Czech, J.
      Die Bevölkerung Polens. Zahl und völkische Zusammensetzung
      Schlesische Gesellschaft für Erdkunde und Geographisches Institut,
        Universität Breslau, Veröffentlichungen, 16
      Breslau, 1932

1371 Loth, Jerzy
      "Aspects of Polish emigration during the last ten years," pp. 48-
        70 in:
      CRCIG, Varsovie, 1934, Vol. 3

1372 Ormicki, Victor
      "Compte rendu des études sur la surpopulation de la Pologne,"
        pp. 604-606 in:
      CRCIG, Varsovie, 1934, Vol. 3

1373 Rewienska, Wanda
      "La densité urbaine en Pologne," pp. 240-249 in:
      CRCIG, Varsovie, 1934, Vol. 3

1374 Ormicki, Victor
      /"The density of the rural agricultural population in Poland, 1931,"/
        (in Polish)
      Wiadomósci Geograficzne, 15(1937), 116-123

1375 Halicka, H.
      /"Population changes in Poland, 1931/33-1946,"/ (in Polish)
      Czasopismo Geograficzne, 17(1946), 123-133

1376 Mauco, Georges
      "La population en Pologne,"
      AG, 55(1946), 230-233

1377 Stålberg, Helge
      /"Conditions of population and economic geography of new Poland,"/
      (in Swedish)
      Svensk Geografisk Årsbok, 23(1947), 96-104

1378 Leonhard, H.
      /"Proportion of men to women in Poland,"/ (in Polish)
      Czasopismo Geograficzne, 19(1948), 113-120

1379 Uhorczak, Franciszek
      /"Population density in Poland,"/ (in Polish)
      Ziemia, 39(1948), 37-45

1380 Migacz, Wladyslaw
      /"Territorial differentiation in the contribution of the principal
      age groups to the population structure of Poland in 1945,"/ (in
      Polish)
      Czasopismo Geograficzne, 21-22(1950-51), 251-279

1381 Zubrzycki, Jerzy
      "Emigration from Poland in the Nineteenth and Twentieth Centuries,"
      Population Studies, 6(1953), 248-272

1382 Mauldin, W. Parker and Akers, Donald S.
      The population of Poland
      U. S. Bureau of the Census, International Population Statistics
         Reports, Series P-90, No. 4
      Washington, 1954

1383 Litterer, Miroslawa
      /Changes in distribution and composition of the population of People's
         Poland in the years 1946-1950/ (in Polish)
      Polska Akademia Nauk, Instytut Geografii, Prace Geograficzne
      Warszawa, 1955

1384 Welpa, Boguslaw
      /"Age composition of the population of People's Poland in 1950,"/
      (in Polish)
      Prace Geograficzne, No. 16(1955), 59-113

1385 Jelonek, Adam
      /The number of inhabitants of Polish cities and settlements in the
         years 1810-1955/ (in Polish)
      Polska Akademia Nauk, Instytut Geografii, Dokumentacja Geograficzna,
         No. 5
      Warszawa, 1956

1386 Kostanick, Huey Louis
      "Postwar population shifts in Poland,"
      California Council of Geograph Teachers, Bulletin, 5(1957), 2-6

1387 Barnett, Clifford R., et al.
      "Geography and population," pp. 33-44 in:
      Poland: its people, its society, its culture
      New Haven, HRAF Press, 1958

1388 Jelonek, Adam
      /"Changes in the age and sex structure of the population of Poland
        in the period from 1946 to 1950,"/ (in Polish)
      Przegląd Geograficzny, 30(1958), 439-458

1389 North, Geoffrey
      "Poland's population and changing economy,"
      GJ, 124(1958), 517-527

1390 Osborne, Richard H.
      "Changes in the urban population of Poland,"
      Geography, 44(1959), 201-204

      (Also see 54, 891, 893, 1801, 1840, 1841, 1846)

                            b. Regional

1391 Praesent, Hans
      "Die Bevölkerungsgeographie des Cholmer Landes (poln. Chelm),"
      PM, 64(1918), 54-62

1392 Romer, Eugenjusz
      La population polonaise dans les pays limitrophes baltiques, mari-
        times et lacustres
      Travaux Géographiques Publiés sous la Direction de Eugenjusz Romer,
        Fasc. II
      Lwów, 1919

1393 Sawicki, Lud.
      "Die Verteilung der Bevölkerung in den Westkarpaten in allgemeinen,"
      Bulletin de l'Academie des Sciences de Cracovie, Nov., 1919, 886-905

1394 Mrazkówna, Marja
      "The distribution of the population in the Duchy of Cracov,"
      Przegląd Geograficzny, 2(1920-21), 105-127

1395 Penck, Albrecht
      "Die Deutschen im polnischen Korridor,"
      Gesellschaft für Erdkunde zu Berlin, Zeitschrift, Series 4, 20(1921),
        169-185

1396 Kubijowicz, Włodzimierz
      /Distribution of cultures and of population in the eastern Car-
        pathians/ (in Polish)
      Conferences Géographiques Cracoviennes, No. 7
      Kraków, 1924

1397 Zaborski, Bogdan
      Carte des confessions d'une partie due département de Léopol avec des
        remarques générales sur ce type de carte
      Warszawa, Uniwersytet, Zakład Geograficzny, Prace Wykonane, No. 11
      Warszawa, 1928

1398 Kubijowicz, Włodzimierz
      /Distribution of cultures and population in the northern Carpathians/
        (in Czech)
      Recueil de l'Université de Komenski à Bratislava, No. 60
      Bratislava, 1932

1399 Rewienska, Wanda
      /"The distribution of cities and villages in northeastern Poland,"/
      (in Polish)
      Przegląd Geograficzny, 18(1938), 101-132

1400 Ormicki, Victor
      /"Density of the rural population in the District of Bialystok,"/ (in
      Polish)
      Wiadomósci Geograficzne, 17(1939), 30-35

1400a Czarkowska, Wanda and Leszczyska, Wanda
      /"Demographic problems of the Nowy Sącz region,"/ (in Polish)
      Czasopismo Geograficzne, 31(1960), 261-278

1401 Gluziński, J. and Krynicka, T.
      /"The development of the population inhabiting the coastal districts
      of Poland in the years 1946-1958,"/ (in Polish)
      Zeszyty Geograficzne, 2(1960), 135-158

1402 Kosiński, Leszek
      "Problems of settling the Polish Western and Northern Territories,"
      Przegląd Geograficzny, 32, Supplement (1960), 193-209

                       6540: IBERIAN PENINSULA

1403 Quelle, Otto
      "Die spanisch-portugiesische Auswanderung,"
      Ibero-Amerikanisches Archiv, 1920, 141-172

1404 Gavira, José
      "La población costera de la Península y su distribución,"
      Real Sociedad Geográfica, Boletín, 86(1936), 451-463

1405 Fernandez, Felipe
      "El más antiquo mapa de población de la Peninsula Ibérica,"
      Estudios Geográficos, No. 65(1956), 704-706

                           6560: SPAIN

                           a. National

1406 Petermann, A. and Gumprecht, T. E.
      "Die Städtbevölkerung von Spanien,"
      Mitteilungen aus Justus Perthes' Geographischer Anstalt, 2(1856),
      393-399

1407 Pasanisi, Fr. M.
      "La popolazione della Spagna nel 1897,"
      BSGI, Serie 3, 12(1899), 515-529

1408 Girard, A.
      "L'émigration espagnole,"
      AG, 21(1912), 418-425

1409 Quelle, Otto
      "Anthropogeographische Studien aus Spanien,"
      Geographische Gesellschaft in Hamburg, Mitteilungen, 30(1917), 69-186

1410 Sorre, Maximilien
      "La population de l'Espagne d'après le recensement de 1920,"
      AG, 33(1924), 177-182

1411 Monbeig, Pierre
      "L'état actuel des migrations espagnols,"
      AG, 40(1931), 198-201

1412 Gavira, José
      "Bemerkungen zu einer Karte über die Bevölkerungsdichte Spaniens,"
      Zeitschrift für Erdkunde, 5(1937), 640-644

1413 Ruiz Almansa, Javier
      "Crecimiento y repartición de la población de España," pp. 141-183 in:
      Instituto Balmes de Sociología
      Estudios Demográficos
      Madrid, 1945

1414 Ruiz de Gordejuela, Adolfo Melón
      "Geografía del censo de la población,"
      Estudios Geográficos, 6(1945), 67-120

1415 Ruiz de Gordejuela, Amando Melón
      "Los modernas y actuales censos de población en España," pp. 432-442
      in:
      CRCIG, Lisbonne, 1949, Vol. 3

1416 Dominguez Ortiz, António
      "La población española a lo largo de nuestra historia,"
      Real Sociedad Geográfica, Boletín, 76(1950), 250-285

1417 Hoyos Sáinz, Luis de
      La densidad de población y el acrecentamiento en España; hechos,
         causas, aplicaciones e interpretaciones
      Madrid, Instituto Juan Sebastián Elcano, 1952

1418 Hoyos Sáinz, Luis de
      "Relación provincial del rendimento agricola y la densidad de
         población,"
      Real Sociedad Geográfica, Boletín, No. 88(1952), 703-726

1419 Ruiz de Gordejuela, Amando Melón
      "La población de España en 1950. Datos y comentarios,"
      Estudios Geográficos, 13(1952), 441-454

1420 Quelle, Otto
      "Densidad de población y tipos de poblamiento de distintas regiones
         españolas,"
      Estudios Geográficos, 13(1952), 699-720

1421 Abascal Garayoa, Angel
      "La evolución de la población urbana española en la primera mitad
         del siglo XX,"
      Geográphica; Revista de Información y Enseñanza, 3(1956), 47-57

1422 Casas Torres, José M.
      "Un plan para el estudio de la geografía de la población española,"
      Revista Internacional de Sociología, 15(1957), 73-113
      Also: Geográphica; Revista de Información y Enseñanza, 4(1957),
      30-47

      (Also see 310, 572)

                              b. Regional

1423 Sorre, Maximilien
      "Groupement des populations dans la Catalogne septentrionale,"
      AG, 20(1911), 69-73

1424 Dantin Cerceda, Juan
      Distribución geográfica de la población en Galicia
      Madrid, Centro de Estudios Historicos, 1925

1425 Urabayen, L. de
      "Algunos observaciones sobre la distribución de la población de
      Navarra en 1920,"
      Revue Internationale des Etudes Basques, 16(1925), 539-550

1426 Dantin Cerceda, Juan
      "La poblacion de la Mancha Española en el centro de su maximo
      endorréismo. Contribución al conocimiento de habitat rural en
      España," pp. 61-72 in:
      CRCIG, Paris, 1931, Vol. 3

1427 Lefebvre, Theodore
      "La répartition et le mouvement de la population actuelle," pp. 684-
      716 in:
      Les modes de vie dans les Pyrénées Atlantiques orientales
      Paris, Colin, 1933

1428 Vila, P.
      "Le peuplement en Catalogne. Le problème de l'eau," pp. 537-546 in:
      CRCIG, Amsterdam, 1938, Vol. 1.

1429 Dantin Cerceda, Juan
      "El medio físico aragones y el reparto de su población," pp. 1-112 in:
      Consejo Superior de Investigaciones Científicas, Instituto "J. Sebas-
      tian Elcano," Madrid
      Primera Reunión de Estudios Geográficos Celebrada en la Universidad
      de Jaca, Agosto, 1941
      Madrid, 1942

1430 Llobet, Salvador
      "Evolución del pobliamento y población de la comarca de Vallés,"
      Estudios Geográficos, 3(1942), 751-832

1431 Ramos, Demetrio
      "Desplazamiento de población en el Jarama, Henares y Tajo Medio,"
      Estudios Geográficos, 5(1944), 815-879

1432 Jiménez de Gregorio, Fernando
      "La población en la Jara Toledana,"
      Estudios Geográficos, 11(1950), 201-250

1433 Jiménez de Gregorio, Fernando
      "Los núcleos de población de la Jara Toledana,"
      Real Sociedad Geográfica, Boletín, 87(1951), 343-377

1434 Quelle, Otto
      "Densidad de población en la region occidental de la provincia de
      Guadalajara,"
      Estudios Geográficos, 12(1951), 583-600

1435 Quelle, Otto
      "La densidad de población en la Provincia de Murcia,"
      Estudios Geográficos, 13(1952), 357-374

1436 Quelle, Otto
      "Densidad de población de la Provincia de Toledo,"
      Estudios Geográficos, 13(1952), 161-177

1437 Rubio, M.
      "Un intento de representación cartográfica del poblamiento de los
      alcededores de Barcelona,"
      Estudios Geográficos, 14(1953), 595-628

1438 Jiménez de Gregorio, Fernando
      "La población en la Jara Toledana. La población en el siglo XIX.
      La población en el siglo XX,"
      Estudios Geográficos, 15(1954), 209-245 and 16(1955), 585-636

1439 Abascal Garayoa, Angel
      Los origenes de la población actual de Pamplona
      Spain, Consejo Superior de Investigaciones Científicas, Instituto
      Juan Sebastian Elcano, Departamento de Geografía Aplicada, Revista
      Geográfica, Numero Monográfico
      Zaragoza, 1955

1440 Torres-Balbas, L.
      "Extensión y demografía de las ciudades hispano-musulmanes,"
      Studia Islamica, 3(1955), 35-60

1441 Higueras Arnal, Antonio
      "Geodemografía de la provincia de Logroño (1900-1950),"
      Geográphica; Revista de Información y Enseñanza, 3(1956), 86-109

1442 Jiménez de Gregorio, Fernando
      Notas para una geografía de la población murciana
      Murcia, 1956

1443 Mavrichi, M.
      /"Map of the population of Mallorca,"/ (in Swedish)
      Ymer, 76(1956), 154-155

1444 Voltés, Pedro
      "La población de Cataluña en el primer cuarto del siglo XVIII,"
      Estudios Geográficos, 17(1956), 165-184

1445   Ferrer Regales, Manuel
       "La población," pp. 103-114 in:
       El campo de Cariñena; estudio geográfica
       Spain, Consejo Superior de Investigaciones Científicas, Instituto
         Juan Sebastian Elcano, Departamento de Geografía Aplicada, Publica-
         ción 16
       Zaragoza, 1957

1146   Floristán, A. and Bosque, J.
       "Movimentos migratorios en la provincia de Granada,"
       Estudios Geográficos, 18(1957), 361-402

1447   Jiménez Castillo, Margarita
       La población de Navarra; estudio geográfico
       Instituto Juan Sebastian Elcano, Departamento de Geografía Aplicada
       Zaragoza, 1958

1448   Tortajada Pérez, José
       "El poblamiento antiguo de la huerta de Murcia,"
       Estudios Geográficos, 19(1958), 465-486

1449   Bolos y Capdevila, María
       "La immigración en Barcelona en los dos últimos decenios,"
       Estudios Geográficos, 20(1959), 209-249

1450   Pardo Perez, María Pilar
       La población de Zaragoza (capital y provincia); estudio geográfico
       Spain, Consejo Superior de Investigaciones Científicas, Instituto
         Juan Sebastian Elcano, Departamento de Geografía Aplicada, Serie
         Regional, 7, Número general, 22
       Zaragoza, 1959

1451   Jiménez de Gregorio, Fernando
       "La población en La Jara cacereña,"
       Estudios Geográficos, 20(1959), 21-80 and 21(1960), 313-369

1452   Muñoz Fernández, Antonio
       "La emigración en la provincia de Jaén, 1900-1955,"
       Estudios Geográficos, 21(1960), 455-495

                            6690: PORTUGAL

1453   Ribeiro, Orlando, ed.
       Distribuição da população de Portugal
       Lisboa, Instituto para a Alta Cultura, Centro de Estudos Geográficos,
       1946

1454   Ribeiro, Orlando and Cardigos, Norberto
       Geografia da população em Portugal
       Lisboa, Instituto para a Alta Cultura, Centro de Estudos Geográficos,
       1946

1455   Schwalbach, Luiz
       A população portugesa
       Universidade de Coimbra, Faculdade de Letras, Revista, 24
       Coimbra, 1948

1456 Amorim Girão, Aristides de
      "Povoamento humano," pp. 213-280 and "Movimento e mobilidade da
      população," pp. 281-309 in:
      Geografia de Portugal, 2nd ed., Vol. 2
      Porto, Portucalense Editora, 1949-51

1457 Amorim Girão, Aristides de
      "Densidade da população por frequensias,"
      Universidade de Coimbra, Faculdade de Letras, Centro de Estudos
        Geográficos, Boletim, 1(1950), 25-57
      Also: CRCIG, Lisbonne, 1949, Vol. 1, pp. 226-238

1458 Universidade de Coimbra, Centro de Estudos Geográficos
      "Aglomeração e dispersão do povoamento dem Portugal,"
      Universidade de Coimbra, Faculdade de Letras, Centro de Estudos
        Geográficos, Boletim, 2(1951), 103-108

1459 Velho, Fernando and Amorim Girão, Aristides de
      "O mais antigo censo de população de Portugal (1527),"
      Universidade de Coimbra, Faculdade de Letras, Centro de Estudos
        Geográficos, Boletim, 8-9(1954), 56-68

1460 Amorim Girão, Aristides de
      "População rural e população urban em Portugal (ensaio de classi-
        ficação),"
      Universidade de Coimbra, Faculdade de Letras, Centro de Estudos
        Geográficos, Boletim, 12-13(1956), 67-76

1461 Amorim Girão, Aristides de, ed.
      Plates 12-19 /Population/ in:
      Atlas de Portugal, 2nd ed.
      Coimbra, Faculdade de Letras, Instituto de Estudos Geográficos, 1958

                              6710: ITALY

                              a. National

1462 Yver, G.
      "L'émigration italienne,"
      AG, 6(1897), 123-132

1463 Denis, Pierre
      "Les migrations périodiques à l'intérieur de l'Italie,"
      AG, 17(1908), 79-83

1464 Rambaud, Jacques
      "L'émigration italienne,"
      Revue de Géographie, 3(1909), 525-549

1465 Dingelstedt, Victor
      "Italian emigration,"
      SGM, 26(1910), 337-353

1466   Lorin, Henri
       "Un rapport sur l'émigration italienne,"
       Société de Géographie Commerciale de Bordeaux, Bulletin, 34(1911),
          121-125

1467   Marinelli, Olinto
       "Il nuovo censimento ed alcuni desideri dei geografi,"
       RGI, 18(1911), 212-219

1468   Roster, G.
       /"Einfluss der Klimas auf verbreitung und Verteilung der Bevölkerung
          Italiens,"/ (in Italian)
       R. Accademia dei Georgofili di Firenze, Atti, Serie 5, No. 9
       Firenze, 1912

1469   Rühl, A.
       "Die geographischen Ursachen der italienischen Auswanderung,"
       Gesellschaft für Erdkunde zu Berlin, Zeitschrift, Series 4, 11(1912),
          655-671

1470   Scano, Giulio
       "Distribuzione, aumento e densità della popolazione italiana in
          rapporto all'altimetria dei centri abitati,"
       RGI, 27(1920), 37-42, 28(1921), 103-108, 29(1922), 197-203, 30(1923),
          50-56, 158-165, and 31(1924), 159-175

1471   Schiarini, G. Pompilio
       "La popolazione del Regno d'Italia nel cinquantennio 1871-1921.
          Rilievi e raffronti,"
       BSGI, Serie 5, 11(1922), 375-386

1472   Giusti, Ugo
       "Lo sviluppo della popolazione italiana tra il 1911 e il 1921 nei
          centri urbani e nel complesso del Regno,"
       L'Universo, 6(1925), 97-115

1473   Almagìa, Roberto
       "La carta della densità di popolazione in Italia,"
       RGI, 40(1933), 125-134

1474   Pollastri, Francisco
       "La densità della popolazione data con espressioni maggiormente
          realistiche,"
       L'Universo, 18(1937), 479-487

1475   Toniolo, Antonio Renato
       "Studies of depopulation in the mountains of Italy,"
       GR, 27(1937), 473-477

1476   Gley, Werner
       "Die Entwicklung der italienischen Auswanderung,"
       Zeitschrift für Erdkunde, 6(1938), 768-772

1477   Sestini, Aldo
       "Popolazione dei principali centri italiani,"
       RGI, 45(1938), 163-168

1478 Aartsen, J. P. van
      /"Regional growth of population in Italy,"/ (in Dutch)
      TGE, 30(1939), 25-32

1479 Livi, L.
      "La geografia della natalità italiana,"
      Razza e Civiltà, 1(1940), 657-676

1480 Nice, Bruno
      "La popolazione straniera in Italia,"
      L'Universo, 25(1944), 119-129

1481 Giusti, Ugo
      "L'emigrazione italiana potenziale. Aspetti economico-geografico.
        Prospettive," pp. 198-208 in:
      Atti, XIV Congresso Geografico Italiano, Bologna, 1947
      Bologna, 1949

1482 Pracchi, Roberto
      "Schema di uno studio geografico dell'emigrazione italiana," pp. 471-
        472 in:
      Atti, XIV Congresso Geografico Italiano, Bologna, 1947
      Bologna, 1949

1483 Roselli, Bruno
      "Direttive geografiche per il nuovo censimento dell popolazione,"
        pp. 109-119 in:
      Atti, XIV Congresso Geografico Italiano, Bolgna, 1947
      Bologna, 1949

1484 Giannitrapani, Luigi
      "Lo spopolamento montano e le sue consequenze attuale,"
      L'Universo, 32(1952), 13-27

1485 Toschi, Umberto
      "Una rappresentazione italiana di distribuzione della popolazione
        col metodo dei volumi,"
      RGI, 61(1954), 144-147

1486 Wise, Michael J.
      "Population pressure and national resources; some observations upon
        the Italian population problem,"
      EG, 30(1954), 144-156

1487 Almagià, Roberto
      "La carta della distribuzione della popolazione in Italia,"
      La Ricerca Scientifica (Roma), 26(1956), 2043-2048

1488 Ruocco, Domenico
      Alcuni saggi di carte della popolazione con considerazione
        metodiche preliminare
      Roma, Consiglio Nazionale delle Ricerche, 1956

1489 Almagià, Roberto and Ruocco, Domenico
      "Nuovi saggi per una carta della popolazione d'Italia," pp. 38-52 in:
      Atti, XVII Congresso Geografico Italiano, Bari, 1957, Vol. 3

1490   Barbieri, Giuseppe
       "I 'mestieri degli emigranti' e alcune caratteristiche correnti di
          emigrazione della montagna italiana,"
       Suppl. à RGI, 45(1958), 45-65

1491   Almagià, Roberto
       "Centro di Studio per la Geografia Antropica. Attività svolta negli
          anni 1957-58,"
       Ricerca Scientifica, 29(1959), 481-483

1492   Sestini, Aldo
       "Densità tipiche di popolazione in Italia secondo le forme di
          utilizzazione del suolo,"
       RGI, 66(1959), 231-241

1493   Pinna, Mario
       La carta della densità della popolazione in Italia (Cens. 1951)
       Roma, Consiglio Nazionale delle Ricerche, 1960

       (Also see 108, 783, 929, 1156, 1654, 2280, 2331.)

                                   b. Regional

                               6720: Northern Italy

1494   Bianchi, Franco
       "Sulla distribuzione della popolazione nella provincia di Como,"
       RGI, 14(1907), 79-89

1495   Aicardi, Giacomo
       "Nota preliminare sulla distribuzione delle popolazione nella
          riviera ligure,"
       RGI, 18(1911), 546-554

1496   Ricci, Leonardo
       "Nota preliminare sulla distribuzione altimetrica della popolazione
          nel bacino del Noce (Adige),"
       RGI, 18(1911), 150-156

1497   Aicardi, Giacomo
       "La popolazione nella Riviera Ligure dal 1861 al 1901,"
       RGI, 20(1913), 58-65

1498   Anfossi, G.
       "Appunti sulla distribuzione altimetrica della popolazione in
          alcune valli Alpine,"
       RGI, 24(1917), 319-330

1499   Marinelli, Olinto
       "The regions of mixed population in northern Italy,"
       GR, 7(1919), 129-148

1500   Roletto, Giorgio B.
       "La densité de population des Alpes occidentales (versant italien)
          d'après le recensement de 1911,"
       RGA, 10(1922), 281-304

1501 Giannitrapani, Luigi
      "La popolazione e i centri abitati della pianura Padano-Veneta secondo
        gli ultimi censimenti,"
      L'Universo, 4(1923), 9-23

1502 Landini, Piero
      "La distribuzione della popolazione nella provincia di Novara,"
      La Geografia, 11(1923), 145-176

1503 Rondelli, Ugo
      "La decadenza demografica della montagna piemontese,"
      L'Universo, 10(1929), 295-303

1504 Toniolo, Antonio Renato
      "Per uno studio sistematico sullo spopolamento delle vallate Alpine
        italiane," pp. 175-184 in:
      Atti, XI Congresso Geografico Italiano, Napoli, 1930, Vol. 2
      Napoli, 1930

1505 Toniolo, Antonio Renato
      "Lo spopolamento montano nella Venezia Tridentina,"
      BSGI, Serie 6, 8(1931), 99-111

1506 Brauzzi, L.
      "La distribuzione della popolazione sulla 'Riviera Bresciana' del Lagi
        di Garda,"
      RGI, 40(1933), 224-237

1507 Nangeroni, L. Giuseppe
      "Cenni generali sulla distribuzione della popolazione nella Regione
        Benacense,"
      BSGI, Serie 7, 1(1936), 275-301

1508 Candida, Luigi
      "Aspetti geografici della variazioni di popolamento nella Venezia nel
        trentennio 1901-31," pp. 48-61 in:
      CRCIG, Amsterdam, 1938, Vol. 2

1509 Morandini, Giuseppe
      "La distribuzione della popolazione sparsa e dei centri nella Venezia
        Tridentina,"
      RGI, 48(1941), 313-333

1510 Gambi, Lucio
      "Una carta della distribuzione della popolazione in Romagna,"
      L'Universo, 27(1947), 781-791

1511 Gambi, Lucio
      "Riflessi della seconda guerra mondiale sopra le condizione demo-
        grafiche dell'Italia nord e centro peninsulare,"
      BSGI, Serie 8, 2(1949), 124-135

1512 Gortani, M.
      "I fattori geografi dello spopolamento in Friuli," pp. 498-499 in:
      Atti, XIV Congresso Geografico Italiano, Bologna, 1947
      Bologna, 1949

1513   Mansuelli, G. A.
       "La distribuzione della popolazione emiliana nell'età del ferro,"
          pp. 522-524 in:
       Atti, XIV Congresso Geografico Italiano, Bologna, 1947
       Bologna, 1949

1514   Sestini, Aldo and Storai, Tina
       "Carta della densità di popolazione in Emilia con curve isometriche
          equidistanti," pp. 456-460 in:
       Atti, XIV Congresso Geografico Italiano, Bologna, 1947
       Bologna, 1949

1515   Bonetti, Eliseo and Schiffrer, C.
       "Popolamento urbano e popolamento rurale in Istria,"
       RGI, 57(1950), 129-144

1516   Ortolani, Mario
       "Richerche sul popolamento della Pianura ferrarese,"
       BSGI, Serie 8, 3(1950), 209-237

1517   Ortolani, Mario
       "Un territorio sovrapopolato: la partecipanza agraria di Cento
          (pianura emiliana),"
       RGI, 57(1950), 209-222

1518   Bertossi, Thea and Chiesa, A.
       "La densità della popolazione in Lombardia,"
       L'Universo, 31(1951), 521-530

1519   Candida, Luigi
       "Il fenomeno emigratorio nella Valle Varaita,"
       RGI, 59(1952), 211-219

1520   Capello, Carlo Felice
       "Lineamenti generali della distribuzione delle sedi e della popolazione
          nelle Alpi Occidentali Italiane," pp. 401-423 in:
       Atti, XV Congresso Geografico Italiano, Torino, 1950, Vol. 1
       Torino, 1952

1521   Fumagalli, Savina
       "Popolazione e ambiente naturale delle valli saluzzesi," pp. 440-449
          in:
       Atti, XV Congresso Geografico Italiano, Torino, 1950, Vol. 1
       Torino, 1952

1522   Ferrantini, Alberto
       "Variazioni della popolazione nel Piemonte, Valle d'Aosta e Liguria
          dal 1848 al 1948," pp. 431-439 in:
       Atti, XV Congresso Geografico Italiano, Torino, 1950, Vol. 1
       Torino, 1952

1523   Pracchi, Roberto
       "Lo spopolamento montano è in regresso? Sondaggio sullo spopolamento
          della montagna lombarda secondo i dati del censimento 1951,"
       BSGI, Serie 8, 6(1953), 183-206

1524   Raptschinsky, B.
       /"The German minority in Italy,"/ (in Dutch)
       TESG, 45(1954), 77-80

1525   Acher, Gilbert
       "Les migrations italiennes à travers les Alpes,"
       AG, 64(1955), 340-358

1526   Toldo, A. and Castelli, M.
       "Il Delta Padano. Evoluzione della popolazione prima e dopo il 1951,"
       Aggiornamenti Sociali, 7(1956), 81-92, 147-158

1527   Carone, G.
       Distribuzione territoriale della popolazione della regione alpina
       Trento, Arti Grafiche "Saturnia," 1957

1528   Cerutti, Augusta V.
       "Considerazioni intorno alla densità della popolazione in Valle d'Aosta,"
       pp. 351-356 in:
       Atti, XVII Congresso Geografico Italiano, Bari, 1957, Vol. 3
       Bari, Cressati, 1957

1529   Vanni, Manfredo
       "L'immigrazione a Torino dall'Italia meridionale,"
       RGI, 64(1957), 1-8

1529a Capello, Carlo F.
       "Sedi umane e popolazione nella Valle d'Aosta," pp. 73-86 in:
       Studi geografici pubblicati in onore del Prof. Renato Biasutti
       Supplemento al Vol. 65 della Rivista Geografica Italiana
       Firenze, 1958

1930   Gabert, Pierre
       "L'immigration italienne à Turin,"
       Association de Géographes Français, Bulletin, Nos. 276-277 (1958),
       30-45

1531   Leidlmair, Adolf
       Bevölkerung und Wirtschaft in Südtirol
       Innsbruck, Universitätsverlag Wagner, 1958

1532   Lendl, Egon
       "Die italienische Zuwanderung nach Südtirol,"
       Geographischen Gesellschaft in Wienn, Mitteilungen, 100(1958), 160

1533   Piccardi, Silvio
       "Contributo allo studio dello spopolamento montano nella Valle
          d'Aosta,"
       L'Universo, 38(1958), 985-990

1534   Siedentop, Irmfried
       "Südtirols Bevölkerung,"
       Zeitschrift für Wirtschaftsgeographie, 3(1959), 150-154

1535   André, Jacques
       "Densité et répartition de la population en Vénétie romaine,"
       Annales de Bretagne, 67(1960), 103-106

6740: Central Italy

1536 Errera, Carlo
      "Sull'aumento della popolazione in alcune parte della Toscana negli
         ultimi secoli,"
      RGI, 5(1898), 212-215

1537 Mori, Attilio
      "L'aumento della popolazione in Toscana negli ultimi secoli,"
      RGI, 5(1898), 38-49

1538 Romei, Pia
      Distribuzione degli abitanti in Toscana: monografia antropogeo-
         grafica
      Firenze, Ricci, 1901

1539 Bonacci, Giovannia
      "La densità di popolazione nel Lucchese e il senatore Francesco
         Gianni,"
      RGI, 12(1905), 146-154

1540 Germano, E.
      "Distribuzione della popolazione nel gruppo del Vulture,"
      L'Opinione Geografica, 6(1910), 73-78

1541 Dainelli, Giotto
      "L'aumento della popolazione toscana nel secolo XIX (Studi sulla
         distribuzione della popolazione, II),"
      Memorie Geografiche, 6, No. 19(1912), 226-336

1542 Dainelli, Giotto
      "La distribuzione della popolazione in Toscana (Studi sulla
         distribuzione della popolazione, II),"
      Memorie Geografiche, 11, No. 33(1917), 1-260

1543 Riccardi, Riccardo
      "L'aumento della popolazione in Sabina dal 1656 al 1911,"
      La Geografia, 9(1921), 203-220

1544 Riccardi, Riccardo
      "La distribuzione della popolazione in Sabina,"
      BSGI, Serie 5, 11(1922), 5-42

1545 Galavotti, Albertina
      "La diminuzione demografica della montagna (osservazioni sulla montagna
         toscana),"
      RGI, 37(1930), 87-93

1546 Emiliani, Cl.
      "La distribuzione della popolazione nel baciono dell'Esino,"
      BSGI, Serie 6, 9(1932), 142-163

1547 Pracchi, Roberto
      "La distribuzione della popolazione nel triangolo lariano,"
      RGI, 48(1941), 184-204

1548 Mori, Assunto
      "Le migrazioni stagionali dei pescatori nell'alto Terrino in relazione
        col popolamento recenti dei centri costieri,"
      BSGI, Serie 8, 1(1948), 223-237.

1549 Bevilacqua, Eugenia
      "Carta della distribuzione della popolazione sparsa e dei centri nelle
        Marche," pp. 438-441 in:
      Atti, XIV Congresso Geografico Italiano, Bologna, 1947
      Bologna, 1949

1550 Riccardi, Mario
      "Carta della distribuzione della popolazione sparsa e dei centri in
        Abruzzo,"
      BSGI, Serie 8, 3(1950), 149-161

1551 Bevilacqua, Eugenia
      I centri abitati più elevati dell'Appennino, con particolare riguardo
        a quelli dell'Abruzzo
      Università di Padova, Istituto di Geografia, Pubblicazioni, 2
      Padova, 1951-52

1552 Gigli, Fernanda
      "La densità di popolazione in Toscana nei secoli XVI e XVIII,"
      RGI, 61(1954), 265-276

1553 Pecora, Aldo
      "Sullo spopolamento montano negli Abruzzi,"
      BSGI, Serie 8, 8(1955), 508-524

1554 Lisoni, Maria Luisa
      "L'emigrazione della Lunigiana,"
      RGI, 63(1956), 204-210

1555 Alessandri, Maria Luisa
      "La densità di popolazione nella Toscana meridionale negli ultimi
        secoli,"
      RGI, 64(1957), 224-243

1556 Bugelli, Delmas A.
      The Montagna Pistoiese: population-supporting characteristics of an
        Italian Apennine region
      University Microfilms, Publication No. 21,601
      Ann Arbor, 1957

1557 Almagià, Roberto
      "Sul popolamento di un cantone montano dell'Abruzzo," pp. 1-11 in:
      Studi geografici pubblicati in onore del Prof. Renato Biasutti.
      Supplemento al Vol. 65 della Rivista Geografica Italiana
      Firenze, 1958

1558 Cozzolini, Anna M.
      Le variazioni della popolazione in Toscana dal 1911 al 1951
      Università di Pisa, Istituto di Geografica, Pubblicazioni, 5
      Pisa, Goliardica, 1958

1559 Luisi, Francesca
      "Variazione recenti della popolazione nell'Appennino settentrionale
      e zone contermini,"
      Universita di Pisa, Istituto di Geografia, Pubblicazioni, 6(1959),
      87-109

                          6750: Southern Italy

1560 Bonacci, Giovanni
      "La Calabria e l'emigrazione,"
      RGI, 15(1908), 417-431

1561 Colamonico, Carmelo
      "La distribuzione della popolazione nella Puglia centrale e meridionale
      secondo la natura geologica del suolo,"
      BSGI, Serie 5, 5(1916), 201-234, 274-305, 403-429

1562 De Grazia, Paolo
      "La diminuzione della popolazione in Basilicata,"
      BSGI, Serie 5, 10(1921), 411-440

1563 Punzo, Concetta
      "La distribuzione altimetrica delle popolazione nella Campania,"
      BSGI, Serie 5, 12(1923), 19-43

1564 Bella, Paride de
      "La Calabria e l'emigrazione,"
      BSGI, Serie 6, 1(1924), 549-608

1565 Pagano, Salvatore
      "Qualche esempio di movimenti di popolazione in Calabria,"
      L'Universo, 8(1927), 939-960

1566 Franciosa, Luchino
      "La distribuzione della popolazione nella Lucania in rapporto alle
      condizione litologiche del suolo,"
      BSGI, Serie 7, 11(1946), 65-78

1567 Franciosa, Luchino
      "La distribuzione planimentrica e altimetrica della popolazione nella
      Basilicata,"
      BSGI, Serie 8, 1(1948), 269-283

1568 Franciosa, Luchino
      "La popolazione sparsa e i centri della Basilicata,"
      BSGI, Serie 8, 4(1951), 128-143

1569 Dickinson, Robert E.
      The population problem of Southern Italy. An essay in social geography
      Maxwell School Series, 2
      Syracuse, Syracuse University Press, 1955

1570 Belli, V.
      "Distribuzione attuali della popolazione in Puglia secondo la
      distanza dal mare, con le variazione nell'ultimo quarantennio,"
      pp. 285-290 in:
      Atti, XVII Congresso Geografico Italiano, Bari, 1957, Vol. 3
      Bari, Cressati, 1957

1571 Ruocco, Domenico
      "Breve nota sul censimento del 1951, con particolare riguardo alla
      Campania," pp. 274-278 in:
      Atti, XVII Congresso Geografico Italiano, Bari, 1957, Vol. 3
      Bari, Cressati, 1957

                              6760:   Sardinia

1572 Anfossi, G.
      "Distribuzione altimetrica della popolazione in Sardegna,"
      La Geografia, 4(1915), 179-192

1573 Anfossi, G.
      "Ricerche sulla distribuzione della popolazione in Sardegna,"
      BSGI, Serie 5, 4(1915), 165-195, 277-297

1574 Alivia, G.
      La distribuzione della popolazione della Sardegna tra la montagna ed
         il litorale
      Comitato Italiano per lo Studio dei Problemi della Popolazione
      Roma, 1932

1575 Le Lannou, Maurice
      "La population et l'économie de la Sardaigne,"
      AG, 43(1934), 89-93

1576 Alivia, G.
      "Il popolamento della Sardegna," pp. 41-46 in:
      CRCIG, Amsterdam, 1938, Vol. 2

1577 Le Lannou, Maurice
      "La population," pp. 332-346 in:
      Pâtres et paysans de la Sardaigne
      Tours, Arrault, 1941

1578 Kallay, Ferencz P.
      Repopulation of Sardinia
      Doctoral dissertation, University of Michigan
      Ann Arbor, 1955

1579 Vardabasso, Silvana
      "Il popolamento delle coste della Sardegna attraverso i tempi,"
         pp. 601-618 in:
      Atti, XVI Congresso Geografico Italiano, Padova-Venezia, 1954
      Faenza, 1955

1580 Pinna, Mario and Corea, Leocadia
      La distribuzione della popolazione e i centri abitati della Sardegna
      Università di Pisa, Istituto di Geografia, Pubblicazione, 3-4
      Pisa, Goliardica, 1957

1581 Pinna, Mario
      "La distribuzione della popolazione in Sardegna,"
      L'Universo, 38(1958), 95-108

1582 Terrosu Asole, Angela
      "Il movimento migratorio dei siciliani in Sardegna,"
      BSGI, Serie 8, 11(1958), 353-360

6770: Sicily

1583 Marinelli, Olinto
      "Distribuzione della popolazione della Sicilia rispetto alla
        distanza dal mare," pp. 221-227 in:
      Atti, II Congresso Geografico Italiano, Roma, 1896

      (Also see 1582.)

1584 Orinò, Sebastiano
      Distribuzione geografica degli uomini insigni della Sicilia Parte 1
      Palermo, Reber, 1902

1585 Almagià, Roberto
      "Distribuzione della popolazione in Sicilia secondo la costituzione
        geologica del suolo,"
      RGI, 14(1907), 1-15

1586 Mori, Attilio
      "La distribuzione della popolazione in Sicilia e le sue variazioni
        negli ultimi quattro secoli,"
      Memorie Geografiche, 12, No. 36(1918), 125-314

1587 Beloch, K.
      Bevölkerungsgeschichte Italiens. I. Grundlagen, Sizilien, Königsreich
        Neapel
      Berlin, 1937

1588 Ricci, Riccardo
      "Nuovo carta della distribuzione della popolazione sparsa e dei centri
        in Sicilia,"
      BSGI, Serie 7, 4(1939), 815-834

1589 Alexandersson, Gunnar
      /"Population and economic geography of Sicily,"_7 (in Swedish)
      Ymer, 70(1950), 257-284

1590 Riccardi, Mario
      "Carta delle variazione della popolazione in Sicilia dal 1901 al
        1951,"
      BSGI, Serie 8, 11(1958), 339-352

6790: MALTA

1591 Fallot, Ernest
      "Démographie maltaise,"
      Société de Géographie et d'Etudes Coloniales de Marseille, Bulletin,
        29(1905), 160-169

1592 Robinson, George W. S.
      "The distribution of population in the Maltese Islands,"
      Geography, 33(1948), 69-78

6800: BALKAN PENINSULA

1593   Cvijić, Jovan
       La péninsule balkanique; géographie humaine
       Paris, Colin, 1918

1594   Pallis, A. A.
       "Racial migrations in the Balkans during the years 1912-1924,"
       GJ, 66(1925), 315-331
1595   Čubrilović, V.
       /"Political factors in population change in the Balkans from 1860
          to 1880,"/ (in Serbian)
       Srpsko Geografsko Društvo, Glasnik, 16(1930), 26-49

6810: GREECE

1596   Ardaillon, E.
       "Répartition des chrétiens et des musulmans dans l'île de Crète,"
       AG, 6(1897), 255-257

1597   Oppel, A.
       "Die Griechen nach Zahl, Verbreitung und Abstammung,"
       Globus, 71(1897), 249-255

1598   Philippson, Alfred
       "Die Bevölkerungszunahme in Griechenland,"
       Geographische Zeitschrift, 3(1897), 409-411

1599   Baldacci, Antonio
       "La popolazione dell'Epiro,"
       BSGI, Serie 4, 1(1900), 102-104

1600   Rambaud, Jacques
       "L'émigration grecque,"
       AG, 19(1910), 177-182

1601   Ancel, Jacques
       "Les migrations de peuples dans la Grèce actuelle,"
       AG, 34(1925), 277-280

1602   Blanchard, Raoul
       "The exchange of populations between Greece and Turkey,"
       GR, 15(1925), 449-456

1603   Fels, Edwin
       "Die griechische Völkerwanderung,"
       Geographische Zeitschrift, 33(1927), 576-588

1604   Lehmann, Herbert
       Uber die potentielle Volkskapazitat der Peloponnes. Ein Beitrag zur
          Bonitierung der Erdoberfläche
       Doctoral dissertation, University of Berlin
       Berlin, 1927

1605 Ogilvie, Alan G.
      "Population density in Greece,"
      GJ, 101(1943), 251-260

1606 Armao, Ermanno
      "Superficie e popolazione delle isole del Mar Egeo,"
      BSGI, Serie 7, 12(1947), 266-274

1607 Celli, Silvano
      "Densità di popolazione dei centri abitati nelle Isole Eolie,"
      pp. 434-437 in:
      Atti, XIV Congresso Geografico Italiano, Bolgna, 1947
      Bologna, 1949

1608 Allbaugh, Leland G.
      "Human resources," pp. 54-65 in:
      Crete; a case study of an underdeveloped area
      Princeton, Princeton University Press, 1953

1609 Salmon, Pierre
      "La population de la Grèce antique. Essai de démographie appliquée
      à l'antiquité,"
      Société Royale Belge de Géographie, Bulletin, 77(1955), 34-61

1610 Common, Robert
      "Some recent developments in Greece,"
      TESG, 49(1958), 253-266

1611 Common, Robert
      "Population changes on the Salonika Campagna,"
      Canadian Geographer, No. 13(1959), 31-40

1612 Riccardi, Mario
      "Il recente sviluppo demografico ed economico della Grecia,"
      BSGI, Serie 9,1(1961), 181-205

                          6830: ALBANIA

1613 Almagià, Roberto
      "Un computo approssimato della popolazione dell'Albania,"
      RGI, 28(1921), 122-125

1614 Louis, Herbert
      "Die Bevölkerung Albanien," pp. 36-47 in:
      Albanien: eine Landeskunde
      Stuttgart, Engelhorn, 1927

1615 Popp, Marian
      "Les confessions en Albanie,"
      Societatea Romănă de Geografie, Buletinul, 50(1931), 216-236

1616 Bonasera, Francesco
      "Gli italiani in Albania," pp. 441-443 in:
      Atti, XIV Congresso Geographico Italiano, Bologna, 1947
      Bologna, 1949

6840: YUGOSLAVIA

1617 Daneš, Georg V.
        Bevölkerungsdichtigkeit der Hercegovina
        Travaux Géographiques Tchéques, 3
        Praha, 1903

1618 Gravisi, Giannandrea
        "Distribuzione altimetrica della popolazione dell'Istria,"
        Alpi Giulie (Trieste), 9(1904), 122-126

1619 Gravisi, Giannandrea
        "Distribuzione della popolazione dell'Istria secondo la costituzione
          geologica del suolo,"
        RGI, 12(1905), 19-29

1620 Gravisi, Giannandrea
        "Nazionalità e densità di popolazione in Istria,"
        BSGI, Serie 4, 5(1905), 149-152

1621 Krebs, Norbert
        Densità e aumento della popolazione nell'Istria e in Trieste
        Estratto all'Archeografo Triestino, Vol. 30
        Trieste, 1905
        Also: Archeografo Triestino, 1, No. 3(1905), 1-26

1622 Oestreich, Karl
        "Die Bevölkerung von Makedonien,"
        Geographische Zeitschrift, 11(1905), 268-292

1623 Gravier, Gaston
        /"The density of population in Serbia,"/ (in Serbian)
        Srpsko Geografsko Društvo, Glasnik, 3-4(1914), 32-38

1624 Marcić, Lucijan
        /"Migration in the islands of Zara and Sibenik,"/ (in Serbian)
        Srpsko Geografsko Društvo, Glasnik, 15(1929), 61-64

1625 Baš, F.
        "Die Verbreitung der Protestanten im Prekmurje,"
        Geografski Vestnik, 5-6(1930), 78-92

1626 Popp, Nicolae M. A.
        "La minorité roumano-albanaise de Yougoslavie,"
        Societatea Română de Geografie, Buletinul, 50(1931), 353-375

1627 Roglic, Josip
        /"Agriculture and population in the Makarska littoral,"/ (in Serbian)
        Srpsko Geografsko Društvo, Glasnik, 17(1931), 29-37

1628 Milojević, Borivoje Z.
        "Le surpeuplement de la région dinarique montagneuse," pp. 599-602 in:
        CRCIG, Varsovie, 1934, Vol. 3

1629 Milojević, Borivoje Z.
        "Le peuplement de la région dinarique montagneuse,"
        Société Belge d'Etudes Géographiques, Bulletin, 5(1935), 124-129

1630 Bukurov, Branislav B.
      /"Migrations after the World War in the region northwest of Potsje,"/
      (in Serbian)
      Srpsko Geograsko Društvo, Glasnik, 25(1939), 54-64

1631 Ilešić, Svetozar
      /"The increase of population in the banovina of Savska from 1880 to
      1931,"/ (in Serbian)
      Geografski Glasnik, 8-10(1939), 85-93

1632 Ilešić, Svetozar
      /"The increase of population in the territory of Yugoslavia,"/ (in
      Serbian)
      Geografski Vestnik, 16(1940), 3-24

1633 Melik, Anton
      /"Density of population in Yugoslavia,"/ (in Serbian)
      Geografski Vestnik, 16(1940), 88-104

1634 Royal Geographical Society
      "Land and population of Yugoslavia,"
      GJ, 97(1941), 265-266

1635 Ortolani, Mario
      "La distribuzione della popolazione in Dalmazia,"
      BSGI, Serie 7, 8(1943), 208-218

1636 Ilešić, Svetozar
      /"The density of rural population in Carinthia,"/ (in Slovenian)
      Geografski Vestnik, 18(1946), 22-34

1637 Filipovič, Milenko
      /"Alimentary migrations,"/ (in Serbian)
      Srpsko Geografsko Društvo, Glasnik, 27(1947), 76-93

1638 Zrimec, Stane
      /"Population density map, Yugoslavia, 1948,"/ (in.Serbian)
      Geografski Vestnik, 20-21(1948-1949), 317-326

1639 Nikolić, Rajko
      /"Economy, settlement, and population of the loess plateau of Titelski
      Breg,"/ (in Serbian)
      Srpsko Geografsko Društvo, Glasnik, 29(1949), 119-140

1640 Lipoglavšek-Rakovec, Sl.
      /"The Slovenian emigrants,"/ (in Slovenian)
      Geografski Vestnik, 22(1950), 3-58

1641 Zrimec, Stane
      /"Mouvement de la population de la Slovénie de 1931 à 1948,"/ (in
      Slovenian)
      Geografski Vestnik, 22(1950), 61-93

1642 Jutronić, Andre
      /"The population and settlements on the islands of Middle Dalmatia
      from the beginning of the fifteenth century to the middle of the
      nineteenth century,"/ (in Serbian)
      Srpsko Geografsko Društvo, Glasnik, 32(1952), 129-137

1643 Jutronić, Andre
      /"Population changes in the islands of central Dalmatia during the
      last one hundred years,"/ (in Serbian)
      Geografski Glasnik, 14-15(1952-53), 65-70

1644 Klemenčič, Vladimir
      /"Mouvement de la population dans la Carinthie slovène entre 1934 et
      1951,"/ (in Slovenian)
      Geografski Vestnik, 24(1952), 115-134

1645 Klemenčič, Vladimir
      /"Significance of the population censuses of 1948 and 1953 for the
      geography of the population of Slovenia,"/ (in Slovenian)
      Geografski Vestnik, 26(1954), 187-190

1646 Myers, Paul F. and Campbell, Arthur A.
      The population of Yugoslavia
      U. S. Bureau of the Census, International Population Statistics
      Reports, Series P-90, No. 5
      Washington, 1954

1647 Trifunoski, Jovan F.
      /"Population movements in Macedonia,"/ (in Serbian)
      Srpsko Geografsko Društvo, Glasnik, 35(1955), 140-142

1648 Crkvenčić, Ivan
      /"Hrvatsko Zagorje, foyer d'émigration,"/ (in Serbian)
      Geografski Glasnik, 18(1956), 33-45

1649 Witthauer, Kurt
      "Bevölkerungsdichte und -zunahme. Beziehungen der Zahlenwerte am
      Beispiel Jugoslawien,"
      PM, 100(1956), 159-162

1650 Milojević, Borivoje Z.
      "Population," pp. 86-92 in:
      Yugoslavia; geographical survey
      Belgrade, Committee for Cultural Relations with Foreign Countries, 1958

                            6880: RUMANIA

1651 Martonne, Emmanuel de
      "Recherches sur la distribution géographique de la population en
      Valachie,"
      Societatea Română de Geografie, Buletinul, 23(1902), 1-161
      Also: Paris, Colin, 1903

1652 Dimitrescu, A. G.
      Bevölkerungsdichte der Moldau, nach natürlichen Gebieten berechnet
      Bucuresti, Baer, 1909

1653 Mihailescu, Vintila
      /"Contribution to the study of the population and human establishments
      of the Romanian plain between 1853 and 1899,"/ (in Rumanian)
      Societatea Română de Geografie, Buletinul, 41(1922), 96-111

1654   Schiarini, G. Pompilio
       "L'emigrazione italiana in Romania,"
       BSGI, Serie 5, 12(1923), 437-442

1655   Girard, C.
       "Le peuplement de la Bucovine,"
       AG, 34(1925), 226-234

1656   Mihailescu, Vintila
       /"Mode of population grouping in Dobruja,"/ (in Rumanian)
       Societatea Română de Geografie, Buletinul, 47(1928), 373-376

1657   Somesan, Laurian
       /"The population of the Călimani area,"/ (in Rumanian)
       Cluj, Universitatea, Institut de Geografie, Travaux, 6(1936-38), 10-70

1658   Manig, Marianne
       Die Volksdichte Rumäniens
       Doctoral dissertation, University of Frankfurt
       Würzburg, Triltsch, 1937

1659   Beynon, Erdmann D.
       "The eastern outposts of the Magyars,"
       GR, 31(1941), 63-78

1660   Nimigeanu, G.
       /"Population density in southern Bukovina,"/ (in Rumanian)
       Revista Geografică (Bucuresti), 4(1946), 334-347

1661   Suret-Canale, Jean
       "Les nationalités en Roumanie d'après le recensement de 1948," pp. 429-
          443 in:
       Université de Rennes, cinquantienne anniversaire du Laboratoire de
          Géographie (1902-1952), volume jubilaire
       Rennes, 1952

1662   Herbst, Constantin
       /"Quantitative evolution and changes in the distribution of the urban
          population of the R.P.R. during the period 1930-1956,"/ (in Rumanian)
       Probleme de Geografie (Bucuresti), 5(1957), 217-230

1663   Tufescu, Victor
       /"The growth of population in Rumanian towns in 1948-1956,"/ (in
          Rumanian)
       Studi si Cercetări de Geologie-Geografie (Cluj), 8(1957), 55-70

1664   George, Pierre and Suret-Canale, Jean
       "Informations démographiques et économiques sur la Roumanie,"
       AG, 67(1958), 89-94

1665   Haiduc, N.
       /"Some aspects of the urban population's territorial distribution in
          our country,"/ (in Rumanian)
       Probleme Economic (Bucuresti), 11(1958), 31-42

1666   Rumania, Directiune Centrala de Statistica
       /"Population density in the People's Republic of Rumania,"/ (in
          Rumanian)
       Revista de Statistica (Bucuresti), 7(1958), 47-60

1667 Slepyan, S. G.
      /"Changes in the population of Rumania in connection with industriali-
      zation,"/ (in Russian)
      Akademiia Nauk S.S.S.R., Moskva, Izvestiia, Seriia Geograficheskaia,
      9, No. 1(1959), 98-103

1668 Roubitschek, Walter
      "Zur Bevölkerungs- und Agrarstruktur Rumäniens,"
      PM, 104(1960), 23-33

1669 Tufescu, Victor, et al.
      "Géographie de la population de la R.P. Roumaine," pp. 129-141 in:
      Académie de la République Populaire Roumaine, Institut de Géologie,
      Géophysique et Géographie
      Recueil d'études géographiques concernant le territoire de la
      République Populaire Roumaine, 1960
      Bucuresti, 1960

      (Also see 1318, 1849, 1850, 1851, 1852)

                         6890: BULGARIA

1670 Ichirkov, A.
      "Die Bevölkerung in Bulgarien und ihre Siedlungsverhältnisse,"
      PM, 57(1911), 117-122, 179-187

1671 Ichirkov, A.
      /"Density of population in Bulgaria,"/ (in Bulgarian)
      Naučen Pregled (Sofia), 2, No. 2(1930), 59-68

1672 Beaver, Stanley H.
      /"Distribution of the population in Bulgaria,"/ (in Bulgarian)
      Bulgarsko Geografsko Druzhestvo, Izvestiia, 4(1936), 110-117

1673 Kosack, Hans-Peter
      "Ein Beitrag zur Methodik der Bevölkerungskarten: Nationali-
      tätenkarte Bulgariens,"
      Gesellschaft für Erdkunde zu Berlin, Zeitschrift, Series 4, 36(1937),
      348-372

1674 Popov, Vl.
      /"The center of the state and the center of population in Bulgaria,"/
      (in Bulgarian)
      Bulgarsko Geografsko Druzhestvo, Izvestiia, 5(1937), 132-144

1675 Penkov, Ig.
      /"Distribution of inhabited places and population in Bulgaria with
      relation to the elevation above sea level,"/ (in Bulgarian)
      Bulgarsko Geografsko Druzhestvo, Izvestiia, 6(1938), 85-102

1676 Barten, H.
      "Die Entwicklung der Bevölkerung Bulgariens in der letzten Zeit,"
      Zeitschrift für Geopolitik, 16, No. 5(1939)

1677 Barten, H.
      "Bevölkerungsentwicklung und Bevölkerungsprobleme in Bulgarien,"
      Zeitschrift für Erdkunde, 9(1941), 176-180

1678   Batakliev, Ivan
       "Binnen- und Auswanderungen der Bulgaren und ihre völkische und
          staatliche Bedeutung,"
       Zeitschrift für Erdkunde, 9(1941), 129-142

1679   Tanoglu, Ali
       "The recent emigration of the Bulgarian Turks,"
       Istanbul, Üniversite, Coğrafya Enstitüsü, Review, 2(1955), 3-35

       (Also see 1622, 1896, 1898)

                          6910:   SCANDINAVIA

1680   Jonasson, Olaf
       "The relation between the distribution of population and of cultivated
          land in the Scandinavian countries, especially in Sweden, based on
          some recently published maps and agricultural literature,"
       EG, 1(1925), 107-123

1681   O'Dell, Andrew C.
       "Population," pp. 508-517 in:
       The Scandinavian world
       London, Longmans, Green, 1957

1682   Mead, William R.
       "The human setting," pp. 68-84 in:
       An economic geography of the Scandinavian states and Finland
       London, University of London Press, 1958

       (Also see 1801)

                          6920:   DENMARK

1683   Anderson, C. E.
       "Die dänische Volkszählung von 1940,"
       PM, 88(1942), 219-222

1684   Aagesen, Aage
       "Die Bevölkerung Dänemarks,"
       Geographische Rundschau, 8(1956), 424-431

1685   Aagesen, Aage
       /"The population geography of northern Schleswig,"_/ (in Danish)
       Geografisk Tidsskrift, 57(1958), 109-126

1686   Aagesen, Aage
       "The population of Denmark," pp. 310-322 in:
       Niels Kingo Jacobsen, ed.
       Guidebook Denmark; contributions to problems discussed in symposia
          and excursions
       Nineteenth International Geographical Congress
       København, Universitets Geografiske Institut, 1960
       Also: Geografisk Tidsskrift, 59(1960), 163-175

6925:   FAEROE ISLANDS

1687 Denmark, Statistike Departement
      /Population and industry of the Faeroe Islands/ (in Danish)
      Statistical Communications, 4th Series, 103
      København, 1937

6930:   ICELAND

1688 Malmstrom, Vincent H.
      "Population," pp. 123-132 in:
      A regional geography of Iceland
      National Academy of Sciences-National Research Council, Publ. 584
      Washington, 1958

1689 Thorarinsson, Sigurdur
      "Population changes in Iceland,"
      GR, 51(1961), 519-533

6940:   NORWAY

1690 Magnus, Hagbart
      "Die Bewegung der norwegischen Bevölkerung in den Jahren 1891-1896,"
      Geographische Zeitschrift, 4(1898), 410-411

1691 Neukirch, Karl
      "Die Bevölkerung Norwegens nach der Zählung vom 3. Dezember 1900,"
      Geographische Zeitschrift, 7(1901), 514-525

1692 Hammer, K. V.
      "L'émigration norvégienne,"
      La Géographie, 24(1911), 170-173

1693 Söderlund, Alfred
      /The distribution of population in Norway/ (in Norwegian)
      Oslo, Fabritius & Sonners, 1923

1694 Söderlund, Alfred
      "The population map of Norway and other population maps," pp. 274-
          278 in:
      CRCIG, Varsovie, 1934, Vol. 1

1695 Sommers, Lawrence M.
      "Möre og Romsdal County, Norway: population distribution,"
      Journal of Geography, 50(1951), 309-317

1696 Sund, Tore
      /"The distribution of population in the 'Bergen Counties,' 1946.
        Comments on a population map,"/ (in Norwegian), pp. 189-198 in:
      /Festschrift for I. Wedervang on his 60th birthday, July 21, 1951/
      Oslo, Bedriftsøkonomisk Forlag, 1951

1697 Lunde, A. A.
      Norway: a population study
      Ann Arbor, University Microfilms, 1955

1698 L'Orange, Hans
      /"New population map of Norway,"/ (in Norwegian)
      Statistike Meldinger (Oslo), 73(1955), 56-66

1699 Rödevand, Øivind
      /"Depopulation in remote districts of Norway,"/ (in Danish)
      Kulturgeografi, 7(1955), 65-69

1700 Helvig, Magne
      "Norwegen: Der Wechsel in der Beschäftigungslage und seine Wirkungen
          auf die Bevölkerung," pp. 293-304 in:
      Emil Meynen, ed.
      Geographisches Taschenbuch und Jahrweiser zur Landeskunde 1960/61
      Wiesbaden, 1960

      (Also see 376, 426)

                          6950: SWEDEN

                          a. National

1701 Stolpe, Per
      /"On the interrelations between population distribution and geological
          formations in Sweden,"/ (in Swedish)
      Ymer, 24(1904), 281-296

1702 Rabot, Charles
      "La distribution de la population en Suède en fonction de la constitu-
          tion géologique du sol,"
      La Géographie, 11(1905), 359-367

1703 Didczun, Max
      Der Einfluss der geographischen Beschaffenheit und der wirtschaft-
          lichen Entwicklung auf die Siedelungen und die Wohndichte der
          Bevölkerung Schwedens
      Doctoral dissertation, University of Königsberg
      Königsberg, Kemsies, 1908

1704 Flodström, J.
      /"Concerning questions of racial distinctions within the population
          of Sweden,"/ (in Swedish)
      Ymer, 35(1915), 213-266

1705 De Geer, Sten
      /Distribution of population in Sweden. Description of a map at the
          scale of 1:500,000/ (in Swedish)
      Stockholm, Wahlström & Widstrand, 1919

1706 De Geer, Sten
      "La distribution de la population en Suède,"
      La Géographie, 37(1922), 517-524

1707 De Geer, Sten
      "A map of the distribution of population in Sweden: method of prepara-
      tion and general results,"
      GR, 12(1922), 72-83

1708 Von Prosch, C.
      "Schwedische Arbeitserfolge in der Darstellung der Bevölkerungs-
      verteilung,"
      Geographische Zeitschrift, 28(1922), 105-112

1709 William-Olsson, William
      /"The development of agglomerations and of the total population in
      Sweden, 1880-1935,"/ (in Swedish)
      Ymer, 58(1938), 243-280

1710 Höijer, Ernst
      /"The state of the population from a general and geographical point
      of view,"/ (in Swedish)
      Ymer, 64(1944), 114-131

1711 Godlund, Sven
      /"Development and structure of the Swedish population,"/ (in Swedish)
      Geografiska Notiser, 7(1949), 11-15

1712 Enequist, Gerd
      /"A map of the habitations of Sweden,"/ (in Swedish)
      Ymer, 70(1950), 181-206

1713 Quensel, Carl Erik
      /"The regional distribution of marriages in different types of
      parishes in Sweden,"/ (in Swedish)
      Svensk Geografisk Årsbok, 26(1950), 26-44

1714 Leighly, John B.
      "Population and settlement: some recent Swedish studies,"
      GR, 42(1952), 134-137

1715 Ahlberg, Gösta
      /Population growth and urbanization in Sweden, 1911-50/ (in Swedish)
      Stockholm, Stockholms Kommunalförvaltning, 1953

1716 Ahlberg, Gösta
      Population trends and urbanization in Sweden, 1911-1950
      Lund Studies in Geography, Series B, Human Geography, No. 16
      Lund, G. W. K. Gleerup, 1956

1717 Hannerberg, David, ed.
      Migration in Sweden: a symposium
      Lund Studies in Geography, Series B, Human Geography, No. 13
      Lund, G. W. K. Gleerup, 1957

1718 Nordström, Olof
      /"Population changes in Sweden 1805-1950,"/ (in Swedish)
      Svensk Geografisk Årsbok, 35(1959), 123-132

1719 Winberg, Isak P.
      /"Regional differences in the development in population in Sweden,"/
      (in Swedish)
      Ymer, 79(1959), 22-43

1720   Enequist, Gerd and Norling, Gunnar, eds.
       Advance and retreat of rural settlement. Papers of the Siljan Sym-
          posium at the XIXth International Geographical Congress
       Geografiska Annaler, 42, No. 4
       Stockholm, 1960

1720a Winberg, Isak P.
       /"Regional differences of some demographic factors,"/ (in Swedish)
       Ymer, 81(1961), 105-127

       (Also see 115, 315, 426)

                                   b. Regional

1721   De Geer, Sten
       /"Distribution of population in Gottland,"/ (in Swedish)
       Ymer, 28(1908), 240-253

1722   Stolpe, Per
       /"Concerning some questions of the distribution of population in
          Gottland,"/ (in Swedish)
       Ymer, 28(1908), 413-419

1723   Sjögren, Otto
       /Distribution of population in a part of northern Uppland/ (in Swedish)
       Studier i Svensk Bebyggelsegeografi, 1
       Uppsala, 1913

1724   Swedberg, Sven
       /"Geographic factors in the distribution of population in Söderman-
          land in 1910,"/ (in Swedish)
       Ymer, 23(1913), 385-411

1725   Hannerberg, David
       /The rural area of Närke, 1600-1820. Population and population move-
          ment, agriculture and grain production/ (in Swedish)
       Stockholm, Stiftelsen Saxons Närkesarkiv, 1941

1726   Uhnbom, Ivar
       /"Population development in Norrland from ancient times to the present
          period,"/ (in Swedish) pp. 255-270 in:
       /Norrland; nature, population, and industry/
       Stockholm, Industriens Utredningsinstitut, 1942

1727   William-Olsson, William
       /"The population of Norrland,"/ (in Swedish) pp. 271-282 in:
       /Norrland; nature, population, and industry/
       Stockholm Industriens Utredningsinstitut, 1942

1728   Hägerstrand, T.
       /"The movements of rural population. Migration studies on the basis
          of the parish registers of Asby, 1840-1944,"/ (in Swedish)
       Svensk Geografisk Årsbok, 23(1947), 114-142

1729   Jonasson, Olof G.
       /Population and food resources in central Sweden within the traffic
          area of the Göteborg-Dalarne-Gävle, 1865-1940; a geographical study
          of a railroad/ (in Swedish)
       Göteborg, Gumpert, 1950

1730 Molin, Kerstin
      /"Deserted habitations and depopulation in the parish of Järnboås,"/
      (in Swedish)
      Svensk Geografisk Årsbok, 26(1950), 102-118

1731 Friberg, Nils
      /Population of Dalecarlia in the 17th Century/ (in Swedish)
      Geografiska Annaler, Vol. 35, pp. 3-4
      Stockholm, 1953

1732 Birck, E.
      /"Studies concerning agriculture and population in Pedersöre Parish,
      Österboten, 1750-1850,"/ (in Swedish)
      Fennia, 79(1953), No. 3

1733 Edestam, Anders
      /"The population of Dalsland, Sweden in the years 1880 and 1950,"/
      (in Swedish)
      Svensk Geografisk Årsbok, 31(1955), 156-198

1734 Norborg, Knut and Nordström, Olof
      /"Bevölkerungsentwicklung und Rationalisierung der Landwirtschaft in
      Ostsmåland,"/ (in Swedish)
      Svensk Geografisk Årsbok, 31(1955), 86-104

1735 Friberg, Nils
      "The growth of population and its economic-geographical background in
      a mining district in central Sweden, 1650-1750; a methodological
      study,"
      Geografiska Annaler, 38(1956), 395-440

1736 Wendel, Bertil
      /"Resettlement of the population in Scania, 1951-1955,"/ (in Swedish)
      Svensk Geografisk Årsbok, 33(1957), 128-136

1737 Winberg, Isak P.
      /"Net migration, and rationalisation in agriculture in the thinly
      populated districts of southern and central Sweden,"/ (in Swedish)
      Ymer, 77(1957), 190-199

1738 Odeving, Bruno
      /"Population trends in Scania; a methodological study,"/ (in Swedish)
      Svensk Geografisk Årsbok, 34(1958), 145-148

1739 Nordström, Olof
      "Population, settlement and agriculture in south and central Sweden,"
      Svensk Geografisk Årsbok, 36(1960), 46-57

                            6960: FINLAND

1740 Noevius, E. R.
      "La densité de la population en Finlande, d'après une methode carto-
      graphique nouvelle,"
      Fennia, 18(1901), No. 3

1741   Layec, A.
       "Un complement à l'atlas finlandais. Carte de densité de la popula-
       tion,"
       Société Bretonne de Géographie, Bulletin, 20(1902), 244-248

1742   Fontell, A. G.
       "Die natürliche Bevölkerungszunahme in Finnland,"
       Fennia, 21(1904), No. 4

1743   Westerlund, F. W.
       /"Is our demographic problem also a racial problem?"/ (in Swedish)
       Fennia, 42(1921), No. 4

1744   Borremans, Louis
       "L'émigration finlandaise,"
       Société Royale Belge de Géographie, Bulletin, 53(1929), 139-141

1745   Borremans, Louis
       "La population de la Finlande,"
       Société Royale Belge de Géographie, Bulletin, 54, fasc. 2(1930), 103-
       109

1746   Niemelä, Paavo
       Die Verteilung der Bevölkerung im Hügelland von Salo in Südwest-
       Publicationes Instituti Geographici Universitatis Turkuensis, No. 18
       Turku, 1939

1747   Smeds, Helmer and Mattila, Jorma
       /"On the development of urban and rural areas in Finland since 1880.
       A study in the geography of population,"/ (in Swedish)
       Geografiska Annaler, 23(1941), 210-238

1748   Smeds, Helmer
       /"The center of population in Finland,"/ (in Swedish)
       Terra, 54(1942), 180-186

1749   Evers, Wilhelm
       "Bevölkerung," pp. 58-78 in:
       Suomi-Finnland; Land und Volk im hohen Norden
       Stuttgart, Franckh'sche Verlagshandlung, 1950

1750   Smeds, Helmer
       /"Are Finland's rural areas overpopulated?"/ (in Swedish)
       Publicationes Instituti Geographici Universitatis Helsingiensis,
       No. 14(1951), 71-108

1751   Jaatinen, Stig
       /The center of population in Finland,/ (in Swedish)
       Publicationes Instituti Geographici Universitatis Helsingiensis, No. 15
       Helsinki, 1952

1752   Kanervo, Erkki
       "The displaced population," pp. 381-400 in:
       Suomi; a general handbook on the geography of Finland
       Helsinki, Geographical Society of Finland, 1952

1753   Smeds, Helmer
       "A new population and settlement map of Finland," pp. 505-507 in:
       CRCIG, Washington, 1952

1754 Tunkelo, A.
      "Population," pp. 315-334 in:
      Suomi; a general handbook on the geography of Finland
      Helsinki, Geographical Society of Finland, 1952

1755 Enkola, Kurt
      Kulturgeographische Betrachtungen über die Bevölkerungsentwicklung
         Südwestfinnlands in den Jahren 1840-1940
      Publicationes Instituti Geographici Universitatis Turkuensis, No. 27
      Turku, 1953

1756 Jaatinen, Stig
      /"Regionale Züge in der Bevölkerungsentwicklung Ålands 1900-1950,"/
         (in Swedish)
      Fennia, 76, No. 4(1953), 1-88

1757 Smeds, Helmer
      /Plan for a new population map of Finland; population distribution
         according to the 1950 census/ (in Swedish)
      Publicationes Instituti Geographici Universitatis Helsingiensis, No.17
      Helsinki, 1953

1758 Vries, J. de
      /"The displaced population in Finland,"/ (in Dutch)
      K. Nederlandsch Aardrijkskundig Gennotschap, Tijdschrift, Series 2,
         70(1953), 526-531

1759 Ajo, Reino
      "New aspects of geographic and social patterns of net migration rate;
         a pilot study based on Finnish statistics for the year 1951,"
      Svensk Geografisk Årsbok, 30(1954), 153-167

1760 Jaatinen, Stig
      /"On the population and economic-geographical development of the Åland
         Islands 1900-1950,"/ (in Swedish)
      Terra, 66(1954), 37-51

1761 Platt, Raye R., ed.
      "Population and social structure," pp. 42-94 in:
      Finland and its geography; an American Geographical Society handbook
      New York, Duell, Sloan and Pearce, 1955

1762 Smeds, Helmer
      The distribution of urban and rural population in Southern Finland 1950
      Publicationes Instituti Geographici Universitatis Helsingiensis, No. 25
      Helsinki, 1957

1763 Jaatinen, Stig
      /Population distribution and cultivated area, 1950, in the Finnish
         skerrygard/ (in Swedish)
      Helsinki, Svenska Handelshögskolan, Ekonomisk-Geografiska
         Institutionen, Meddelanden, Nr. 13
      Helsinki, 1958

1764 Klövekorn, Martin
      "Die finnlandschwedische Bevölkerung und die Sprachverhältnisse in
         Finnland,"
      Erdkunde, 12(1958), 161-182

1765 Jutikkala, Eino
      "Geographical distribution of emigration in Finland," pp. 460-467 in:
      International Union for the Scientific Study of Population
      Internationaler Bevölkerungskongress, Wien 1959
      Wien, Winkler, 1959

1766 Klövekorn, Martin
      Die sprachliche struktur Finnlands 1880-1950. Veränderungen im
         sprachlichen Charakter der finnlandschwedischen Gebiete und deren
         bevölkerungs-, wirtschafts- und sozialgeographische Ursachen
      Bidrag till kännendom af Finlands natur och folk, H. 105
      Helsinki, 1960

1767 De Geer, Eric
      "Migration in the archipelago of southwestern Finland during the last
         hundred years,"
      Fennia, 84(1960), 66-90

      (Also see 331, 381, 1806)

6965: EASTERN EUROPE

1768 Krebs, Norbert
      "Die Ostgrenze des deutschen Volkstums im Spiegel der Bevölkerungs-
         verschiebung,"
      Deutsches Archiv für Landes- und Volksforschung, 1(1937), 793-807

1769 Moore, Wilbert E.
      Economic demography of eastern and southern Europe
      Geneva, League of Nations, 1945

1770 Schlenger, Herbert
      "Beziehungen zwischen Kulturgeographie und Bevölkerungsentwicklung
         in Ost-Mitteleuropa seit dem Anfang des 19. Jahrhunderts. Ein
         Beitrag zur Sozialgeographie," pp. 501-505 in:
      CRCIG, Washington, 1952

7000: UNION OF SOVIET SOCIALIST REPUBLICS

a. Bibliography

1771 Matveev, G. P.
      /"Dissertations on the geography of population and cities,"/ (in
         Russian)
      Voprosy Geografii, No. 45(1959), 267-269

1772 Varlamov, V. S.
      /"Population geography in new monographs on economic regions and
         Union Republics,"/ (in Russian)
      Voprosy Geografii, No. 45(1959), 253-258

      (Also see 1794)

b. National

7000-7010:   U.S.S.R. and Russia in Europe

1773 Untilov, V.
      /"Einige Bemerkungen in Bezug auf die Dichte der Bevölkerung im
      europaische Russland soweit der physikalisch-geographisch Bedingungen
      abhängt,"/ (in Russian)
      Zemlevedenie; Geograficheskii Zhurnal, 4(1895), 125-140

1774 Semenov-Tian-Shanskii, Veniamin Petrovich
      /Russia; a full geographical description of our fatherland . . . /
      (in Russian), 11 vols.
      St. Petersburg, 1899-1913

1775 Barré, Paul
      "Le peuplement et la colonisation de la Russie d'Europe,"
      Revue de Géographie, 50(1902), 141-162

1776 Velekii, S. N.
      /"The population of Ufa Guberniya,"/ (in Russian)
      Imperatskoe Russkoe Geograficheskoe Obshchestvo, Izvestiia, 38(1902),
      546-614

1777 Aïtoff, D.
      "Peuples et langues de la Russie d'après les données du premier
      recensement russe exécuté en 1897,"
      AG, 15(1906), 9-25

1778 Woeikof, A.
      "Le groupement de la population rurale en Russie,"
      AG, 18(1909), 13-23

1779 Veynberg, B. P.
      /"Positions of the center of density of Russia's population from 1613
      to 1913"/ (in Russian)
      Imperatskoe Russkoe Geograficheskoe Obshchestvo, Izvestiia, 51(1915),
      385-418

1780 Hettner, Alfred
      "Besiedelung und Bevölkerung," pp. 115-142 in:
      Russland: eine geographische Betrachtung von Volk, Staat und Kultur
      Leipzig and Berlin, Teubner, 1916

1781 LeConte, René
      "L'immigration allemande dans l'Empire des Tsars,"
      Mouvement Géographique, 33(1920), 565-572

1782 LeConte, René
      "La répartition des Allemands en Russie,"
      Mouvement Géographique, 33(1920), 593-596

1783 Friederichsen, Max
      "Die dasymetrische (dichtermessende) Karte des Europäischen Russlands,"
      PM, 70(1924), 214-215

1784 U.S.S.R., Institut Izucheniye Poverchnost i Nedra
      /Dasymetric map of European Russia/ (in Russian)
      Leningrad, 1926

1785 Semenov-Tianschansky, B.
      "Russia. Territory and population. A perspective on the 1926
         census,"
      GR, 18(1928), 616-640

1786 Soulas, Jean
      "Le développement des grandes villes en URSS au cours du premier plan
         quinquennal,"
      AG, 47(1938), 400-405

1787 Plaetschke, Bruno
      "Ergebnisse der vorjährigen Sowjetrussischen Volkszählung in geograph-
         ischer Betrachtung,"
      PM, 86(1940), 191-201

1788 Prokopovich, S. N.
      "Changes in the location of population and industry of the USSR,"
      Quarterly Bulletin of Soviet Russian Economics, 1940, 122-142

1789 Konstantinov, Oleg A.
      /"Changes that have occurred in the geographical distribution of the
         large cities of the Soviet Union,"/ (in Russian)
      Geograficheskoe Obshchestvo, S.S.S.R., Izvestiia, 73(1941), 23-30

1790 Plaetschke, Bruno
      "Fragen der Bevölkerungsbewegung und Siedlungspolitik in der Sowjet-
         union,"
      Geographischer Anzeiger, 42(1941), 132-139

1791 Konstantinov, Oleg A.
      /"Geographical differences in the dynamics of urban population in the
         USSR,"/ (in Russian)
      Geograficheskoe Obshchestvo, S.S.S.R., Izvestiia, 76(1943), 11-24

1792 Harris, Chauncy D.
      "The cities of the Soviet Union,"
      GR, 35(1945), 107-121

1793 Harris, Chauncy D.
      "Ethnic groups in cities of the Soviet Union,"
      GR, 35(1945), 466-473

1794 Lorimer, Frank
      The population of the Soviet Union: history and prospects
      Geneva, League of Nations, 1946

1795 Saushkin, Iu. G.
      /"The geographical study of the rural population of places in the
         Soviet Union,"/ (in Russian)
      Voprosy Geografii, No. 5(1947), 53-66

1796 Lyalikov, N. I.
      /"Essays on the geography of population of the USSR,"/ (in Russian)
      Geografiia v Shkole, 1948, No. 2, 15-23 and No. 3, 4-14

1797 Balzak, S. S., Vasyutin, V. F., and Feigin, Ya. G., eds.
      "The population of the USSR and its distribution," pp. 167-200 in:
      Economic geography of the USSR
      New York, Macmillan, 1949

1798 Pokshishevskii, Vadim V.
      /The geography of the migration of population in Russia/ (in Russian)
      Doctoral dissertation, University of Moskva
      Moskva, 1949

1799 Rashin, G.
      /"Changes in the territorial distribution of_the population of Russia
         during the 19th and early 20th centuries,"/ (in Russian)
      Voprosy Geografii, No. 20(1950)

1800 Biehl, Max
      "Binnenwanderungen in der Sowjetunion,"
      Zeitschrift für Geopolitik, 25(1954), 677-684

1801 Seraphim, Peter-Heinz
      "Bevölkerungsverschiebungen im baltischen Raum,"
      Zeitschrift für Geopolitik, 25(1954), 405-411

1802 Davidovich, V. G.
      /"Observations on the typology_of population by groups of cities and
         localities in the U.S.S.R.,"/ (in Russian)
      Voprosy Geografii, No. 38(1956), 27-77

1803 Kovalev, S. A., Liamin, E. A., and Pekel, A. I.
      /"Observations on the migratory relations among the cities of the
         U.S.S.R.,"/ (in Russian)
      Voprosy Geografii, No. 38(1956), 196-210

1804 Langbein, Otto
      "Städtische Bevölkerung und Grosstädte der USSR,"
      Geographische Gesellschaft in Wien, Mitteilungen, 98(1956), 250-256

1805 Preobraženskii, A. J.
      "Karten und Bevölkerungsverteilung aus der Zeit vor der Revolution
         und aus der Sowjetzeit," in:
      Heinrich Täubert, ed.
      Probleme der Kartographie; Aufsätze aus der sowjetische Literatur
      Gotha, Haack, 1956

1806 Rashin, A. G.
      /The population of Russia during 100 years (1811-1913)/ (in Russian)
      Moskva, 1956

1807 Saushkin, Iu. G.
      "Geography of urban and rural population of the USSR," pp. 28-43 in:
      Economic geography of the Soviet Union
      Oslo, Oslo University Press, 1956

1808 Beaujeu-Garnier, Jacqueline
      "La population de l'U.R.S.S.,"
      L'Information Géographique, 21(1957), 13-21

1809 Cole, John P.
      "Urban population change in the U.S.S.R., 1939-1956,"
      TESG, 48(1957), 80-83

1810 Kovalev, S. A.
      /"Shifts in the geography of the population of the USSR in a 40-year
        period,"/ (in Russian)
      Geografiia v Shkole, 1957, No. 5, 11-22

1811 Schubnell, Hermann
      Die Bevölkerung der Sowjetunion. Eine Analyse und Deutung der
        demographischen Lage und Entwicklung
      Deutsche Akademie für Bevölkerungswissenschaft an der Universität
      Hamburg, Veröffentlichung Reihe A., Nr. 2
      Hamburg, 1957

1812 Täubert, Heinrich
      "Die Bevölkerung der Sowjetunion und die Veränderungen ihrer geograph-
        ischen Verteilung,"
      PM, 101(1957), 315-318

1813 Yatsunskii, V. K.
      /"Changes in the distribution of the population of European Russia in
        1724-1816,"/ (in Russian)
      Istoriya SSR, 1957, No. 1

1814 Konstantinov, Oleg A.
      /The current status of the division of the population of places in the
        USSR into urban and rural/ (in Russian)
      Akademiia Nauk S.S.S.R., Izvestiia, Seriia Geograficheskaia, 1958, No. 6
      Moskva, 1958

1815 Davidovich, V. G., Kovalev, S. A., and Pokshishevskii, Vadim V.
      /"Concerning the basis for a classification of the population of
        places in the U.S.S.R. (in connection with the problems of economic
        geography),"/ (in Russian)
      Akademiia Nauk, S.S.S.R., Izvestiia, Seriia Geograficheskaia, 9,
        No. 4(1959), 106-116

1816 Khorev, B. S.
      /"Survey of the work of the Committee on the Geography of Population
        and Cities of the Moskva Branch of the Geographic Society of the
        U.S.S.R., 1945-1957,"/ (in Russian)
      Voprosy Geografii, No. 45(1959), 227-245

1817 Konstantinov, Oleg A.
      /"Some conclusions about the geography of cities and the urban popula-
        tion of the USSR based on the results of the 1959 census,"/ (in
        Russian)
      Akademiia Nauk S.S.S.R., Izvestiia, Seriia Geograficheskaia, 9,
        No. 6(1959), 44-56
      Also: Soviet Geography; Review and Translation, 1, No. 7(1960), 59-75
        (in English translation)

1818 Roof, Michael K. and Leedy, Frederick A.
      "Population redistribution in the Soviet Union,"
      GR, 49(1959), 208-221

1819 Smoliar, I. M.
      /"Distribution of population in the new oil regions of the U.S.S.R.,"_7
      (in Russian)
      Nauchnye Doklady Vysshei Shkoly: Geologo-Geograficheskie Nauki 1959,
        No. 2, 172-177

1820 Witthauer, Kurt
      "Vorläufige Ergebnisse der Volkszählung 1959 in der Sowjetunion,"
      PM, 103(1959), 215-223

1821 Listengurt, F. M.
      /"Some changes in the population geography of the U.S.S.R. from 1939
        to 1956,"/ (in Russian)
      Ekonomicheskaya Geografiia S.S.S.R., 1960, No. 5, 69-76

1822 Pokshishevskii, Vadim V.
      /"Outline of the colonization of the wooded-steppe regions of the
        Russian plains,"/ (in Russian)
      Ekonomicheskaya Geografiia, S.S.S.R., 1960, No. 5, 3-68

1823 Pokshishevskii, Vadim V.
      "The role of population geography in problems of economic regionaliza-
      tion of the USSR,"
      Soviet Geography: Review and Translation, 1, No. 7(1960), 28-35

1824 Shimkin, Demitri B.
      "Demographic changes and socio-economic forces within the Soviet
        Union, 1939-1959," pp. 224-262 in:
      Milbank Memorial Fund
      Population trends in eastern Europe, the USSR and mainland China
      New York, 1960

                              c. Regional

                          7030: Estonia

1825 Tammekann, Aug.
      Outlines of the distribution of population in Estonia
      Tartu, Universität, Institutum Geographicum, Publicationes
      Tartu, 1929

1826 Nuut, J.
      /On the density of farm population in Estonia/
      Tartu, Universität, Institutum Geographicum, Publicationes, 8 (in Estonian)
      Tartu, 1934

1827 Tammekann, Aug.
      "Erläuterungen zu den Karten der Bevölkerungsverteilung in Estland,"
      pp. 365-366 in:
      CRCIG, Varsovie, 1934, Vol. 3

1828 Kant, Edgar
      Bevölkerung und Lebensraum Estlands, Ein anthropo-ökologischer
        Beitrag zur Kunde Baltoskandias
      Tartu, Cooperativa Accademica, 1935

1829   Kant, Edgar
       Problems of environment and population in Estonia
       Eesti Loodusteaduse Ariiv, 2nd series
       Tartu, 1935

1830   Laasi, A.
       /Population, settlement, and communications of the Province of
         Läänemaa/ (in Estonian)
       Tartu, Universität, Institutum Geographicum, Majandus Geograafia
         Seminar, Publicationes, No. 23
       Tartu, 1939

1831   Kant, Edgar
       /"Concerning internal migration in Estonia in connection with com-
         plementary areas of Estonian towns,"/ (in Swedish)
       Svensk Geografisk Årsbok, 22(1946), 83-116

1832   Kant, Edgar
       /"Studies concerning the density of the farm population in prewar
         Estonia and Latvia, together with some methodological questions,"/
         (in Swedish)
       Svensk Geografisk Årsbok, 25(1949), 165-197

1833   Kant, Edgar
       Quelques problèmes concernant la représentation de la densité des
         habitations rurales; exemples pris en Estonie
       Lund Studies in Geography, Series B, Human Geography, No. 2
       Lund, 1950

                              7040: Latvia

1834   Anderle, Joseph
       "Population," pp. 69-109 in:
       Latvia, Vol. 1
       Subcontractor's Monograph HRAF41
       New Haven, Human Relations Area Files, 1956

       (Also see 1276, 1832).

                              7050: Lithuania

1835   Czekanowski, Jan
       Les problèmes nationaux et confessionels en Lithuanie et Ruthénie
       Travaux Géographiques Publiés sous la Direction de Eugenjusz Romer,
         Fasc. 1
       Lwow, 1918

1836   Pakštas, Kazys
       "L'émigration Lituanienne et ses causes," pp. 51-64 in:
       CRCIG, Amsterdam, 1938, Vol. 2

1837   De Porte, A. W.
       "The population of Lithuania," pp. 14-27 in:
       Benedict V. Maciuika, ed.
       Lithuania in the last 30 years
       Subcontractor's Monograph HRAF18
       New Haven, Human Relations Area File, 1955

171   U. S. S. R.: Regional

7090: Byelorussia

1838 Hurwicz, Abraham A., ed.
      "The population of Belorussia," pp. 19-55 in:
      Belorussia
      Subcontractor's Monograph HRAF19
      New Haven, Human Relations Area File, 1955

7100: Ukraine

1839 Rudnyckyj, St.
      "Die Verbreitung der Ukrainer,"
      Kartographische und Schulgeographische Zeitschrift, 4(1915), 161-165

1840 Pawlowski, Stanislas
      La population catholique romaine dans la partie polono-ruthène de la
          Galicie
      Travaux Géographiques Publiés sous la Direction de Eugenjusz Romer,
          Fasc. 3
      Lwow, 1919

1841 Rühle, Edward
      /Land utilization and population distribution in western Polesie/ (in
          Polish)
      Warszawa, Uniwersytet, Zakład Geograficzny, Prace Wykonane, 14
      Warszawa, 1930

1842 Kubijowicz, Vladimir
      Die Verteilung der Bevölkerung in der Ukraine
      Berlin, Geslleschaft der Freunde des Ukrainischen Wissenschaftlichen
          Instituts, 1934

1843 Przepiórski, W.
      "L'influence de la structure géologique sur la répartition de
          l'habitat humain, étudiée dans la région du Polésie," pp. 542-544 in:
      CRCIG, Varsovie, 1934, Vol. 3

1844 Sedlmeyer, Karl A.
      "Die Bevölkerung Karpatorusslands,"
      Geographischer Anzeiger, 35(1934), 297-302

1845 Sedlmeyer, Karl A.
      "Die Landflucht in Karpatorussland,"
      Geographische Wochenschrift, 2(1934), 826-832

1846 Iesman, M.
      /Density of dwellings in the voivodship of Volhynia/ (in Polish)
      Wilno, Uniwersytet, Zakład Geograficzny, Prace, 1
      Wilno, 1936

1847 Hurwicz, Abraham A., et al.
      "The population of the Ukraine," pp. 51-59 in:
      Ukraine
      Subcontractor's Monograph HRAF20
      New Haven, Human Relations Area File, 1955

1848 Anuchin, V. A.
      /"Population and major population centers,"7 (in Russian), pp. 93-
      _192 in:
      /Geography of Soviet Transcarpathia7
      Moskva, 1956

      (Also see 1397, 1655)

                            7110: Moldavia

1849 Pelivan, I. G.
      "Bevölkerungsbewegung in Bessarabien 1812-1918,"
      Societatea Română de Geografie, Buletinul, 38(1919), 244-251

1850 Murgoći, G. M.
      La population de la Bessarabie. Etude démographique
      Paris, 1920

1851 Berg, Lev Semeonovich
      /The population of Bessarabia7 (in Russian)
      Trudy Komissiia Izucheniiu Plemennoe Sostava Naseleniia Rossiya pri
      A.N., No. 6
      Petrograd, 1923

1852 Roblin, Michel
      "La population de la Bessarabie,"
      Société de Géographie et d'Etudes Coloniales de Marseille, Bulletin,
      57(1936), 56-66

      (Also see 1653)

                            7120: Caucasus

1853 Dingelstadt, Victor
      "La population du Caucase et la ville de Tiflis,"
      Globe (Genève), 33(1893), 61-89

1854 Von Erckert, R.
      "Die Bevölkerung des kaukasischen Gebietes,"
      Deutsche Rundschau für Geographie und Statistik, 16(1893), 124-128

1855 Weinberg, Richard
      "Die Bevölkerung des Kaukasus in statistischer und ethnischer
         Beziehung,"
      Deutsche Rundschau für Geographie und Statistik, 28(1906), 244-259

1856 Kluge, Th.
      "Die historische Entwicklung der Bevölkerungsverhältnisse in Russisch-
         Armenien und angrenzenden Gebieten,"
      PM, 68(1922), 141-143

1857 Dzhaoshvili, V. Sh.
      /"Population geography of Kakhetia,"7 (in Georgian)
      Akademiia Nauk Gruzinskoi S.S.R., Institut Geografii Imeni Vakhushti,
         Trudy, 15(1954), 597-604

1858 Pipes, Richard
      "Demographic and ethnographic changes in Transcaucasia, 1897-1956,"
      Middle East Journal, 13(1959), 41-63

                              7270: Siberia

1859 Gondatti, N.
      /"Zusammensetzung der Bevölkerung des Anadyr-Bezirkes,"7 (in Russian)
      Imperatorskoe Russkoe Geograficheskoe Obshchestvo, Priamurskii Otdel,
          Zapiski, 3(1897), 166-178

1860 Klose, F.
      "Die Bevölkerungsverteilung in Nordostasien,"
      PM, 80(1934), 209-213

1861 Hopper, Bruce
      "Population factors in Soviet Siberia," pp. 89-118 in:
      Isaiah Bowman, ed.
      Limits of land settlement
      New York, Council of Foreign Relations, 1937

1862 Pokshishevskii, Vadim V.
      /The settlement of Siberia7 (in Russian)
      Irkutsk, 1951

1863 Mikami, Masatoshi
      /"Cultivation and population of Siberia,"7 (in Japanese)
      Jimbun Chiri. Human Geography, 4(1952), 94-108

1864 Kosmatchev, K. P.
      /"The rural population of the region between the Lena and the Anga,"7
      (in Russian)
      Voprosy Geografii, No. 41(1957), 193-205

1865 D'iakonov, F. V.
      /"Population and its distribution in southwestern Yakutia,"7 (in
          Russian)
      Akademiia Nauk S.S.S.R., Iakutskii Filial, Trudy, Seriia Ekonomi-
          cheskaia, 1959, No. 2, 9-24

1866 Bone, Robert M.
      "The early Siberian migration,"
      Journal of Geography, 59(1960), 112-117

                              7400: ASIA

1867 Fochler-Hauke, Gustav
      "Jüngere Wanderungsbewegungen und Umvolksungsvorgänge in Asien,"
      Zeitschrift für Geopolitik, 18(1941), 547-559

1868 Hauser, Philip M., ed.
      Urbanization in Asia and the Far East
      Calcutta, Research Centre on the Social Implications of Industrializa-
      tion in Southern Asia, 1957

1869 East, W. Gordon and Spate, O. H. K.
      "The demographic aspect," pp. 28-38 in:
      The changing map of Asia; a political geography, 3rd ed.
      London, Methuen, 1958

1870 United Nations, Bureau of Economic and Social Affairs, Population
      Division
      Future population estimates by sex and age. Report IV. The popula-
        tion of Asia and the Far East, 1950-1980
      New York, 1959

1871 Ward, Marion W.
      "Recent population growth and economic development in Asia,"
      Pacific Viewpoint, 1(1960), 205-224

                        7402: MONSOON ASIA

1872 Taeuber, Irene B.
      "Migration and the population potential of Monsoon Asia,"
      Milbank Memorial Fund Quarterly, 25(1947), 21-43

1873 United Nations, Department of Economic and Social Affairs
      Future population estimates by sex and age. Report III. The popula-
        tion of south-east Asia (including Ceylon and China: Taiwan) 1950-
        1980
      Population Studies, No. 30
      New York, 1958

1874 Thompson, Warren S.
      Population and progress in the Far East
      Chicago, University of Chicago Press, 1959

1875 Zelinsky, Wilbur
      "The population prospect in Monsoon Asia,"
      Journal of Geography, 60(1961), 312-321

                        7420: MIDDLE EAST

1876 Hogarth, D. G.
      "The distribution of man," pp. 146-167 in:
      The nearer East
      New York, Appleton, 1902

1877 Worthington, Edgar Barton
      "Population and social studies," pp. 181-195 in:
      Middle East science; a survey of subjects other than agriculture
      London, H.M.S.O., 1946

1878 Fisher, W. B.
      "Population problems in the Middle East,"
      Journal of the Royal Central Asian Society, 36(1949), 208-220

1879 Fisher, W. B.
      "Peoples," pp. 77-112 in:
      The Middle East; a physical, social, and regional geography
      London, Methuen, 1950

1880 Bonné, Alfred
      "Land and population in the Middle East,"
      Middle East Journal, 5(1951), 39-56

1881 Raptschinsky, B.
      /"The Arab refugees,"/ (in Dutch)
      TESG, 48(1957), 133-141

1882 Bruk, Solomon I. and Pershitz, A. I.
      /"The Arab peoples of Asia,"/ (in Russian)
      Geografiia v Shkole, 1960, 31-46

1883 Cressey, George B.
      "Population patterns," pp. 33-41 in:
      Crossroads; land and life in southwest Asia
      New York, Lippincott, 1960

                              7430: TURKEY

1884 Selenoy, G. L. and Von Siedlitz, N.
      "Die Verbreitung der Armenier in der asiatischen Türkei und in
        Transkaukasien,"
      PM, 42(1896), 1-10

1885 Braun, F.
      "Die Siedlungen und die Bevölkerung der thrakischen Halbinsel,"
      Geographische Zeitschrift, 31(1925), 144-162, 204-219

1886 Lefebvre, Th.
      "La densité de la population en Turquie en 1914 et en 1917,"
      AG, 37(1928), 520-526

1887 Caucig, Franz von
      "Bevölkerungsfragen Anatoliens,"
      Zeitschrift für Geopolitik, 13(1936), 234-241

1888 Gley, Werner
      "Einige Ergebnisse der türkischen Volkszählung 1935,"
      Zeitschrift für Erdkunde, 5(1937), 282-286

1889 Pallis, A. A.
      "The population of Turkey in 1935,"
      GJ, 91(1938), 439-445

1890 Louis, Herbert
      Die Bevölkerungskarte der Türkei
      Berliner Geographische Arbeiten, 20
      Berlin, Mier und Glasemann, 1940

1891 Tanoglu, Ali
      "La densité de la population agricole en Turquie,"
      Revue de la Faculté des Sciences Economiques de l'Université
         d'Istanbul, 6(1945), 40-43

1892 Planhol, Xavier de
      "Les migrations de travail en Turquie,"
      RGA, 40(1952), 583-600

1893 Brice, W. C.
      "The population of Turkey in 1950,"
      GJ, 120(1954), 347-352

1894 Darkot, Besim
      "Sur les mouvements démographiques en Turquie,"
      University of Istanbul, Geographical Institute, Review, International
         Edition, 2(1955), 37-44

1895 Darkot, Besim
      /"The sixth population census of Turkey,"/ (in Turkish)
      Türk Coğrafya Dergisi, Nos. 15-16(1955), 85-103

1896 Kostanick, Huey Louis
      "Turkish resettlement of refugees from Bulgaria,"
      Middle East Journal, 9(1955), 41-52

1897 Inandik, Hâmit
      "La population et l'habitat dans la région d'Adapazari--NW de
         l'Anatolie,"
      University of Istanbul, Geographical Institute, Review, International
         Edition, 3(1956), 31-46

1898 Kostanick, Huey Louis
      Turkish resettlement of Bulgarian Turks, 1950-1953
      University of California Publications in Geography, Vol. 8, No. 2
      Berkeley and Los Angeles, 1957

1899 Selen, Hâmit Sadi
      /Population distribution in Turkey according to the census of Octo-
         ber 23, 1955/ (in Turkish)
      Ankara, Dŏgus Matbaasi, 1957

1900 Taeuber, Irene B.
      "Population and modernization in Turkey,"
      Population Index, 24(1958), 101-122

1901 Tümertekin, Erol
      "The distribution of sex ratios with special reference to internal
         migration in Turkey,"
      University of Istanbul, Geographical Institute, Review, International
         Edition, 4(1958), 9-16

1902 Tanoglu, Ali
      "Die Verteilung der Bevölkerung in der Turkei,"
      University of Istanbul, Geographical Institute, Review, International
         Edition, 5(1959), 94-106

1903   Tunçdilek, Necdet and Tümertekin, Erol
       /The population of Turkey; population density, population increase,
          internal migration, and urbanization/ (in Turkish)
       University of Istanbul, Geographical Institute, Monograph Series,
          No. 25
       Istanbul, Matbaasi, 1959

       (Also see 1602)

                              7450:   CYPRUS

1904   Taeuber, Irene B.
       "Cyprus: the demography of a strategic island,"
       Population Index, 21(1954), 4-20

1905   Melamid, Alexander
       "The geographical distribution of communities in Cyprus,"
       GR, 46(1956), 355-374

1906   Vaumas, Etienne de
       "La répartition de la population à Chypre et le nouvel état chypriote,"
       RGA, 47(1959), 457-529

                              7460:   SYRIA

1907   Bernard, Augustin
       "Les populations de la Syrie et de la Palestine d'après les derniers
          recensements,"
       AG, 33(1924), 73-79

1908   Francolini, Bruno
       "Note etniche e demografiche sulla Siria e il Libano,"
       BSGI, Serie 8, 2(1949), 220-224

1909   Nouss, Izzat
       La population de la République syrienne. Etude démographique et
          géographique
       Doctoral dissertation, University of Paris
       Paris, 1952(?)

1910   Vaumas, Etienne de
       "La population de la Syrie,"
       AG, 64(1955), 74-80

       (Also see 1924)

                              7470:   LEBANON

1911   Vaumas, Etienne de
       "La répartition de la population au Liban, introduction à la géographie
          humain de la République Libanaise,"
       Société de Géographie d'Egypte, Bulletin, 26(1953), 5-76

1912   Vaumas, Etienne de
       "La répartition confessionnelle au Liban et l'équilibre de l'Etat
          libanais,"
       RGA, 44(1955), 511-604

       (Also see 1908, 1924)

                              7500:   ISRAEL

1913   Brawer, Abraham J.
       "Il ripopolamento della Palestina con gli Ebrei,"
       L'Universo, 7(1926), 533-565

1914   Casto, E. R. and Dotson, O. W.
       "Urban population of Palestine,"
       EG, 14(1938), 68-72

1915   Gottmann, Jean
       "La capacité de peuplement de la Palestine: aspects géographiques du
          problème," pp. 91-97 in:
       CRCIG, Amsterdam, 1938, Vol. 2

1916   Kallner, H.
       "Population and economic development in Palestine, based on the census
          reports of 1922 and 1931," pp. 436-440 in:
       CRCIG, Amsterdam, 1938, Vol. 2

1917   Thorslund, Sixten
       /"The development of Palestine's population and economic geography
          after the First World War,"/ (in Swedish)
       Ymer, 70(1950), 138-159

1918   Beaujeu-Garnier, Jacqueline
       "L'immigration dans l'Etat d'Isräel,"
       AG, 61(1952), 57-61

1919   Lawrence, Norman
       Israel: Jewish population and immigration
       U. S. Bureau of the Census, International Population Statistics
          Reports, Series P-90, No. 2
       Washington, 1952

1920   Smith, S. G.
       "The boundaries and population problems of Israel,"
       Geography, 37(1952), 152-165

1921   Bianchini, Mario
       "La distribuzione attuale della popolazione in Israele,"
       BSGI, Serie 8, 7(1954), 368-399

1922   Vaumas, Etienne de
       "La population de l'Etat d'Israel,"
       AG, 63(1954), 70-80

1923   Raptschinsky, B.
       /"The growth of the Israeli nation,"/ (in Dutch)
       TESG, 48(1957), 248-258

1924 Maryanski, Andrzej
      /"Certain population problems of Israel and of neighboring countries,"/
        (in Polish)
      Czasopismo Geograficzne, 29(1958), 85-98

1925 Gottman, Jean
      "La colonisation et peuplement en Palestine avant 1940," pp. 15-68 in:
      Etudes sur l'Etat d'Israël et le Moyen-Orient
      Paris, Colin, 1959

1926 Tasma, R.
      "Changes in the Jewish population pattern of Israel, 1948-1957,"
      TESG, 50(1959), 170-182

1927 Amiran, David H. K. and Shahar, A.
      "The towns of Israel; the principles of their urban geography,"
      GR, 51(1961), 348-369

      (Also see 1907)

                              7510: JORDAN

1928 Konikoff, A.
      "The population," pp. 16-27 in:
      Transjordan: an economic survey
      Jerusalem, Jewish Agency, 1946

1929 Issawi, Charles and Dabezies, Carlos
      "Population movements and population pressure in Jordan, Lebanon,
        and Syria,"
      Milbank Memorial Fund Quarterly, 29(1951), 385-401

                           7530: SAUDI ARABIA

1930 Hazard, Harry W.
      "Size and distribution of population," pp. 18-26 in:
      Saudi Arabia
      Subcontractor's Monograph HRAF50
      New Haven, Human Relations Area File, 1956

                              7550: ADEN

1931 Pike, Ruthien W.
      "Land and people of the Hadramaut, Aden Protectorate,"
      GR, 30(1940), 627-648

                              7610: IRAQ

1932 Lebon, J. H. G.
      "Population distribution and the agricultural regions of Iraq,"
      GR, 43(1953), 223-228

1933 Adams, Doris G.
      Iraq's people and resources
      University of California Publications in Economics, Vol. 18
      Berkeley, University of California Press, 1958

1934 Phillips, Doris G.
      "Rural-to-urban migration in Iraq,"
      Economic Development and Cultural Change, 7(1959), 405-421

                          7620: IRAN

1935 Bausani, Alessandro
      "Notizie sulle popolazioni dell'Iran secondo una recente opera,"
      BSGI, Serie 7, 6(1941), 202-211

1936 Furon, R.
      "L'Iran; démographie et géographie économique en rapport avec la
        structure géologique,"
      Association de Géographes Français, Bulletin, Nos. 151-152(1943), 1-7

1937 Planhol, Xavier de
      "Pressione demografica e vita di montagna nella Persia settentrionale,"
      BSGI, Serie 9, 1(1960), 90-96

                       7630: AFGHANISTAN

1938 Wilber, Donald N.
      "Size and geographical distribution of population," pp. 35-66 in:
      Afghanistan, Vol. 1
      Subcontractor's Monograph, HRAF53
      New Haven, Human Relations Area File, 1956

1939 Humlum, Johannes
      "La population," pp. 81-100 in:
      La géographie de l'Afghanistan
      Aarhus, Universitet, Geografisk Institut, Skrifter, No. 10
      København, Gyldendal, 1959

1940 Amerkhail, Najibullah
      "A census design for Afghanistan,"
      Population Review, 5(1961), 46-62

                        7640: PAKISTAN

1941 Heins, H.
      "Uber die Bevölkerungsdichte im nordwestlichen Indien,"
      PM, 55(1909), 152-156

1942 Heins, H.
      Die Volksdichte im nordwestindischen Flachlande und ihr Zusammenhang
        mit den Bewässerungsverhältnissen
      Doctoral dissertation, University of Göttingen
      Göttingen, 1909

1943 Ul-Hasan, Reyaz
"Alcune notizie sulle condizioni demografiche ed economiche del Pakistan,"
BSGI, Serie 8, 1(1948), 238-241

1944 Ahmad, Kazi S.
"Distribution of population in Pakistan,"
Pakistan Geographical Review, 8(1953), 94-112

1945 Ahmad, Kazi S.
"A geographical study of the refugee population and some of its problems,"
Pakistan Geographical Review, 10, No. 2(1955), 1-18

1946 Ahmad, Kazi S.
"Urban population in Pakistan,"
Pakistan Geographical Review, 10, No. 1(1955), 1-16

1947 Elahi, M. Karam
"Food supply and population growth in Pakistan,"
Pakistan Geographical Review, 12(1957), 1-38

1948 Ahmad, Nafis
"The urban pattern in East Pakistan,"
Oriental Geographer, 1(1957), 33-41

1949 Ahmad, Nafis
"Population: distribution, patterns and trends," pp. 273-311 in:
An economic geography of East Pakistan
London, Oxford University Press, 1958

1950 Husain, Hyder
"Some aspects of the rural-urban composition of population in East Pakistan,"
Pakistan Geographical Review, 13(1958), 24-51

1951 Siddiqi, Akhtat Husain
"Population and settlements along the Baluchistan coast,"
Oriental Geographer, 2(1958), 131-139

7650: BRITISH INDIA

1952 Baines, J. A.
"The geographical distribution of population in India,"
Journal of the Royal Statistical Society, 67(1904), 661-670

1953 Dallas, W. L.
"The variation of the population of India compared with the variation of rainfall in the decennium 1891-1901,"
Quarterly Journal of the Royal Meteorological Society, 30(1904), 273-285

1954 Michaelsen, H.
"Die Bevölkerungbewegung in Indien und ihre Beziehung zum Niederschlag und zur Kultur,"
Gesellschaft für Erdkunde zu Berlin, Zeitschrift, Series 4, 13(1914), 716-726

1955 Sion, Jules
      "Les populations de l'Inde d'après les derniers recensements (1911-
         21),"
      AG, 35(1926), 330-351

1956 Dennery, Etienne
      "L'émigration indienne,"
      AG, 37(1928), 328-353

1957 Klose, F.
      "Die Bevölkerung von Indien 1931,"
      PM, 79(1933), 299-301

1958 Shirras, G. F.
      "The Census of India, 1931,"
      GR, 25(1935), 434-448

1959 Baker, John N. L.
      "Some problems of population in India,"
      SGM, 52(1936), 231-240

1960 Geddes, Arthur
      "The population of Bengal, its distribution and changes: a contribu-
         tion to geographical method,"
      GJ, 89(1937), 344-368

1961 Gorrie, R. Maclagan
      "The relationship between density of population and the method of land
         utilization in British India," pp. 405-416 in:
      CRCIG, Amsterdam, 1938, Vol. 2

1962 Pelzer, Karl J.
      "Present day plantation labour migration in India," pp. 65-75 in:
      CRCIG, Amsterdam, 1938, Vol. 2

1963 Krebs, Norbert
      "Die Verteilung der Bevölkerung," pp. 91-103 in:
      Vorderindien und Ceylon; eine Landeskunde
      Stuttgart, Engelhorn, 1939

1964 Ahmad, Kazi S.
      "Environment and the distribution of population in India,"
      Indian Geographical Journal, 16(1941), 117-134

1965 Geddes, Arthur
      "Half a century of population trends in India: a regional study of
         net change and variability, 1881-1931,"
      GJ, 98(1941), 228-252

1966 Geddes, Arthur
      "The population of India: variability of change as a regional
         demographic index,"
      GR, 32(1942), 562-573

1967 Brush, John E.
      "The distribution of religious communities in India,"
      AAAG, 39(1949), 81-98

1968 Hoffman, Lawrence A.
      Population and economic development in India and Pakistan
      Doctoral dissertation, Johns Hopkins University
      Baltimore, 1950

1969 Davis, Kingsley
      The population of India and Pakistan
      Princeton, Princeton University Press, 1951

1970 Learmonth, Andrew T. A.
      "Regional differences in natality and in mortality in the sub-continent
        of Indo-Pakistan, 1921-1940," pp. 195-205 in:
      CRCIG, Washington, 1952

1971 Spate, O. H. K.
      "Population and its problems," pp. 97-121 in:
      India and Pakistan; a general and regional geography, 2nd ed.
      London, Methuen, 1957

      (Also see 2136)

                        7651:   REPUBLIC OF INDIA

                             a. National

1972 Hoffman, Lawrence A.
      "India: main population concentrations,"
      GJ, 111(1948), 89-100

1973 Raza, Moonis
      "Is India over-populated?"
      The Geographer, 3(1950), 36-40

1974 India, Census Commissioner
      "The land and the people--1951," pp. 2-40 in:
      Census of India, 1951. Volume I. India. Part I-A. Report
      Delhi, 1953

1975 Buschmann, K. H.
      "Settlements and habitations in India,"
      Geographical Review of India, 16(1954), 19-39

1976 Kuriyan, George
      "India's population problem,"
      Focus, 5, No. 2(1954)

1977 Kuriyan, George
      "Bevölkerung und Nahrungsmittelversorgung in der Indischen Union,"
      Geographische Rundschau, 7(1955), 382-386

1978 Gosal, Gurdev Singh
      A geographical analysis of India's population
      Doctoral dissertation, University of Wisconsin
      Madison, 1956

1979 Marmoria, C. B.
      "Growth of population in India,"
      Geographical Review of India, 19, No. 4(1957), 13-26

1980 Witthauer, Kurt
      "Zur Bevölkerungsverteilung und -dynamik in Vorderindien,"
      PM, 101(1957), 129-137

1981 Trewartha, Glenn T. and Gosal, Gurdev Singh
      "The regionalism of population change in India,"
      Cold Spring Harbor Symposia on Quantitative Biology, 22(1957), 71-81

1982 Datta, Jatindra Mohan
      "Geographical distribution of the Brahmans in India,"
      Modern Review (Calcutta), 103(1958), 318-320

1983 Dayal, P.
      "Population growth and rural-urban migration in India,"
      National Geographical Journal of India, 5(1959), 179-185

1984 Gosal, Gurdev Singh
      "The occupational structure of India's rural population; a regional
         analysis,"
      National Geographical Journal of India, 5(1959), 137-148

1985 Gosal, Gurdev Singh
      "The regionalism of sex composition of India's population,"
      Rural Sociology, 26(1961), 122-137

1986 Khan, Mohammad Naseer
      "Population distribution in India,"
      Mankind Quarterly, 1(1961), 160-164

      (Also see 2033)

                          b. Regional

1987 Böllert, P.
      "Die Volksdichte in der oberen Ganges-Ebene,"
      PM, 57(1911), 176-179
      Also: Doctoral dissertation, University of Göttingen
      Göttingen, 1911

1988 Kopp, Karl
      "Die Verteilung der Bevölkerung in der Provinz Bombay mit Ausschluss
         des Sindh auf Grund des Census of India 1901,"
      Deutsche Geographische Blätter, 38(1916-17), 1-100
      Also: PM, 62(1916), 212-215

1989 Borchers, Marie
      Die Bevölkerungsdichte im südlichen Indien nach dem Census of India
         1901
      Doctoral dissertation, University of Göttingen
      Göttingen, 1917
      Also: PM, 63(1917), 363-368

1990 McPherson, H.
      "Bihar and Orissa, its fiscal, agrarian and population problems,"
      SGM, 47(1931), 65-77

1991 Srinivasaraghavan, K.
      "The population of the Tanjore District,"
      Journal of the Madras Geographical Association, 12(1937), 137-145

1992 Ganguli, Birendrananth
      Trends of agriculture and population in the Ganges Valley
      London, Methuen, 1938

1993 Ganguli, B. N.
      "Agricultural water-supply and density of population in the Ganges
          Delta,"
      Indian Journal of Economics, 18(1938), 309-323

1994 Geddes, Arthur
      "The delta of Orissa; population and agriculture," pp. 381-396 in:
      CRCIG, Amsterdam, 1938, Vol. 2

1995 Gorrie, R. Maclagan
      "Pressure of population and misuse of land in the Punjab,"
      SGM, 54(1938), 284-295

1996 Kuriyan, George
      "Population and its distribution in Kerala,"
      Journal of the Madras Geographical Association, 13(1938), 125-146

1997 Rajagopal, M. P.
      "Population of Tinnevelly District,"
      Journal of the Madras Geographical Association, 15(1940), 277-288

1998 Rajagopal, M. P.
      "Population of Chitoor District,"
      Indian Geographical Journal, 16(1941), 340-354

1999 Younus, Mohammad
      A resume of the trends of population and crop production in the U.P.
          after 1931,"
      Indian Geographical Journal, 16(1941), 135-144

2000 Muzaffar, Ali S.
      "Population and settlement in the Ghaggar Plain,"
      Indian Geographical Journal, 17(1942), 157-182

2001 Chatterjee, Shiba P. and Ganguli, A. T.
      "Geographical interpretation of the distribution of population in two
          typical districts of India,"
      Calcutta Geographical Review, 5(1943), 116-125

2002 Mukerji, B. N.
      "A study of the effect of irrigation on the pressure of population of
          the United Provinces,"
      Calcutta Geographical Review, 5(1943), 18-21

2003 Raisinghani, G. S. and Pithawalla, Maneck B.
      "The problem of population and food planning in Sind; a study in
          applied geography,"
      Calcutta Geographical Review, 7(1945), 35-65

2004 Bose, S. C.
      "Density and pattern of population in the lower Damodar Basin,"
      Calcutta Geographical Review, 8(1946), 45-52

2005 Singh, Rama L.
      "The trend of the growth of population in the United Provinces,"
      National Geographical Society of India, Bulletin, 3(1947), 17-29

2006 Ahmad, Enayat
      "The distribution of population in the United Provinces,"
      The Geographer, 2(1950), 13-22

2007 Bidvai, B. K.
      "The variation of population in Amravati District,"
      Geographical Review of India, 1(1951), 9-14

2008 Gupta, Debangshu Sen
      "Immigration pattern in the Assam Valley,"
      Calcutta Geographical Review, 12, No. 2(1951)
      Also: Geographical Review of India, 13(1951), 21-27

2009 Mayer, Adrian C.
      Land and society in Malabar
      Institute of Pacific Relations, International Secretariat
      Bombay, Oxford University Press, 1952

2010 Bhat, Laxminarayan S.
      "A population map of the upper Panchaganga Basin,"
      Bombay Geographical Magazine, 1(1953), 52-55

2011 Janaki, V. A.
      "Geographical basis for the distribution and pattern of rural settle-
          ment in Kerala,"
      Journal of the Maharaja Sayajiarao University of Baroda, 2(1953), 41-
      54

2012 Nath, Deba Prasad
      Regional geography of Nowgong District, with special reference to
          population
      Master's thesis, Calcutta University
      Calcutta, 1953

2013 Crane, Robert I., et al.
      "Demography and patterns of settlement," pp. 133-175 in:
      Jammu and Kashmir State
      Subscontractor's Monograph HRAF24
      New Haven, Human Relations Area File, 1955

2014 Anantapadmanabhan, N.
      "Density of rural population in relation to land use in Tamil Nad,"
      Bombay Geographical Magazine, 4(1956), 41-49

2015   Datta, Jatindra Mohan
       "Urbanization in Bengal,"
       Geographical Review of India, 18(1956), 19-23

2016   Kayastha, S. L.
       "Demographic features of the Himalayan Beas Basin,"
       National Geographical Journal of India, 2(1956), 14-35

2017   Khan, Mohammad Naseer
       "Distribution of population in Allahabad District,"
       National Geographical Journal of India, 2(1956), 213-216

2018   Varma, Kripa Nath
       Population problems in the Ganges Valley
       Doctoral dissertation, Clark University
       Worcester, 1956

2019   Varma, Sat Dev
       "Density and patterns of population in the Punjab,"
       National Geographical Journal of India, 2(1956), 193-202

2020   Singh, Ujagir
       "Demographic structure of Allahabad,"
       National Geographical Journal of India, 4(1958), 163-188

2021   Sinha, Bichitrananda
       "Population analysis of Orissa,"
       National Geographical Journal of India, 4(1958), 200-220

2022   Rasmussen, Tor Fr.
       "Population and land utilization in the Assam Valley,"
       Journal of Tropical Geography, 14(1960), 51-76

2023   Ahmad, Enayat
       "The rural population of Bihar,"
       GR, 51(1961), 253-276

7710: ANDAMAN ISLANDS

2024   Sen, Probhat Kumar
       "Some aspects of the recent colonization in the Andamans,"
       Geographical Review of India, 16(1954), 33-41

2025   Sen, Probhat Kumar
       "A study of the population of the Andamans,"
       Indian Geographer, 4(1959), 115-135

7720: BURMA

2026   Sundrum, R. M.
       Population statistics of Burma
       Economics Research Project, Statistical Paper No. 3
       Rangoon, University of Rangoon, 1957

7740: PORTUGUESE INDIA

2027 Correia Fernandes, Avertano
      "Emigração Indo-Portugesa,"
      Sociedade de Geografia de Lisboa, Boletim, 56(1938), 277-306

      (Also see 1980)

7750: CEYLON

2028 Joachim, A. W. R.
      "The relationship between the density of population and the method of
         land utilization in colonial regions (Ceylon)," pp. 347-   in:
      CRCIG, Amsterdam, 1938, Vol. 1

2029 Taeuber, Irene B.
      "Ceylon as a demographic laboratory: preface to analysis,"
      Population Index, 15(1949), 293-304

2030 Cook, Elsie K.
      "Population," pp. 223-232 in:
      Ceylon; its geography, its resources and its people, 2nd ed.
      London, Macmillan, 1951

2031 Kohomaban-Wickrema, Pearl Mildred Corea
      A population study of Ceylon with special reference to the Western
         Province
      Master's thesis, Clark University
      Worcester, 1956

2032 Sarkar, N. K.
      The demography of Ceylon
      Colombo, Ceylon Government Press, 1957

2033 Bartz, Fritz
      Fischer auf Ceylon. Ein Beitrag zur Wirtschafts- und Bevölkerungs-
         geographie des indischen Subkontinents
      Bonner Geographische Abhandlungen, H. 27
      Bonn, F. Dümmlers Verlag, 1959

2034 Gorrie, R. Maclagan
      "Irrigation and population in Ceylon, India and Pakistan,"
      Journal of the Royal Society of Arts, 118(1960), 354-369

      (Also see 1963, 1980)

7760: NEPAL

2035 Hagen, Toni
      "Regions and populations of Nepal,"
      Geographica Helvetica, 12(1957), 22-33.

2036 Karan, Pradyumna P.
      "Population and settlement," pp. 47-62 in:
      Nepal; a cultural and physical geography
      Lexington, University of Kentucky Press, 1960

      (Also see 1980)

                          7800: FAR EAST

2037 Gauthier, Camille
      "L'émigration chinoise dans les pays de l'Extrême-Orient,"
      Société de Géographie Commerciale de Paris, Bulletin, 15(1893), 641-
         648

2038 Pelzer, Karl J.
      "Population and land utilization," Part I in:
      Frederick V. Field, ed.
      An economic survey of the Pacific Area
      New York, Institute of Pacific Relations, 1941-42

2039 Lasker, Bruno
      Asia on the move; population pressure, migration, and resettlement in
         eastern Asia under the influence of want and war
      New York, Holt, 1945

2040 Balfour, Marshall C., et al.
      Public health and demography in the Far East
      New York, Rockefeller Foundation, 1950

                          7820: CHINA

                          a. Bibliography

2041 U. S. Bureau of the Census, Foreign Manpower Research Office
      The population and manpower of China: an annotated bibliography
      International Population Reports, Series, P-90, No. 8
      Washington, 1958

                          b. National

2042 Popov, P. S.
      /"Population change in China,"/ (in Russian)
      Imperatorskoe Russkoe Geograficheskoe Obshchestvo, Izvestiia, 32(1896),
         226-228

2043 Köhler, E. M.
      "Kritische Studien zur Bevölkerungsfrage Chinas,"
      Deutsche Rundschau für Geographie und Statistik, 22(1900), 337-347

2044 Rockhill, W. W.
      "The 1910 census of the population of China,"
      Bulletin of the American Geographical Society, 44(1912), 668-673

2045   Roxby, P. M.
       "The distribution of population in China,"
       GR, 15(1925), 1-24

2046   Schmitthenner, H.
       "Ist China übervölkert?"
       Geographische Zeitschrift, 32(1926), 505-515

2047   Torgasheff, Boris P.
       "Town population in China,"
       China Critic, 3(1930), 317-322

2048   Mosolff, Hans
       Die chinesische Auswanderung
       Rostock, 1932

2049   Weng, Wen-hao
       /"The distribution of population and land utilization in China,"/ (in
       Chinese)
       Tu Li P'ing Lun, No. 3(1932), 9-12, No. 4(1932), 11-13

2050   Fong, Wen-hao
       Distribution of population and land utilization in China
       New York, Institute of Pacific Relations, 1933

2051   Hu, Huan-yong
       /"The distribution of the Chinese population,"/ (in Chinese)
       Ti-Li Hsüeh-Pao (Journal of the Geographical Society of China), 2,
       No. 2(1935), 4-5

2052   Tu, C. W.
       /"Is China overpopulated?"/ (in Chinese)
       Ti-Li Hsüeh-Pao (Journal of the Geographical Society of China) 2,
       No. 1(1935)

2053   Chang, Ch'i-yun
       /"Geographic distribution of the Chinese people,"/ (in Chinese)
       K'o Hsüeh Ti Min Tsu Fu Hsing, Feb., 1937, 38-112

2054   Liu, Ping Jên
       /"The population and food supply during the Han dynasties,"/ (in
       Chinese)
       Yü Kung Pan-Yüeh-K'an (Chinese Historical Geography), 7(1937), 171-
       181

2055   Seiffert, G.
       "Volk und Raum in China. Eine biologische Betrachtung,"
       Zeitschrift für Geopolitik, 14(1937), 717-734

2056   Shen, Ju-sheng
       /"The distribution of the cities of China,"/ (in Chinese)
       Ti-Li Hsüeh-Pao (Journal of the Geographical Society of China),
       4(1937), 915-935

2057   Freeman, Thomas W.
       "Recent and contemporary Chinese migrations," pp. 11-22 in:
       CRCIG, Amsterdam, 1938, Vol. 2

2058 Ueda, Sinzo
      /"Population of China,"_/ (in Japanese)
      Chigaku Zasshi. Journal of Geography, 54(1942), 459-470

2059 Wang, Chang
      /"Geographic analysis of Chinese population density,"_/ (in Chinese)
      Hu Cheng Tao Pao, 1(1945), 129-144

2060 Chen, Ta
      Population in modern China
      Chicago, University of Chicago Press, 1946

2061 Jaffe, A. J.
      "A review of the censuses and demographic statistics of China,"
      Population Studies, 1(1947), 208-337

2062 Alexander, John W.
      "The prewar population of China: distribution and density,"
      AAAG, 38(1948), 1-5

2063 Taeuber, Irene B.
      "Current estimates of the size and distribution of China's population,"
      Population Index, 14(1948), 3-20

2064 Keyes, Fenton
      "Urbanism and population distribution in China,"
      American Journal of Sociology, 56(1951), 519-527

2065 Trewartha, Glenn T.
      "Chinese cities: number and distribution,"
      AAAG, 41(1951), 331-347

2066 Trewartha, Glenn T.
      "Chinese cities; origins and functions,"
      AAAG, 42(1952), 69-93

2067 Dresch, Jean
      "Population et ressources de la Chine nouvelle,"
      AG, 64(1955), 171-201

2068 Kuan-hai, Lung
      /Population of China/ (in Chinese)
      Taipei, 1955

2069 Skibbe, Bruno
      "Die Veränderung der Volksdichte in China: zu einigen Ergebnissen der
         Volkszählung 1953,"
      PM, 99(1955), 298-302

2070 Kan, Lao
      "Population and geography in the two Han dynasties," pp. 83-102 in:
      E-tu Zen Sun and John De Francis, eds.,
      Chinese social history: translations of selected studies
      American Council of Learned Societies, Studies in Chinese and Related
         Civilizations, No. 7
      Washington, 1956

2071 Taeuber, Irene B. and Orleans, Leo A.
      "A note on the population statistics of Communist China,'
      Population Index, 22(1956), 274-276

2072 Bruk, Solomon Ilyich
      /"The population of the Chinese People's Republic,"/ (in Russian)
      Geografiia v Shkole, 1957, No. 2, 18-31

2073 Maryanski, Andrzej
      /"The development of the Chinese population in the course of the last
        fifty years,"/ (in Polish)
      Czasopismo Geograficzne, 28, No. 1(1957), 29-47

2074 Trewartha, Glenn T.
      "New maps of China's population,"
      GR, 47(1957), 234-239

2075 Bruk, Solomon Ilyich
      /The population of China, M.P.R., and Korea; explanatory note for an
        ethnographic map/ (in Russian)
      Academy of Sciences, U.S.S.R., Institute of Ethnography
      Moskva, 1959

2076 Chandrasekhar, Sripati
      China's population: census and vital statistics
      Hong Kong and London, Oxford University Press, 1959

2077 Hung, Fu
      "The population China and present means of subsistence," pp. 332-340 in:
      Proceedings of IGU Regional Conference in Japan 1957
      Tokyo, 1959

2078 Orleans, Leo A.
      "The recent growth of China's urban population,"
      GR, 49(1959), 43-57

2079 Ho, Ping-Ti
      Studies on the population of China, 1368-1953
      Harvard East Asian Studies, 4
      Cambridge, Harvard University Press, 1959

2080 Shabad, Theodore
      "The population of China's cities,"
      GR, 49(1959), 32-42

2081 Durand, John D.
      "The population statistics of China, A.D. 2-1953,"
      Population Studies, 13(1960), 209-256

2082 Orleans, Leo A.
      "Population redistribution in Communist China," pp. 141-150 in:
      Milbank Memorial Fund
      Population trends in eastern Europe, the USSR, and mainland China
      New York, 1960

      (Also see 334, 602, 1770a, 2136, 2187, 2192, 2217, 2219, 2241, 2263)

c. Regional

2083 Chu, K'o-chen
      /"On population densities of Kiangsu and Chekiang,"/ (in Chinese)
      Eastern Miscellany, 23(1926), 91-112

2084 Wang, Hai-po
      /Problems of migration in the Northeast/ (in Chinese)
      Shanghai, 1932

2085 Hu, Huan-yung
      /"The cultivated areas and population density of Kiangning District,"/
         (in Chinese)
      Ti-Li Hsüeh-Pao (Acta Geographica Sinica), 1(1934), 1-26

2086 Hu, Huan-yung
      /"The agricultural regions and population density of Anhwei Province,"/
         (in Chinese)
      Ti-Li Hsüeh Pao (Acta Geographica Sinica), 2(1935), 53-62

2087 Chang, En-hu
      /"A preliminary study of the population density and its problems in
         Hopei,"/ (in Chinese)
      Ti-Hsüeh Tsa-Chih (Geographical Journal), No. 181(1937), 91-112

2088 Tao, Shao-yuan
      The distribution of population in the three lower Yangtze provinces
      Master's thesis, University of Chicago
      Chicago, 1938

2089 Hurlbut, Floy
      "The origin and distribution of present population," pp. 30-55 in:
      The Fukienese: a study in human geography
      N.p., author, 1939

2090 Kiuchi, Sinzo
      /"On the population and land utilization of Shansi, China,"/ (in
         Japanese)
      Chigaku Zasshi. Journal of Geography, 55(1943), 121-136

2091 Köhler, Günther
      "Karte der Bevölkerungsdichte der Provinz Schensi,"
      Deutsches Institut für Länderkunde, Wissenschaftliche Veröffent-
         lichungen, N.s., 11(1952), 120-127

2092 Pan, Chia-lin and Taeuber, Irene B.
      "The expansion of the Chinese: north and west,"
      Population Index, 18(1952), 85-108

2093 Köhler, Günther
      "Besiedlung und Binnenwanderung in Chinas Nordwesten,"
      PM, 98(1954), 269-271

2094 Hu, Huan-yung
      /"The population density of Nan-Tung District, Kiangsu,"/ (in Chinese)
      Ti-Li Hsüeh-Pao (Acta Geographica Sinica), 24(1958), 79-83

2095   Davis, Sydney George
       "Population growth and pressure in South China and Hong Kong,"
           pp. 296-301 in:
       Proceedings of IGU Regional Conference in Japan 1957
       Tokyo, 1959

                           7830: MANCHURIA

2096   Lattimore, Owen
       "Chinese colonization in Manchuria,"
       GR, 22(1932), 177-195

2097   Lee, Hoon K.
       "Korean migrants in Manchuria,"
       GR, 22(1932), 196-204

2098   Tanaka, Kaoru
       "Emigration to Manchuria in the light of climatological geography,"
       Journal of the Kobe University of Commerce, 1(1939), 85-108

2099   Beal, E. G., Jr.
       "The 1940 census of Manchuria,"
       Far Eastern Quarterly, 4(1945), 243-262

2100   Taeuber, Irene B.
       "Manchuria as a demographic frontier,"
       Population Index, 11(1945), 260-274

2101   Anuchin, V. A.
       /Geographic sketches of Manchuria/ (in Russian)
       Moskva, 1948

2102   Glushakov, P. I.
       /"Population,"/ (in Russian) pp. 70-84 in:
       /Manchuria/
       Moskva, 1948

2103   Wynne, Waller, Jr.
       The population of Manchuria
       U. S. Bureau of the Census
       Washington, 1958

                   7860: MONGOLIAN PEOPLE'S REPUBLIC

2104   Poppe, Nicholas and Murphy, G. G. S.
       "Size and geographical distribution of population," pp. 133-150 in:
       Mongolian People's Republic (Outer Mongolia). Vol. I
       Subcontractor's Monograph, HRAF39
       New Haven, Human Relations Area File, 1956

195   Korea

2105 Thiel, Erich
      Die Mongolei: Land, Volk und Wirtschaft der Mongolischen Volks-
         republik
      Osteuropa-Institutes München
      Müchen, Isar Verlag, 1958

      (Also see 2075)

                              7890: TIBET

2106 Kao, Ch'ang-chu
      /Conditions in Tibet/ (in Chinese)
      Taipei, 1953

2107 Beger, Bruno
      "Das Hochland Tibet und seine Bevölkerung,"
      Geographische Rundschau, 7(1955), 41-46

                              7900: KOREA

2108 Chosen, Government-General
      /Atlas of population phenomena in Korea/ (in Japanese)
      Seoul, 1927

2109 Lee, Hoon K.
      Land utilization and rural economy in Korea
      Chicago, University of Chicago Press, 1936

2110 Lautensach, Hermann
      "Das japanische Bevölkerungselement in Korea,"
      Geographischer Anzeiger, 43(1942), 371-375

2111 Taeuber, Irene B.
      "Korea in transition: demographic aspects,"
      Population Index, 10(1944), 229-242

2112 Lautensach, Hermann
      Korea; eine Landeskunde auf Grund eigner Reisen und der Literatur
      Leipzig, Koehler, 1945

2113 Taeuber, Irene B.
      "The population potential of postwar Korea,"
      Far Eastern Quarterly, 5(1945-46), 289-307

2114 Taeuber, Irene B. and Barclay, George
      "Korea and the Koreans in the northeast Asian region,"
      Population Index, 16(1950), 278-297

2115 Zaichikov, V. T.
      "Population," pp. 35-53 in:
      Geography of Korea
      New York, Institute of Pacific Relations, 1952

2116 Trewartha, Glenn T. and Zelinsky, Wilbur
      "Population distribution and change in Korea, 1925-1949,"
      GR, 45(1955), 1-26

2117 McCune, Shannon
      "The Korean population pattern," pp. 56-66 in:
      Korea's heritage; a regional & social geography
      Rutland, Vermont, Charles E. Tuttle Co., 1956

2118 Lee, Chun Myun
      Recent population patterns and trends in the Republic of Korea
      Doctoral dissertation, University of Michigan
      Ann Arbor, 1960

      (Also see 2075, 2097)

                          7905: RYUKYU ISLANDS

2119 Inamine, Ichiro
      The economy and population of the Ryukyu Islands
      Naha, 1953

2120 Taeuber, Irene B.
      "The population of the Ryukyu Islands,"
      Population Index, 21(1955), 233-263

                          7910: TAIWAN

2121 Kano, T.
      /"Forschungen über die Verteilung der Eingeborenenbevölkerung und die
        Höhenlage der Eingeborenensiedlungen in Formosa,"/ (in Japanese)
      Chirigaku Hyoron. Geographical Review of Japan, 14(1938), 649-667,
        761-796

2122 Taeuber, Irene B.
      "Colonial demography: Formosa,"
      Population Index, 10(1944), 147-157

2123 Ch'en, Cheng-hsiang
      /Land utilization in Taiwan/ (in Chinese)
      Taipei, 1950

2124 Ch'en, Cheng-hsiang and Tuan, Chi-hsien
      /Population of Taiwan/ (in Chinese)
      National Taiwan University, Institute of Agricultural Geography
      Taipei, 1951

2124a Barclay, George W.
      Colonial development and population in Taiwan
      Princeton, Princeton University Press, 1954

2125 Barclay, George W.
      A report on Taiwan's population
      Princeton, Princeton University Press, 1954

2126 Ch'en, Cheng-hsiang
        "Population and settlement in Formosa,"
        TESG, 45(1954), 176-180

2127 Ch'en, Cheng-hsiang
        /The demographic geography of Taiwan/ (in Chinese)
        Fu-Min Institute of Agricultural Geography, Research Report, No. 65
        Taipei, 1956

2128 Ch'en, Cheng-hsiang and Sun, Te-hsiung
        /Population distribution and change in Taiwan/ (in Chinese)
        Fu-Min Geographical Institute of Economic Development, Research
          Report, No. 78
        Taipei, 1958
        Also: Chirgaku Hyoron. Geographical Review of Japan, 31(1958), 644-
          658 (in Japanese)

2129 Ch'en, Cheng-hsiang
        "Population distribution and change in Taiwan," pp. 290-295 in:
        Proceedings of IGU Regional Conference in Japan 1957
        Tokyo, 1959

                              7950: JAPAN

                          a. Bibliography

2130 Hall, Robert B. and Noh, Toshio
        Japanese geography; a guide to Japanese reference and research
          materials
        University of Michigan Center for Japanese Studies, Bibliographical
          Series, No. 6
        Ann Arbor, University of Michigan Press, 1956

        (Also see 2169)

                          b. National

2131 Schultze, E.
        "Die japanische Auswanderung,"
        PM, 61(1915), 129-133, 175-179, 260-276, 301-308

2132 Jefferson, Mark
        "The distribution of people in Japan in 1913,"
        GR, 2(1916), 368

2133 Coulter, J. Wesley
        "A dot map of the distribution of population in Japan,"
        GR, 16(1926), 283-284

2134 Orchard, John E.
        "The pressure of population in Japan,"
        GR, 18(1928), 374-401

2135 Dennery, Etienne
        "La surpopulation japonaise,"
        AG, 38(1929), 148-168

2136 Dennery, Etienne
      Foules d'Asie. Surpopulation japonaise. Expansion chinoise. Emigra-
          tion indienne
      Paris, Colin, 1930

2137 Mecking, Ludwig
      "Japans Siedlungsraume,"
      Geographische Gesellschaft in München, Mitteilungen, 24(1931), 193-210

2138 Odauti, Tubin
      "Les caractéristiques regionales de la population rurale au Japon,"
          pp. 581-587 in:
      CRCIG, Paris, 1931, Vol. 3

2139 Hall, Robert B.
      "Cities of Japan; notes on distribution and inherited forms,"
      AAAG, 24(1934), 175-200

2140 Odauti, Tubin
      "Les problèmes de la surpopulation au Japon," pp. 596-598 in:
      CRCIG, Varsovie, 1934, Vol. 3

2141 Trewartha, Glenn T.
      "Japanese cities: distribution and morphology,"
      GR, 24(1934), 404-417

2142 Trewartha, Glenn T.
      "Population: density and distribution," pp. 28-33 in:
      A reconnaissance geography of Japan
      Madison, University of Wisconsin Press, 1934

2143 Charcot, J. B.
      "Le problème démographique japonais,"
      Geographie, 63(1935), 230-238

2144 Inouye, Shūji
      "Die Bevölkerungsverteilung Japans 1930,"
      Deutsches Institut für Landeskunde, Wissenschaftliche Veröffent-
          lichungen, N.s., 4(1936), 159-166

2145 Inouye, Shūji
      /"On the density and distribution of population by chō and son for all
          Japan, 1930,"/ (in Japanese) pp. 79-97 in:
      /Materials concerning the present population/
      Tokyo, Tōe Shoin, 1936

2146 Freeman, Thomas W.
      "Recent and contemporary Japanese migration,"
      SGM, 53(1937), 323-335

2147 Hall, Robert B.
      "A map of settlement agglomeration and dissemination in Japan,"
      Michigan Papers in Geography, 7(1937), 365-367

2148   Isida, Tatuziro
       "The population of the Japanese Empire since the Meizi Restoration,
          1868," pp. 1-27 in:
       Papers presented by the Japanese Preparatory Committee at the Geography
          Section of the Seventh Biennial Conference of the W.F.E.A., Tokyo,
          1937
       Tokyo, 1937
2149   Odauti, Tubin
       "Regional movement of population in Japan," pp. 41-50 in:
       CRCIG, Amsterdam, 1938, Vol. 2

2150   Tanakadate, Hidazo
       "Regional analysis of the distribution of population in the mainland
          of Japan," pp. 151-167 in:
       CRCIG, Amsterdam, 1938, Vol. 2

2151   Plasse, Jean de
       "La surpopulation japonaise,"
       Société de Géographie de Lille, Bulletin, 83(1939), 70-73

2152   Izukawa, Senkichi
       /"Population distribution and change in Mino-no-kuni,"/ (in Japanese)
       Jinkō Mondai (Population Problems), 6(1943), 19-48

2153   Trewartha, Glenn T.
       "Population and culture," pp. 121-150 in:
       Japan: a physical, cultural, and regional geography
       Madison, University of Wisconsin Press, 1945

2154   Hoffman, Lawrence A.
       "Japan: main population concentrations,"
       Journal of Geography, 46(1947), 62-69

2155   Ueda, Masao
       /"The areal characteristics of the Japanese population,"/ (in
          Japanese) pp. 85-187 in:
       Nihon, Kōsei-shō, Jinkō Mondai Kenkyūjo
       /The pending population problem/
       Tokyo, Kokumin Kyoiku-sha, 1949

2156   Tachi, Minoru and Ishii, Kiichi
       /Geographical study on population of postwar Japan - population growth
          and density/ (in Japanese)
       /The Fourth Study Meeting of the Population Association of Japan/
       Tokyo, 1950

2157   Tachi, Minoru and Ishii, Kiichi
       /"Geographical study on population of postwar Japan - median density
          of population by prefectures,"/ (in Japanese) pp. 97-102 in:
       Nihon, Kōsei-shō, Jinkō Mondai Kenkyūjo
       /Major results of surveys and research, 1951/
       Tokyo, 1951

2158   Ackerman, Edward A.
       Japan's natural resources and their relation to Japan's economic future
       Chicago, University of Chicago Press, 1953

2159   Hama, Hidehiko
       /"Analysis of changes in population distribution patterns,"/ (in
          Japanese) pp. 367-384 in:
       Nihon, Kōsei-shō, Jinkō Mondai Kenkyūjo
       /Major results of research/
       Tokyo, 1953

2160   Tachi, Minoru and Ueda, Masao
       /"Population,"/ (in Japanese) pp. 181-292 in:
       Kiuchi, Shinzo, ed.
       /Population and commune geography/
       Shinchirigaku Koza (New Geographical Series), Vol. 5
       Tokyo, Asakura Shoten, 1955

2161   Neuvy, Pierre
       "L'evolution de la population japonaise,"
       AG, 65(1956), 40-53

2162   Takayama, Ryuzo
       /"Migration of population in Japan,"/ (in Japanese)
       Jimbun Chiri. Human Geography, 8(1956), 369-377

2163   Tschudi, Aadel Brun
       /"Population change and employment in Japan,"/ (in Danish)
       Kulturgeografi, 8(1956), 181-194

2164   Hidaka, Tatutaro
       "Population density of Japan,"
       Geographical Survey Institute, Bulletin (Tokyo), 5(1957), 31-64

2165   Schwind, Martin
       "Betrachtungen zum japanischen Zensus von 1955,"
       Erdkunde, 1, No. 1(1957), 64-69

2166   Takagi, Hideki
       /"Internal migration in Japan,"/ (in Japanese)
       Chirigaku Hyoron. Geographical Review of Japan, 30(1957), 974-981

2167   Versantvoort, A. A. M.
       /"Recent changes in the population increase of Japan,"/ (in Dutch)
       K. Nederlandsch Aardrijkskundig Genootschap, Tijdschrift, 74(1957),
          204-206

2168   Schiedl, Leopold
       "Das japanische Bevölkerungsproblem," pp. 225-233 in:
       Geographische Forschungen. Festschrift zum 60. Geburtstag von Hans
          Kinzl
       N.p., Schlern-Schriften, 1958

2169   Taeuber, Irene B.
       The population of Japan
       Princeton, Princeton University Press, 1958

2170   Inaba, M. G.
       Japan: some geographical aspects of industrialization population
          correlates
       Doctoral dissertation, Columbia University
       New York, 1959

2171 Tachi, Minoru, Ueda, Masao, and Hama, Hidehiko
      "Regional characteristics of population in Japan," pp. 480-483 in:
      Proceedings of IGU Regional Conference in Japan 1957
      Tokyo, 1959

2172 Tsubouchi, Syoji
      "Population pressure and rural-urban migration in Japan," pp. 512-
          516 in:
      Proceedings of IGU Regional Conference in Japan 1957
      Tokyo, 1959

2173 Josif, Donald W.
      A comparative study of the demographic transition in Japan and England
          and Wales
      Master's thesis, Ohio State University
      Columbus, 1960

2174 Kawabe, Hiroshi
      /"Migration to cities in Japan: 1950-1955,"/ (in Japanese)
      Chigaku Zasshi. Journal of Geography, 70(1961), 16-30

2175 Kawabe, Hiroshi
      /"The internal migration of Japan: 1950-55,"/ (in Japanese)
      Chirigaku Hyoron. Geographical Review of Japan, 34(1961), 96-108

      (Also see 786, 797, 2110)

                              c. Regional

2176 Davis, Darrel H.
      "Japan (Hokkaido). Distribution of population in 1910, 1920, 1930,"
      GR, 24(1934), 388-390

2177 Scheinpflug, Alfons
      "Die japanische Kolonisation in Hokkaido,"
      Gesellschaft für Erdkunde zu Leipzig, Mitteilungen, 53(1935), 5-132

2178 Tanakadate, Hidazo
      /"Topographical analysis of the density of population in Kwanto,"/
          (in Japanese)
      Chigaku Zasshi. Journal of Geography, 50(1938), 541-555

2179 Taeuber, Irene B.
      "Hokkaido and Karafuto: Japan's internal frontiers,"
      Population Index, 12(1947), 6-12

2180 Goda, Eisaku
      /"The migration of the population of Osaka City,"/ (in Japanese)
      Chirigaku Hyoron. Geographical Review of Japan, 27, No. 10, (1954)

2181 Goda, Eisaku
      /"Spheres of migration in Tokyo,"/ (in Japanese)
      Chirigaku Hyoron. Geographical Review of Japan, 27, No. 1, (1954)

2182 Goda, Eisaku
      /"Migration caused by marriage in Omishima Ehime Prefecture,"/ (in
          Japanese)
      Chirigaku Hyoron. Geographical Review of Japan, 28(1955), 532-535

2183 Okamoto, Kaneyoshi
       /"Dispersed settlement and its relation to the surface configuration
         on the deltaic plain of Kanto,"/ (in Japanese)
       Jimbun Chiri. Human Geography, 7(1955), 14-26

2184 Yonetani, Seiji
       /"Center of population in Kyushu,"/ (in Japanese)
       Chirigaku Hyoron. Geographical Review of Japan, 28(1955), 249-254

                   8000: SOUTHEAST ASIA (INDOCHINA)

2185 Wenzler, Josef
       "Die Bevölkerung Südostasiens,"
       Zeitschrift für Geopolitik, 4(1927), 614-620

2186 Pelzer, Karl J.
       Die Arbeiterwanderungen in Südostasien: eine wirtschafts- und
         bevölkerungsgeographische Untersuchung
       Doctoral dissertation, University of Bonn
       Hamburg, Friedrichsen, de Gruyter, 1935

2187 Unger, Leonard
       "The Chinese in southeast Asia,"
       GR, 32(1942), 196-217

2188 Broek, Jan O. M.
       "Diversity and unity in southeast Asia,"
       GR, 34(1944), 175-195

2189 Van Aartsen, J. P.
       /"Population development in southeast Asia,"/ (in Dutch)
       TESG, 39(1948), 665-682, 712-732, 40(1949), 58-79, 105-120

2190 Helbig, Karl
       "Die chinesische Element in Südostasien; Herkunft, Verteilung und
         Aufgaben,"
       Die Erde, 1(1950-51), 54-61

2191 Zelinsky, Wilbur
       "The Indochinese peninsula: a demographic anomaly,"
       Far Eastern Quarterly, 9(1950), 115-145

2192 Purcell, Victor
       The Chinese in southeast Asia
       London and New York, Oxford University Press, 1951

2193 Fryer, Donald W.
       "The 'million city' in southeast Asia,"
       GR, 43(1953), 474-494

2194 Alers, H. J. H.
       /Dilemma in southeast Asia. An anthropogeographic interpretation of
         the Chinese penetration into southeast Asia/ (in Dutch)
       Leiden, E. J. Brill, 1955

2195 Ginsburg, Norton S.
      "The great city in southeast Asia,"
      American Journal of Sociology, 60(1955), 455-462

2196 Bruk, Solomon Ilyich
      /The population of Indochina; explanatory note for an ethnographic map/
      (in Russian)
      U.S.S.R., Academy of Sciences, Institute of Ethnography
      Moskva, 1959

2197 Louka, Kathryn T.
      The role of population in the development of southeast Asia
      Washington, George Washington University, 1960

                          8010: FORMER FRENCH INDOCHINA

2198 Robequain, Charles
      "L'habitat et la répartition des hommes," Vol. 1, pp. 193-221 and
      "Les établissements humaines et les migrations," Vol. 2, pp. 466-
         509 in:
      Le Thanh Hoá; étude géographique d'une province annamite
      Paris and Bruxelles, Van Oest, 1929

2199 Robequain, Charles
      "Notes sur les modifications du peuplement de l'Indochine française
         depuis cinquante ans," pp. 491-500 in:
      CRCIG, Paris, 1931, Vol. 3

2200 Gourou, Pierre
      Les paysans du delta tonkinois: étude de géographie humaine
      Publications de l'Ecole Française d'Extrême-Orient, Vol. 27
      Paris, 1936

2201 Gourou, Pierre
      "Un type de peuplement extrême-oriental: la densité de la population
         dans le delta du Fleuve Rouge,"
      Société Belge d'Etudes Géographiques, Bulletin, 7(1937), 132-144

2202 Gourou, Pierre
      "La densité de la population dans le delta du Tonkin," pp. 68-80 in:
      Congrès International de la Population, Vol. 6
      Paris, 1938

2203 Gourou, Pierre
      "Densité de la population et utilisation du sol en Indochine
         Française," pp. 417-420 in:
      CRCIG, Amsterdam, 1938, Vol. 2

2204 Thompson, Virginia M.
      "The relationship between the density of population and the method
         of land utilization in colonial regions, French Indo-China,"
         pp. 507-517 in:
      CRCIG, Amsterdam, 1938, Vol. 2

2205 Gourou, Pierre
L'utilisation du sol en Indochine Française
Centre d'Etudes de Politique Etrangère; Travaux des Groupe d'Etudes,
Publ. No. XIV
Paris, 1940

2206 Gourou, Pierre
"La population rurale de la Cochinchine,"
AG, 51(1942), 7-25

2207 Marres, Paul
"Le problème du surpeuplement dans l'Indochine et en Extrême-Orient
d'après Pierre Gourou et Charles Robequain,"
AG, 51(1942), 52-57

2208 Robequain, Charles
"People," pp. 21-88 in:
The economic development of French Indo-China
New York, Oxford University Press, 1944

2209 Taeuber, Irene B.
"French Indo-China: demographic imbalance and colonial policy,"
Population Index, 11(1945), 68-81

2210 Pietrantoni, Eric
"La population du Laos de 1912 à 1945,"
Société des Etudes Indochinoises, Bulletin, N.s., 28(1953), 25-38

2211 Larrimore, Ann
"The population characteristics of Laos," pp. 108-136 in:
Area handbook on Laos
Subcontractor's Monograph, HRAF23
New Haven, Human Relations Area File, 1955

2212 Pietrantoni, Eric
"La population du Laos en 1943 dans son milieu géographique,"
Société des Etudes Indochinoises, Bulletin, N.s., 32(1957), 223-243

2213 Steinberg, David J., et al.
"Geography and population," pp. 20-36 in:
Cambodia; its people, its society, its culture
New Haven, Human Relations Area File, 1957

8020: THAILAND

2214 Credner, Wilhelm
Siam, das Land der Tai
Stuttgart, 1935

2215 Barton, Thomas Frank
"Thailand's population density and distribution,"
Transition (Chicago), 3, No. 2(1960)

8030: MALAYA

2216   Vlieland, C. A.
       "The population of the Malay Peninsula,"
       GR, 24(1934), 61-78

2217   Chapman, F. Spencer
       "The Chinese in Malaya,"
       Geographical Magazine, 23(1951), 401-411

2218   Smith, T. E.
       Population growth in Malaya: an analysis of recent trends
       London, Royal Institute of International Affairs, 1952

2219   Ginsburg, Norton S. and Roberts, Chester F., Jr.
       "Demographic patterns," pp. 47-79 in:
       Malaya
       Seattle, University of Washington Press, 1958

2220   Hodder, B. W.
       "The population of Malaya," pp. 32-44 in:
       Man in Malaya
       London, University of London Press, 1959

8050: MALAY ARCHIPELAGO

2221   Helbig, Karl
       "Das chinesische Element in Bevölkerung und Siedlung Insel-Indiens,"
       Ostasiatische Rundschau, 23(1942), 246-255, 24(1943), 10-18

2222   Helbig, Karl
       "Bevölkerungsverteilung," pp. 54-59 in:
       Die Südostasiatische Inselwelt (Inselindien)
       Stuttgart, Franckh'sche Verlagshandlung, 1949

2223   Robequain, Charles
       "Distribution of population; modes of life," pp. 87-111 in:
       Malaya, Indonesia, Borneo, and the Philippines; a geographical and
          political description of Malaya, the East Indies, and the Philippines
       New York, Longmans, Green, 1958

8060: PHILIPPINES

2224   Fehlinger, H.
       "Die Bevölkerung der Philippinen,"
       Globus, 90(1906), 142-145

2225   Lenk, S.
       Die Bevölkerung der Philippinen; eine anthropogeographische Unter-
          suchung
       Doctoral dissertation, University of Leipzig
       Leipzig, 1932

2226 Cruz, Cornelio C.
     Philippine demography from the geographic point of view
     Manila, Philippine Council, Institute of Pacific Relations, 1933

2227 Cruz, Cornelio C.
     "Population and land utilization in the Philippines," pp. 383-395 in:
     Problems of the Pacific 1933
     Chicago, 1934

2228 Keesing, F. M.
     "Population and land utilization among the Lepanto, northern Philip-
         pines," pp. 543-549 in:
     CRCIG, Amsterdam, 1938, Vol. 2

2229 Kolb, Albert
     "Das heutige Bevölkerungsbild," pp. 392-418 in:
     Die Philippinen
     Leipzig, Koehler, 1942

2230 Taeuber, Irene B.
     "The demography of the Philippines,"
     Population Index, 8(1942), 3-9

2231 Martin, Gene Ellis
     Population and food production in the Philippine Province of Antique
     Master's thesis, University of Washington
     Seattle, 1952

2232 Spencer, Joseph E.
     "Population growth and standards of living," pp. 36-48 in:
     Land and people in the Philippines
     Berkeley and Los Angeles, University of California Press, 1952

2233 Hunt, Chester L.
     Cotabato, melting pot of the Philippines; a study on population dis-
         tribution and integration of a non-homogenous community
     Manila, Unesco National Commission of the Philippines, 1954

2234 Carroll, John J., S. J.
     "Population increase and geographical distribution in the Philippines,"
     Philippine Statistician, 8(1959), 154-173

2235 United Nations, Department of Economic and Social Affairs
     Population growth and manpower in the Philippines
     Population Studies, No. 32
     New York, 1960

     (Also see 283)

8070: INDONESIA

a. National

2236 Most, Otto
      "Die Bevölkerungsverhältnisse in Ostindien. Eine statistisch-
      geographische Studie,"
      Jahresbericht für Nationalökonomie und Statistik (Jena), 31(1906), 815-
      827

2237 Gonggrijp, J. W.
      "Soil management and density of population in the Netherlands Indies,"
      pp. 397-404 in:
      CRCIG, Amsterdam, 1938, Vol. 2

2238 Mohr, E. C. J.
      "The relation between soil and population density in the Netherlands
      Indies," pp. 478-493 in:
      CRCIG, Amsterdam, 1938, Vol. 2

2239 Smits, M. B.
      "Population density and soil utilisation in the Netherlands Indies,"
      pp. 500-506 in:
      CRCIG, Amsterdam, 1938, Vol. 2

2240 Taeuber, Irene B.
      "The demography of the Netherlands Indies,"
      Population Index, 6(1940), 150-154

2241 Ong, Eng-die
      /The Chinese in the Netherlands Indies/ (in Dutch)
      Amsterdam, University of Amsterdam-Assen, 1943

2242 Robequain, Charles
      "La surpopulation et les migrations dirigées dans l'Insulinde,"
      AG, 58(1948), 160-162

2243 Horstmann, Kurt
      "Indonesien; Bevölkerungsproblem und Wirtschaftsentwicklung," pp. 410-
      423 in:
      Geographisches Taschenbuch; Jahrweiser zur Deutscher Landeskunde,
      1958/9
      Wiesbaden, 1958

b. Regional

2244 Niermeyer, J. F.
      /"The population of Java and Madura in 1905,"/ (in Dutch)
      K. Nederlandsch Aardrijkskundig Genootschap, Tijdschrift, 24(1907),
      891-896

2245 Volz, W.
      "Die Bevölkerung Sumatras,"
      Globus, 95(1909), 1-7, 24-29

2246 Regelink, Z.
      /Contribution to the study of the population problem of Java and
          Madura/ (in Dutch)
      Doctoral dissertation, University of Utrecht
      Utrecht, 1931

2247 Van Valkenburg, Samuel
      "Java, a study of population,"
      Papers, Michigan Academy of Science, Arts and Letters, 14(1931) 399-
          415

2248 Lekkerkerker, C.
      /"Java's overpopulation,"/ (in Dutch)
      K. Nederlandsch Aardrijkskundig Genootschap, Tijdschrift, 54(1937),
          866-885

2249 Kuperus, G.
      "The relation between density of population and utilization of soil
          in Java," pp. 465-477 in:
      CRCIG, Amsterdam, 1938, Vol. 2

2250 Lehmann, Herbert
      "Die Bevölkerung der Insel Sumatra,"
      PM, 84(1938), 3-15

2251 Pasteyns, F.
      "Sumatra. La population,"
      Société Royale Belge de Géographie, Bulletin, 63(1939), 267-280

2252 Kuperus, G.
      /"The maximum population of the native agricultural living space in
          Java and Madura about 1930,"/ (in Dutch)
      K. Nederlandsch Aardrijkskundig Genootschap, Tijdschrift, 61(1944), 363-
          409

2253 Pelzer, Karl J.
      "Tanah Sabrang and Java's population problem,"
      Far Eastern Quarterly, 5(1946), 133-142

2254 Meel, H. de
      /The population of West Borneo, 1920-1948,"/ (in Dutch)
      K. Nederlandsch Aardrijkskundig Genootschap, Tijdschrift, 69(1952)

2255 Hanrath, J. J.
      /"The population density of Celebes,"/ (in Dutch)
      TESG, 45(1954), 89-90

2256 Hanrath, J. J.
      /"Transmigration in Indonesia in general and particularly in
          Celebes,"/ (in Dutch)
      TESG, 45(1954), 133-138

2257 Ormeling, H. J.
      "Population growth," pp. 180-186 in:
      The Timor problem; a geographical interpretation of an underdeveloped
          island
      The Hague, J. B. Wolters, 1956

2258 Bennett, Don C.
      Population pressure in east Java
      Doctoral dissertation, Syracuse University
      Syracuse, 1957

2259 Bhatta, J. N.
      /Regarding internal migration in Indonesia, with special reference to
         Sumatra/ (in Indonesian)
      Indonesia, Ministry of Defense, Topographical Service of the Army,
         Geographical Institute, Publication No. 7
      Djakarta, 1957

2260 Bintarto, R.
      "Pressure of population in Klaten and its obvious results,"
      Indonesian Journal of Geography, 1(1960), 45-50

2261 Reksohadiprodjo, Iso and Hadisaputro, Ir. Soedarsono
      "Trends in population change and food (paddy) production,"
      Indonesian Journal of Geography, 1(1960), 15-20

                          8104: BRITISH BORNEO

2262 Ride, Lindsay T.
      "The problem of depopulation with special reference to British North
         Borneo,"
      Population, 1(1934), 36-48

2263 T'ien, Ju-k'ang
      The Chinese of Sarawak
      London, London School of Economics and Political Science, 1953

2264 Grotewold, L.
      "Geography and population," pp. 19-34 in:
      British Borneo
      Subcontractor's Monograph, HRAF14
      New Haven, Human Relations Area File, 1955

                          8140: NEW GUINEA

2265 Murray, H. P.
      "The population problem in Papua--lack of direct evidence: a priori
         considerations," pp. 231-240 in:
      Proceedings of the Pan-Pacific Science Congress, Australia, 1923
      Melbourne, Government Printer, 1926

2266 Vial, L. G.
      "Some statistical aspects of population in the Morobe District, New
         Guinea,"
      Oceania, 8(1937), 283-307

2267 Baal, J. van
      /"The population of southern New Guinea under Dutch rule: 36 years,"/
         (in Dutch)
      Tijdschrift voor Indische Taal-, Land- en Volkenkunde, 79(1939), 309-
         314

2268   Barrie, J. W.
       "Population-land investigation in the Chimbu Subdistrict,"
       Papua and New Guinea Agricultural Journal, 1(1956), 45-51

2269   Reiner, Ernst
       "Neue Bevölkerungszahlen für Neuguinea,"
       PM, 101(1957), 213-215

2270   Koojiman, S.
       "Population research project among the Marind-anim and Jeei-nan
          peoples in Netherlands South New Guinea,"
       Nieuw Guinea Studiën (The Hague), 3(1959), 9-34

2271   Brookfield, H. C.
       "Population distribution and labour migration in New Guinea: a pre-
          liminary survey,"
       Australian Geographer, 7(1960), 233-242

                                8200: AFRICA

                              a. Bibliography

2272   U. S. Bureau of the Census and the Library of Congress
       Population censuses and other official demographic statistics of
          Africa (not including British Africa)
       Washington, 1950

                            b. Population Studies

2273   Wagner, Eduard
       "Die deutsche Bevölkerung der deutschen Schutzgebiete in Afrika,"
       Die Erde, 3(1904), 77-80

2274   LeConte, René
       "L'émigration allemande dans les colonies imperiales d'Afrique (1901
          à 1913),"
       Mouvement Géographique, 34(1921), 594-598

2275   Rehm, Karl
       "Das Problem der Bevölkerungsschätzung Afrikas,"
       Geographischer Anzeiger, 29(1928), 361-371

2276   Binder, Hilde
       "Die Verteilung der Europaer in Afrika,"
       Koloniale Rundschau, 26(1934), 176-179

2277   Troll, Carl
       "Weisser Siedlungsraum in Afrika,"
       Koloniale Rundschau, 27(1936), 437-444

2278   Wellington, John H.
       "Some geographical aspects of the peopling of Africa,"
       South African Journal of Science, 34(1937), 29-60

2279 Mendes Corrêa, Antonio Augusto
      "Computos da população global da Africa,"
      Portugal, Instituto Nacional de Estatistica, Centro de Estudos Demo-
         graficos, Revista, No. 5(1948), 17-35

2280 Francolini, Bruno
      "L'emigrazione italiana in Africa,"
      RGI, 56(1949), 2-22

2281 Badenhorst, L. T.
      "Population distribution and growth in Africa,"
      Population Studies, 5(1951), 23-34

2282 Mai, Erwin
      "Bevölkerungszahl und -verteilung," pp. 75-80 in:
      Der Erdteil Afrika
      Stuttgart, Frankh'sche Verlagshandlung, 1953

2283 Beaujeu-Garnier, Jacqueline
      "Quelques traits de la géographie de la population en Afrique,"
      Cahiers de l'Information Géographique, No. 11(1954), 1-10

2284 Schmidt, Elsa
      Die Bevölkerungskarte von Afrika
      Doctoral dissertation, University of München
      München, Steinbauer, 1959

2285 Schmidt, Else
      "Die Bevölkerungsdichte in Afrika in Beziehung zu dem Natur- und
      Kulturlandschaften. Erlauterungen zu einer neuen Darstellung der
      Bevölkerungsdichte im Masstab 1:10,000,000,"
      Geographischen Gesellschaft in München, Mitteilungen, 45(1960), 5-38

8203: BRITISH AFRICA

2286 U. S. Bureau of the Census and Library of Congress
      Population censuses and other official demographic statistics of
         British Africa. An annotated bibliography
      Washington, 1950

8220: NORTH AFRICA

2287 Bernard, Augustin
      "Le recensement de 1921 dans l'Afrique du Nord,"
      AG, 31(1922), 52-58

2288 LeConte, René
      "L'émigration allemande dans L'Afrique du Nord,"
      Mouvement Géographique, 35(1922), 177-182

2289 Chevalier, Louis
      Le problème démographique Nord-Africain
      Institut National d'Etudes Démographiques, Travaux et Documents,
        Cahier No. 6
      Paris, Presses Universitaires de France, 1947

2290 Paschinger, Herbert
      "Probleme aus Bevölkerung und Wirtschaft in Französisch-Nordafrika,"
      Geographischen Gesellschaft in Wien, Mitteilungen, 93(1951), 106-123

2291 Ortolani, Mario
      "Sulla densità della popolazione nel Sahara occidentale,"
      BSGI, Serie 8, 7(1954), 284-296

2292 Glauert, Günter
      "Zur Bevölkerungs- und Kulturlandschaftsentwicklung der nördlichen
        Sahara,"
      PM, 101(1957), 252-259

2293 Glauert, Günter
      "Veränderungen in der Bevölkerungsstruktur Nordafrikas in den letzten
        Jahrzenten,"
      Die Erde, 88(1957), 298-319

2294 Stephens, Richard W.
      Population factors in the development of North Africa
      Washington, George Washington University, 1960

                          8230: MOROCCO

2295 Larras, N.
      "La population du Maroc,"
      La Géographie, 13(1906), 337-348

2296 René-Leclerc, Ch.
      "La population israélite du Maroc,"
      Société de Géographie de Lille, Bulletin, 48(1907), 133-137

2297 Gadrat, François
      "Le peuplement du Maroc,"
      Société de Géographie de Lyon, Bulletin, Serie 2, 5(1912), 38-60

2298 Célérier, Jean
      "Densité de population et niveaux de vie au Maroc,"
      Revue de Géographie Marocaine, 32(1948), 1-24

2299 Raynal, René
      "Déplacements récents et actuels des populations du bassin de la
        Moulouya (Maroc oriental)," pp. 67-80 in:
      CRCIG, Lisbonne, 1949, Vol. 4

2300 Forichon, R. and Mas, P.
      "Les problèmes de la répartition du peuplement au Maroc,"
      Bulletin Economique et Social du Maroc (Rabat), 21(1957), 471-505

213   Algeria

2301 Ayache, Albert
      "La population ouvrière au Maroc: evaluation et répartition
      géographique,"
      Bulletin Economique et Social du Maroc (Rabat), 22(1959), 301-311

      (Also see 695)

                              8240: ALGERIA

2302 Chesneau, M.
      "La population européenne en Algérie,"
      La Géographie, 2(1900), 502-506

2303 Demontés, V.
      "Densité comparée des populations européennes et des populations
      indigènes en Algérie," pp. 196-214 in:
      Congrès National des Sociétés Françaises de Géographie, Compte Rendu,
      21. Session, Paris 1900
      Paris, 1901

2304 Lorin, Henri
      "Le peuplement français de l'Algérie,"
      Société de Géographie Commerciale de Bordeaux, Bulletin, 25(1902),
      277-284, 321-325

2305 Bernard, Augustin
      "La colonisation et le peuplement de l'Algérie d'après un enquête
      récente,"
      AG, 16(1907), 320-336

2306 Dechaud, Ed.
      "La population de l'Oranie d'après le dénombrement de 1911,"
      Société de Géographie et d'Archéologie d'Oran, Bulletin, 33(1913), 349-
      382

2307 Strasser, Col. --
      "La population de l'Oranie d'après le dénombrement de 1921,"
      Société de Géographie et d'Archéologie d'Oran, Bulletin, 41(1921),
      233-255

2308 Barthelet, --
      "Peuplement et natalité en Algérie et dans l'Afrique du Nord,"
      Société de Géographie d'Alger et de l'Afrique du Nord, Bulletin,
      32(1927), 478-508

2309 Maillet, Ct.
      "Population du département d'Oran d'après le dénombrement de 1926,"
      Société de Géographie d'Alger et de l'Afrique du Nord, Bulletin,
      32(1927), 58-75

2310 Peyronnet, R.
      "A propos du recensement de 1926,"
      Société de Géographie d'Alger et de l'Afrique du Nord, Bulletin,
      32(1927), 468-477

2311 Larnaude, Marcel
      Le groupement de la population berbère dans la Kablie du Djurdjura
      Alger, 1932

2312 Tinthoin, Robert
      "Rapport entre la densité de la population, le mode d'exploitation du
        sol et l'habitat dans le Tell Oranais," pp. 518-527 in:
      CRCIG, Amsterdam, 1938, Vol. 2

2313 Dessoliers, A.
      "La population européenne en Algérie,"
      Société de Géographie et d'Archéologie d'Oran, Bulletin, 70(1948),
        67-81

2314 Larnaude, Marcel
      "La carte de la répartition de la population dans l'Algérie du Nord,
        en 1948,"
      France, Comité des Travaux Historiques et Scientifiques, Section de
        Géographie, Bulletin, 64(1951), 87-93

2315 Isnard, Hildebert
      "Géographie de la faim: surpeuplement de l'Algérie,"
      Economie et Humanisme: Diagnostic Economique et Social, 1952, 38-47

2316 Suter, Karl
      "Etude sur la population et l'habitat d'une région du Sahara
        algérien: Le Touat,"
      RGA, 41(1953), 443-474

2317 Tinthoin, Robert
      "Le peuplement musulman d'Oran,"
      Société de Géographie et d'Archéologie d'Oran, Bulletin, 77(1954),
        5-72

2318 Acher, Gilbert
      "Le peuplement espagnol dans l'Algérie occidentale,"
      Bulletin de Géographie d'Aix-Marseille, N.s., 1(1955), 9-27

2319 Larnaude, Marcel
      La population musulmane de l'Algérie: traits principaux de sa
        géographie
      Cahiers Nord Africains, No. 50
      Paris, 1956

2320 Despois, Jean
      "La répartition de la population en Algérie,"
      Annales; Economies, Sociétés, Civilisations, 15(1960), 915-926

2321 Good, Dorothy
      "Notes on the demography of Algeria,"
      Population Index, 27(1961), 3-32

2322 Planhol, Xavier de
      "La formation de la population musulmane à Bilda,"
      Revue de Géographie de Lyon, 36(1961), 219-229

2323 Suter, Karl
      "Die Bevölkerung Algeriens,"
      Erdkunde, 15(1961), 192-201

8250:   TUNISIA

2324   Saurin, Jules
       "Le peuplement français de la Tunisie,"
       Société de Géographie Commerciale de Bordeaux, Bulletin, 29(1906),
       325-330

2325   Depois, Jean
       "Signification historique d'une carte de la densité de la population
       en Tunisie," pp. 15-22 in:
       Congrès International de la Population, Paris, 1937, Vol. 6
       Paris, Herman, 1938

2326   Clarke, John I.
       "The population of Tunisia; an example of contact between modern
          civilization and the Moslem world,"
       EG, 28(1952), 364-371

2327   Clarke, John I.
       "Emigration from southern Tunisia,"
       Geography, 42(1957), 96-104

2328   Poncet, Jean
       "L'évolution géographique du peuplement tunisien à l'époche récente,"
       AG, 68(1959), 247-253

2329   Wolkowitsch, Maurice
       "L'émigration des Français de Tunisie,"
       AG, 68(1959), 253-257

8260:   LIBYA

a.   Bibliography

2330   Hill, R. W.
       "Human and economic studies, Section E," pp. 76-100 in:
       A bibliography of Libya
       University of Durham, Department of Geography, Research Papers
          Series, No. 1

2330a Ricci, Leonardo
       "Centri abitati e popolazione nomade in Cirenaica,"
       RGI, 29(1922), 21-31

b.   Population Studies

2331   Macchia, A.
       "L'emigrazione italiana in Libia," pp. 478-481 in:
       Atti, Congresso Geografico Italiano, 14., Bologna, 1947
       Bologna, 1949

2332   Pan, Chia-Lin
       "The population of Libya,"
       Population Studies, 3(1949), 100-125

2333   Toni, Youssef T.
       "The population of Cyrenaica,"
       TESG, 49(1958), 1-10

8300: EGYPT

2334 Boinet Bey, A.
       "Le recensement de l'Egypte. Note présenté à la Société Khédiviale
       de Géographie,"
       Société Khédiviale de Géographie, Bulletin, 2e Série, No. 7(1885),
       353-395

2335 Boak, A. E. R.
       "Irrigation and population in the Faiyûm, the garden of Egypt,"
       GR, 16(1926), 353-364

2336 Cleland, Wendell
       The population problem in Egypt
       Lancaster, Pa., Science Press Printing Co., 1936

2337 Mitwalli, Mohammed
       "The population of the Egyptian oases,"
       Société Royale de Géographie d'Egypte, Bulletin, 21(1946), 289-312

2338 James, L.
       "The population problem in Egypt,"
       EG, 23(1947), 98-104

2339 Farid, I. A.
       The population of Egypt; some aspects of its growth and distribution
       Cairo, Renaissance, 1948

2340 Mountjoy, Alan B.
       "A note on the 1947 population of Egypt,"
       Geography, 34(1949), 30-37

2341 Nassif, E.
       "L'Egypte est-elle surpeuplée?"
       Population, 5(1950), 513-532

2342 Mountjoy, Alan B.
       "Egypt's population problem,"
       Institute of British Geographers, Publications, No. 18(1953), 121-135

2343 Awad, Mohammed
       "The assimilation of nomads in Egypt,"
       GR, 44(1954), 240-252

2344 Abou El-Ezz, Mohammed S.
       "Some aspects of migration in Cairo,"
       Société de Géographie d'Egypte, Bulletin, 32(1959), 121-141

8310: SUDAN

2345 Hassoun, Isam Ahmad
       "Western migration and settlement in the Gezira,"
       Sudan Notes and Records, 33(1952), 60-112

2346   Mather, D. B.
       "Migrations in the Sudan," pp. 113-144 in:
       R. W. Steel and C. A. Fisher, eds.
       Geographical essays on British tropical lands
       London, 1956

2347   Lebon, J. H. G.
       "Population distribution and land use in Sudan," in:
       The population of Sudan: report on the sixth annual conference, held in
           the University of Khartoum, 16th and 17th January, 1958
           Khartoum, 1958

2348   Simoons, Frederick J.
       "Problems of the first Sudan population census,"
       GR, 49(1959), 573-575

                            8315:   TROPICAL AFRICA

                             a.   Bibliography

2349   Lorimer, Frank
       Demographic information on tropical Africa
       Boston, Boston University Press, 1961

                          b.   Population Studies

2350   Robequain, Charles
       "La densité de la population dans l'Afrique occidentale et équatoriale,"
       Association de Géographes Français, Bulletin, Nos. 163-166(1944), 96-101

2351   Robequain, Charles
       "La répartition des hommes en Afrique occidentale et équatoriale,"
       Académie des Sciences Coloniales, Compte Rendu des Seances, 12(1944),
           6-15

2352   Robequain, Charles
       "Densités de population et géographie humaine en Afrique noire,"
       AG, 68(1954), 226-230

2353   Trewartha, Glenn T. and Zelinsky, Wilbur
       "Population patterns in tropical Africa,"
       AAG, 44(1954), 135-162

2354   Schultze, Joachim H.
       Beiträge zur Geographie Tropisch-Afrikas
       Deutsche Institut für Länderkunde, Wissenschaftliche Veröffentlichungen,
           Neue Folge 13-14
       Leipzig, 1955

2355   Steel, Robert W.
       "Land and population in British Tropical Africa,"
       Geography, 40(1955), 1-17

2356   Stephens, Richard W.
       Population pressures in Africa south of the Sahara
       Population Research Project, George Washington University
       Washington, 1959

2357   Kimble, George H. T.
       "The pattern of population," pp. 81-123 in:
       Tropical Africa, Vol. I. Land and livelihood
       New York, Twentieth Century Fund, 1960

2357a Barbour, Kenneth Michael and Prothero, R. Mansell, eds.
       Essays on African population
       London, Routledge & Kegan Paul, 1961

2358   Prothero, R. Mansell
       "Population movements and problems of malaria eradication in Africa,"
       Bulletin of the World Health Organization, 24(1961), 405-425

                         8320:   EAST AFRICA

2359   Baker, Samuel J. K.
       "The distribution of native population over East Africa,"
       Africa, 10(1937), 37-54

2360   Seidel, Werner
       Die Verbreitung der Inder in Ost- und Südafrika
       Geographische Gesellschaft zu Rostock, Mitteilungen Beiheft 7
       Rostock, Leopold in Komm., 1937

2361   Kayser, Kurt
       "Bevölkerungsdichte, Wanderarbeit und europaeischer Arbeitsbedarf in
          Ostafrika," pp. 441-457 in:
       CRCIG, Amsterdam, 1938, Vol. 2

2362   Baker, Samuel J. K.
       "The distribution of native population over south-east central Africa,"
       GJ, 108(1946), 198-210

       (Also see 2461)

                         8330:   ETHIOPIA

2363   Cerulli, E.
       "Le popolazioni Sidama secondo due recenti esplorazioni italiane,"
          pp. 99-105 in:
       CRCIG, Varsovie, 1934, Vol. 3

2364   Giaccardi, Albert
       "Le popolazioni del Borana e del Sidama,"
       Rivista delle Colonie, 11(1937), 1549-1563

2365   Perham, Margery
       /Population/ pp. 264-266 in:
       The government of Ethiopia
       London, 1948

2366   Smeds, Helmer
       /"The habitability of the altitudinal zones of the Ethiopian high-
          lands,"/ (in Swedish)
       Ymer, 76(1956), 197-219
       Also: PM, 100(1956), 61

2367   Brooke, Clarke
       "The rural village in the Ethiopian highlands,"
       GR, 49(1959), 58-75

                              8340:   ERITREA

2368   Rossini, Carlo Conti
       "Il censimento delle popolazioni indigene della colonia Eritrea,"
       RGI, 9(1902), 52-64

2369   Castellano, Vittorio
       "La popolazione italiana dell'Eritrea dal 1924 al 1940,"
       Rivista Italiana di Demografia e Statistica, 2(1948), 530-540

                             8350:   SOMALILAND

2370   Puccioni, N.
       "Appunti sulla distribuzione geografica delle popolażione della
           Somalia,"
       BSGI, Serie 5, 8(1919), 149-159

2371   Naldoni, Nardo
       "La colonizzazione italiana della Somalia,"
       L'Universo, 30(1950), 197-212

2372   Hunt, John A.
       A general survey of the Somaliland Protectorate, 1944-1950 (C.D. & W.
           Scheme D. 484)
       London, H.M.S.O., 1951

       (Also see 2373)

                        8400:   BRITISH EAST AFRICA

2373   Kuczynski, Robert R.
       Demographic survey of the British colonial empire. Volume II. East
           Africa, etc.
       London, Oxford University Press, 1949

2374   Rawson, Robert R.
       "Emigration to British east and central Africa,"
       EG, 27(1951), 65-71

                              8410:   KENYA

2375   Prins, A. H. J.
       "The geographical distribution of the north-eastern Bantu population,"
       K. Nederlandsch Aardrijkskundig Genootschap, Tijdschrift, 72(1955),
           232-240

       (Also see 2377)

8420: UGANDA

2376   Middleton, J. F. M. and Greenland, D. S.
       "Land and population in the West Nile District of Uganda,"
       GJ, 120(1954), 446-457

2377   Trewartha, Glenn T.
       "New population maps of Uganda, Kenya, Nyasaland, and Gold Coast,"
       AAAG, 47(1957), 41-58

8430: TANGANYIKA

2378   Uhlig, Carl
       "Natur und Bevölkerung Deutsch-Ostafrikas in ihren Beziehungen zur
          politischen Geographie und zur Wirtschaft des Landes," pp. 243-282
          in:
       Zwölf . . . Studien. Von Schülern A. Hettners
       Breslau, F. Hirt, 1921

2379   Gillman, Clement
       "South-west Tanganyika Territory,"
       GJ, 69(1927), 97-131

2380   Gillman, Clement
       "A population map of Tanganyika Territory,"
       GR, 26(1936), 353-375

2381   Kayser, Kurt
       "Das Problem der Bevölkerungsverteilung in Ostafrika,"
       Koloniale Rundschau, 27(1936), 401-405

2382   Kayser, Kurt
       "Die Eingeborenen-Arbeit als Problem der Bevölkerungs- und Wirt-
          schaftstruktur Deutsch-Ostafrikas,"
       Geographische Zeitschrift, 45(1939), 121-138

2383   Nowack, Ernst
       "Die Bevölkerungsverteilung in Deutsch-Ostafrika und ihre Ursachen,"
       PM, 88(1942), 367-369

2384   United Nations, Department of Economic and Social Affairs, Population
          Division
       The population of Tanganyika
       Population Studies, No. 2
       New York, 1949

2385   Huttlinger, Frank D.
       Tanganyika: a geographical interpretation of native population dis-
          tribution
       Master's thesis, Pennsylvania State College
       State College, 1953

2386 Malcolm, D. W.
      "Population," pp. 9-19 in:
      Sukumaland: an African people and their country; a study of land use
          in Tanganyika
      London, Oxford University Press, 1953

2387 United Nations, Department of Economic and Social Affairs, Population
      Division
      Additional information on the population of Tanganyika (supplement to
          "The population of Tanganyika")
      Reports on the Population of Trust Territories, No. 2
      New York, 1953

2388 Fosbrooke, H. A.
      "Tanganyika's population problem: an historical explanation,"
      Rhodes-Livingstone Journal, No. 23(1958), 54-58

2389 Gulliver, P. H.
      "The population of the Arusha chiefdom: a high density area in East
          Africa,"
      Rhodes-Livingstone Journal, No. 28(1961), 1-21

2390 Tanner, R. E. S.
      "Population changes, 1955-1959, in Musoma District, and their effect
          on land usage,"
      East African Agricultural and Forestry Journal, 26(1961), 164-169

      (Also see 2373)

                              8450: MOZAMBIQUE

2391 Lange, Fritz
      "Die nichteingeborene Bevölkerung in Portugiesisch-Ostafrika; ein
          Beitrag zur kolonialen Bevölkerungslehre,"
      Koloniale Rundschau, 28(1937), 175-200

                              8460: MADAGASCAR

2392 Martonne, Emmanuel de
      "La densité de population à Madagascar,"
      AG, 20(1911), 77-85

2393 Decary, Raymond
      "La population de l'Androy, extrême sud de Madagascar," pp. 42-55 in:
      Congrès International de la Population, Vol. 6
      Paris, Herman, 1938

2394 Decary, Raymond and Castel, Remy
      Modalités et consequences des migrations intérieures récentes des
          populations malgaches
      Gouvernement General de Madagascar et Dependances, Etudes Démo-
          graphiques
      Tananarive, 1941

2395 Gourou, Pierre
      "La population de Madagascar,"
      AG, 53-54(1945), 299-301

2396 Chevalier, Louis
      Madagascar, populations et ressources
      Paris, Presses Universitaires de France, 1952

2397 Decary, Raymond
      "Les conditions physiques du peuplement humain de Madagascar,"
      Institut de Recherche Scientifique de Madagascar, Mémoires, Série C,
          Tome 1, Fasc. 1(1952), 1-12

2398 Lasserre, Guy
      "La démographie de Madagascar,"
      Cahiers d'Outre-Mer, 6(1953), 281-285

2399 Molet, Louis
      Démographie de l'Ankaisinana (Madagascar)
      Institut de Recherche Scientifique de Madagascar, Mémoires, Série C,
          Tome 3
      Tananarive, 1953

2400 Molet, Louis
      "Les populations de l'Ankaizinana (centre nord de Madagascar),"
      AG, 65(1956), 418-436

2401 Deschamps, Hubert
      Les migrations intérieures à Madagascar
      Paris, Berger-Levrault, 1959

8500: SOUTH AFRICA

2402 Waibel, Leo
      "Der Mensch im südafrikanischen Veld,"
      Geographische Zeitschrift, 36(1920), 26-50, 79-89

2403 LeConte, René
      "L'émigration allemande dans l'Afrique du sud,"
      Mouvement Géographique, 34(1921), 601-605

2404 Fitzgerald, W.
      "The population problem of South Africa,"
      SGM, 44(1928), 334-349

2405 Narath, Rudolf
      Die Union von Südafrika und ihre Bevölkerung
      Geographische Schriften, Bd. VI
      Leipzig, Teubner, 1930

2406 Hugo, C. F.
      "A study of the geographical distribution of population within the
          magisterial district of Pretoria and the adjacent portion of the
          District of Brits,"
      South African Geographical Journal, 18(1935), 22-42

2407 Moolman, Jan Hendrik
      /"The distribution of population in southwestern Cape Province,"/
      (in Afrikaans)
      Annale van die Universiteit van Stellenbosch, 19, B, No. 1(1941),
      1-164

2408 Back, C. de
      /"Immigration in South Africa (from 1652 to today),"/ (in Dutch)
      TEG, 38(1947), 271-283

2409 Buchanan, Keith and Hurwitz, N.
      "The Asiatic immigrant community in the Union of South Africa,"
      GR, 39(1949), 440-449

2410 Buchanan, Keith and Hurwitz, N.
      "The 'Coloured' community in the Union of South Africa,"
      GR, 40(1950), 397-414

2411 Alsop, M. H.
      The population of Natal
      Natal Regional Survey, Vol. 2
      Capetown, University of Natal Press, 1952

2412 Badenhorst, L. T.
      "Territorial differentials in fertility in the Union of South Africa--
      1911-1936,"
      Population Studies, 6(1952), 135-162

2413 Fair, T. J. D.
      "Agricultural regions and the European rural farm population of
      Natal,"
      South African Geographical Journal, 34(1952), 3-19

2414 Pollock, N. C.
      "The distribution of native population in Victoria East, Cape
      Province,"
      South African Geographical Journal, 35(1953), 28-32

2415 Fair, T. J. D.
      The distribution of population in Natal
      Natal Regional Survey, Vol. 3
      New York, Oxford University Press, 1955

2416 Wellington, John W.
      "The people," pp. 201-270 in:
      Southern Africa; a geographical study. Volume II. Economic and
      human geography
      Cambridge, Cambridge University Press, 1955

2417 Brookfield, H. C.
      "Urbanization among the South African white population,"
      Geography, 42(1957), 63-64

2418 Nel, Andries
      /"Two maps of population density in South Africa,"/ (in Afrikaans)
      Journal for Geography (Stellenbosch), 1, No. 1(1957), 34-38

2419 Nel, Andries
      /"The depopulation of the countryside of whites, 1946-1951,"/
         (in Afrikaans)
      Journal for Geography (Stellenbosch), 1, No. 2(1958), 48-58

2420 Cole, Monica M.
      "Population," pp. 653-667 in:
      South Africa
      London, Methuen, 1961

8550: FEDERATION OF RHODESIA AND NYASALAND

2421 Baker, Colin
      "The non-African population of the Federation of Rhodesia and
         Nyasaland,"
      Geography, 43(1958), 132-134

8560: SOUTHERN RHODESIA

2422 Scott, Peter
      "Migrant labor in Southern Rhodesia,"
      GR, 44(1954), 29-48

2423 Prescott, J. R. V.
      "Overpopulation and overstocking in the native areas of Matabeleland,"
      GJ, 127(1961), 212-225

8590: SWAZILAND

2424 Doveton, Dorothy M.
      The human geography of Swaziland
      Institute of British Geographers, Publication No. 8
      London, 1937

2425 Scott, Peter
      "Land policy and the native population of Swaziland,"
      GJ, 117(1951), 435-447

      (Also see 2373)

8610: NYASALAND

2426 Dixey, F.
      "The distribution of population in Nyasaland,"
      GR, 18(1928), 274-290

2427 Baker, C. A.
      "Chigaru's: a study of its population,"
      Nyasaland Journal, 2(1958), 60-64

2428 Petterson, Donald R.
      "The European population of Nyasaland,"
      Illinois State Academy of Science, 51(1958), 43-47

2429 Baker, Colin
      "Blantyre District. A geographical appreciation of the growth, dis-
      tribution and composition of its population,"
      Nyasaland Journal, 12(1959), 7-35

      (Also see 2373)

                        8630: CENTRAL AFRICA

2430 Vierkandt, A.
      "Die Volksdichte im westlichen Central-Afrika,"
      Verein für Erdkunde zu Leipzig, Wissenschaftliche Veröffentlichungen,
      2(1895), 63-172

                          8640: ANGOLA

2431 Martin, Kurt
      "Bevölkerung, Wirtschaft und Verwaltung Angolas,"
      Koloniale Rundschau, 30(1939), 71-102

2432 Sarmento, Alexandre
      "População indigena de Angola (sondagens e perspectivas demográficas),"
      Sociedade de Geografia de Lisboa, Boletim, 66(1948), 635-649

2433 Amorim, Fernando B. P. de
      "A concentração urbana em Angola: contribuição para o estudo da
      demografia de Angola,"
      Centro de Estudos Demograficos, Revista, No. 11(1958-59), 87-112

          8650: REPUBLIC OF THE CONGO (LEOPOLDVILLE)

2434 Gilot, Mathieu
      "Ein Beitrag über die Bevölkerung Belgisch-Kongos (nach dem Stand
      von 1939),"
      Beiträge zur Kolonialforschung, 3(1943), 77-87

2435 Gourou, Pierre
      "La géographie humaine du Congo Belge,"
      Université Libre de Bruxelles, Institut de Sociologie Solvay,
         Revue de l'Institut de Sociologie, 23(1950), 5-23

2436 Gourou, Pierre
      Carte de la densité de la population. Atlas général du Congo
      Bruxelles, Institut Géographique Militaire, 1951

2437 Gourou, Pierre
      "La population rurale du Congo belge. Introduction à l'étude de sa
      répartition géographique,"
      Revue de l'Université de Bruxelles, Oct.-Dec., 1954, 5-15

2438   Trewartha, Glenn T. and Zelinsky, Wilbur
       "The population geography of Belgian Africa,"
       AAAG, 44(1954), 163-193

2439   Gourou, Pierre
       La densité de la population rurale au Congo belge
       Académie Royale des Sciences Coloniales, Mémoires, N.s., Tome 1
       Bruxelles, 1955

2440   Klein, W. C.
       /"Migrations du population du Congo belge et de la Nouvelle Guinée
       Nederlandaise et les discussions sur la valorisation du travail
       aux récentes Journées d'Etudes Internationales Africaines de
       Ghent,"/ (in Dutch)
       TESG, 47(1956), 37-48

2441   Fortems, Guy
       La densité de la population dans le Bas-Fleuve et le Mayumbe
       Académie Royale des Sciences d'Outre-Mer, Classe des Sciences
       Naturelles et Médicales, Mémoires in-8°, N.s., Tome 11
       Bruxelles, 1960

2442   Gourou, Pierre
       Cartes de la densité et de la localisation de la population dans la
       province de l'Equateur
       Académie Royale des Sciences d'Outre-Mer and Institut de Géographie
       de l'Université Libre de Bruxelles, Atlas Général du Congo,
       Fascicule No. 624.1
       Bruxelles, 1960

                        8655:   RUANDA-URUNDI

2443   Gourou, Pierre
       La densité de la population au Ruanda-Urundi; esquisse d'une étude
       géographique
       Institut Royal Colonial Belge, Section des Sciences Naturelles et
       Médicales, Mémoires, Tome 21, Fasc. 6
       Bruxelles, 1953

2444   United Nations, Department of Economic and Social Affairs, Population
       Division
       The population of Ruanda-Urundi
       Population Studies, No. 15
       New York, 1953

       (Also see 2438)

                        8670:   FERNANDO PO

2445   Castillo-Fiel, El Conde de
       "La población de Fernando Poo," pp. 83-102 in:
       Conferencia Internacional dos Africanistas Ocidental, Bissau, 1947,
       Vol. 4
       Lisboa, 1952

8675: SAO TOME AND PRINCIPE

2446 Alves Morgado, Nuno
      "Contribuição para o estudo do problema demográfico de S. Tome e
        Principé,"
      Garcia de Orta; Revista da Junta das Missões Geográficas e de In-
        vestigações do Ultramar (Lisboa), 5(1957), 633-658

8680: FORMER FRENCH EQUATORIAL AFRICA

2447 Sautter, Gilles
      "Les paysans noirs du Gabon septentrional; essai sur le peuplement
        et l'habitat du Woleu-N'Tem,"
      Cahiers d'Outre-Mer, No. 14(1951), 1-40

2448 Soret, M.
      "Carte ethno-démographqie de l'Afrique Equatoriale Française.
        Note preliminaire,"
      Institut d'Etudes Centrafricaines, Bulletin, No. 11(1956), 27-52

8730: CAMEROONS

2449 Oetting, W.
      "Die Volksdichte in Alt-Kamerun,"
      Koloniale Rundschau, 26(1934), 116-120

2450 Kuczynski, Robert R.
      The Cameroons and Togoland; a demographic study
      London, Oxford University Press, 1939

2451 Dizian, R.
      Densité de la population, démographie, économie rurale dans les sub-
        divisions de Guider, Kaele et Yagoua (Nord-Cameroun)
      France, Ministère de la France d'Outre-Mer, Office de la Recherche
        Scientifique et Technique Outre-Mer, Institut de Recherches du
        Cameroun, Section de Géographie Humaine
      Yaoundé, 1954

2452 Schramm, Joseph
      "Bevölkerungsverschiebungen in Süd-Kamerun,"
      Erdkunde, 8(1954), 323-324

8735: WEST AFRICA

2453 Harrison-Church, R. J.
      "Population distribution and movements," pp. 163-173 in:
      West Africa: a study of the environment and of man's use of it
      London, Longmans, Green, 1957

2454 Prothero, R. Mansell
      "Population movement in West Africa,"
      GR, 47(1957), 434-437

8750: DAHOMEY

2455 Mercier, P.
      "Densités de population dans le Moyen-Dahomey," pp. 181-191 in:
      CRCIG, Lisbonne, 1949, Vol. 4

8760: TOGO

2456 Froelich, J. C.
      "Densité de la population et méthodes de culture chez les Kabré du
      Nord Togo," pp. 168-180 in:
      CRCIG, Lisbonne, 1949, Vol. 4

      (Also see 2450)

8790: GUINEA

2457 Richard-Molard, J.
      "Les densités de population au Fouta-Dialon et dans les régions
      environnantes," pp. 192-204 in:
      CRCIG, Lisbonne, 1949, Vol. 4

8810: SENEGAL

2458 Rousseau, R.
      "La population du Sénégal en 1926,"
      AG, 38(1929), 399-403

8830: BRITISH WEST AFRICA

2459 Kuczynski, Robert R.
      Demographic survey of the British colonial empire. Volume I. West
          Africa
      London, Oxford University Press, 1948

2460 Steel, Robert W.
      "Some problems of population in British West Africa," pp. 19-50 in:
      Robert W. Steel and C. A. Fisher, eds.,
      Geographical essays on British tropical lands
      London, 1956

8840: NIGERIA

2461 Dent, H. M. and Kendrick, M. G.
      "Two African population maps,"
      Journal of the Manchester Geographical Society, 44(1929), 64-68

2462   Dodge, Stanley D.
       "The distribution of population in northern Nigeria,"
       Papers of the Michigan Academy of Science, Arts and Letters, 14(1930),
          297-303

2463   Niven, C. R.
       "Some Nigerian population problems,"
       GJ, 85(1935), 54-58

2464   Gourou, Pierre
       "Géographie du peuplement en Nigeria méridionale,"
       Société Belge d'Etudes Géographiques, Bulletin, 17(1947), 58-64

2465   Grove, Alfred Thomas
       "Soil erosion and population problems in south-east Nigeria,"
       GJ, 117(1951), 291-306

2466   Buchanan, Keith M. and Pugh, John Charles
       "The human pattern," pp. 58-99 in:
       Land and people in Nigeria
       London, University of London Press, 1955

2467   Mitchel, N. C.
       "The Nigerian town: distribution and definition,"
       University College, Ibadan, Department of Geography, Research Notes,
          7(1955), 1-13

2468   Morgan, William B.
       "Farming practice, settlement pattern, and population density in
          southeastern Nigeria,"
       GJ, 121(1955), 320-333

2469   Prothero, R. Mansell
       "The population census of Northern Nigeria,"
       GR, 45(1955), 579-581

2470   Prothero, R. Mansell
       "The population of Eastern Nigeria,"
       SGM, 71(1955), 165-170

2471   Prothero, R. Mansell
       "Population patterns and migrations in Sokoto Province, Northern
          Nigeria," pp. 49-54 in:
       L. Dudley Stamp, ed.
       Natural resources, food and population in Intertropical Africa; report
          of a symposium held at Makerere College, September, 1955
       London, Geographical Publications, 1956

2472   Grove, Alfred Thomas
       Land and population in Katsina Province
       Kaduna, Government Printer, 1957

2473   Jennings, John H.
       "A population distribution map of the Eastern Region of Nigeria,"
       GJ, 123(1957), 416-417

2474   Prothero, R. Mansell
       "Problems of population mapping in an underdeveloped territory
          (Northern Nigeria),"
       Nigerian Geographical Journal, 3(1959), 1-7

                              8850: GHANA

2475   Dresch, Jean
       "Les migrations des populations des colonies françaises vers la Gold
          Coast,"
       Association de Géographes Français, Bulletin, Nos. 171-172(1945),
          84-92

2476   Steel, Robert W.
       "The population of Ashanti: a geographical analysis,"
       GJ, 112(1948), 64-77

2477   Steel, Robert W.
       "The towns of Ashanti: a geographical study," pp. 81-93
       CRCIG, Lisbonne, 1949, Vol. 4

2478   Hilton, Thomas Eric
       "The distribution and density of population in the Gold Coast Colony
          and southern Togoland," pp. 472-481 in:
       CRCIG, Washington, 1952

2479   Hilton, Thomas Eric
       "The population of the Gold Coast," pp. 43-49 in:
       L. Dudley Stamp, ed.
       Natural resources, food and population in Inter-Tropical Africa;
          report of a symposium held at Makerere College, September, 1955
       London, Geographical Publications, 1956

2480   Rouch, Jean
       Migrations au Ghana (Gold Coast). Enquête 1953-1955
       Paris, Société des Africanistes, 1956

2481   Skorupka, Rev. Joseph A.
       Population distribution in Birim District, Gold Coast, 1948
       Master's thesis, Catholic University of America
       Washington, 1956

2482   Varley, W. J. and White, Henry Patrick
       "Distribution of population," pp. 271-291 in:
       The geography of Ghana
       London, Longmans Green, 1958

2483   Boateng, Ernest Amano
       "Population and settlements," pp. 104-117 in:
       A geography of Ghana
       Cambridge, Cambridge University Press, 1959

2484   Boateng, Ernest Amano
       "Some geographical aspects of the 1960 population census of Ghana,"
       Ghana Geographical Association, Bulletin, 5(1960), 2-8

2485 Hilton, Thomas Eric
      Ghana population atlas: the distribution and density of population
         in the Gold Coast and Togoland under United Kingdom trusteeship
      Edinburgh, Nelson, 1960

      (Also see 2373)

8870: GAMBIA

2486 Jarrett, H. Reginald
      "Population and settlement in the Gambia,"
      GR, 38(1948), 633-636

8880: LIBERIA

2487 Porter, Philip W.
      Population distribution and land use in Liberia
      Doctoral dissertation, London School of Economics
      London, 1957

8950: AUSTRALASIA

2488 Geisler, Walter
      "Die Bevölkerung," pp. 103-125 in:
      Australien und Ozeanien
      Leipzig, Bibliographisches Institut, 1930

8960: AUSTRALIA

2489 Langenstrassen, Bodo
      Die Bevölkerungsverhältnisse der britischen Kolonialstaaten in
         Australien, unter Berücksichtigung der wirtschaftlichen Einflüsse
      Doctoral dissertation, University of Breslau
      Breslau, Grass, Barth & Co., 1912

2490 Taylor, Griffith
      "Uninhabited Australia; and the reasons therefore," pp. 659-664 in:
      Proceedings of Sections, Pan-Pacific Science Congress, Australia, 1923
      Melbourne, 1923

2491 Barkley, Henry
      "Climatic factors affecting the distribution and limits of the popula-
         tion of Australia," pp. 182-221 in:
      P. D. Phillips and G. L. Wood, eds.
      The peopling of Australia
      Melbourne, Macmillan, 1928

2492 Fenner, Ch.
      "A geographical enquiry into the growth, distribution and movement of
          population in South Australia 1836-1927,"
      Royal Society of South Australia, Transactions and Proceedings,
          53(1929), 79-145

2493 Radcliffe-Brown, A. R.
      "Former numbers and distribution of the Australian aboriginals,"
          pp. 671-696 in:
      Official yearbook of the Commonwealth of Australia, 1930
      Canberra, 1930

2494 Holmes, MacDonald
      An atlas of population and production for New South Wales
      Sydney, Angus & Robertson, 1931

2495 Eggleston, F. W. and Packer, G.
      The growth of Australian population
      Melbourne, 1937

2496 Andrews, John
      "Some aspects of the population question in Australia,"
      Australian Geographer, 3(1940), 3-14

2497 Taylor, Griffith
      "The spread of settlement in Australia," pp. 217-236 in:
      Australia
      New York, Dutton, 1943

2498 Connellan, E. J.
      "Population potential of the Northern Territory,"
      Queensland Geographical Journal, N.s., 49(1944-45), 89-111

2499 Borrie, W. D.
      Population trends and policies
      Sydney, 1948

2500 Gentilli, Joseph
      "Australian rural population changes,"
      Economic Record, 25(1949), 37-47

2500a Robinson, Kenneth W.
      "Population and land use in the Sydney District, 1788-1820,"
      New Zealand Geographer, 9(1953), 144-160

2501 Scott, Peter
      "The changing population of Tasmania,"
      Geographical Studies (London), 4(1957), 13-29

2502 Borrie, W. D. and Dedman, Ruth M.
      Population increase and decrease 1947-1954 (Commentary on map in
          'Atlas of Australian Resources')
      Canberra, Department of National Development, 1958

2503   Lawton, Graham H.
       "The growth and distribution of population," pp. 37-47 in:
       Rupert J. Best, ed.
       Introducing South Australia
       Melbourne, Melbourne University Press, 1958

2504   Rose, Arthur J.
       "The geographical pattern of European immigration in Australia,"
       GR, 48(1958), 512-527

2505   Woolmington, Erik R.
       "The distribution of immigrants in the Newcastle region of N.S.W.,"
       Australian Geographer, 7(1958), 85-96

2506   Rose, Arthur J.
       "Irish migration to Australia in the twentieth century,"
       Irish Geography, 4(1959), 79-84

2507   Zubrzycki, Jerzy
       Immigrants in Australia. A demographic survey based upon the 1954
          census
       Australian National University, Social Science Monographs, No. 17
       Melbourne, Melbourne University Press, 1960

                            9080:   NEW ZEALAND

2508   Vergez-Tricom, G.
       "La population en Nouvelle-Zélande,"
       AG, 30(1921), 145-147

2509   Butijn, J. A. A.
       /"New Zealand as an immigration area,"_/ (in Dutch)
       TEG, 32(1941), 123-126

2510   Tocker, A. H.
       "Population policy in New Zealand and elsewhere: a review of objec-
          tives,"
       New Zealand Geographer, 1(1945), 139-148

2511   Cumberland, Kenneth B.
       "Population changes in New Zealand,"
       GJ, 108(1946), 121-123

2512   Calvert, G. N.
       "New Zealand's population prospects,"
       New Zealand Geographer, 3(1947), 1-18

2513   Lethwaite, Gordon
       "The population of Aotearoa: its number and distribution,"
       New Zealand Geographer, 6(1950), 35-52

2514   Metge, Joan
       "The Maori population of northern New Zealand,"
       New Zealand Geographer, 8(1952), 104-124

2515   Rose, Arthur J.
       "The Maori in northwest Nelson about 1840,"
       New Zealand Geographer, 8(1952), 63-68

2516   Cumberland, Kenneth B.
       "Population growth in New Zealand: a review of recent census
            figures,"
       SGM, 69(1953), 97-105

2517   Franklin, Samuel H.
       "Some demographic aspects of New Zealand rural and urban communi-
            ties," pp. 71-78 in:
       New Zealand: inventory & prospect
       Wellington, New Zealand Geographical Society, 1956

2518   Franklin, Samuel H.
       "The pattern of sex ratios in New Zealand,"
       EG, 32(1956), 162-176

2519   Pownall, Leslie L.
       "Evolution of the urban structure of New Zealand,"
       TESG, 47(1956), 63-68

2520   Franklin, Samuel H.
       "The age structure of New Zealand's North Island communities,"
       EG, 34(1958), 64-79

2521   Frazer, R. M.
       "Maoriland and Maori population in the far north,"
       New Zealand Geographer, 14(1958), 19-31

2522   Forrest, James
       "Population and settlement on the Otago Goldfields, 1861-1870,"
       New Zealand Geographer, 17(1961), 64-86

9120:   BERMUDA ISLANDS

See 668

9140:   MADEIRA ISLANDS

2523   Hartnack, Wilhelm
       "Bevölkerungsdichte und Siedelungen," pp. 95-103 in:
       Madeira; Landeskunde einer Insel
       Hamburg, Friedrichsen, de Gruyter, 1930

2524   Ribeiro, Orlando
       "La population," pp. 139-147 in:
       L'Île de Madère; étude géographique
       Lisboa, International Geographical Union, 1949

9150: CANARY ISLANDS

2525 Matznetter, Josef
      "Bevölkerungsbewegung und agrarzonale Struktur," pp. 162-175 in:
      Die Kanarischen Inseln; Wirtschaftsgeschichte und Agrargeographie
      Ergänzungsheft Nr. 266 zu Petermanns Geographischen Mitteilungen
      Gotha, Haack, 1958

9160: CAPE VERDE ISLANDS

2526 Sarmento, Alexandre, Morais, Joaquim José Pais de, and Alves Morgado, Nuno
      "A população de Cabo Verde; ensaio de análise demográfica,"
      Garcia de Orta; Revista da Junta das Missões Geográficas e de Investi-
      gações do Ultramar, 5(1957), 11-41

9172.F3: FALKLAND ISLANDS

See 668

9192.M3: MAURITIUS

2527 Waring, H. E. A.
      "The distribution of the population in Mauritius,"
      SGM, 31(1915), 180-185

2528 Robequain, Charles
      "Destin d'une île à sucre: l'économie et le peuplement de Maurice,"
      AG, 63(1954), 255-273

2529 Brookfield, H. C.
      "Mauritius; demographic upsurge and prospect,"
      Population Studies, 11(1957), 102-122

2530 Brookfield, H. C.
      "Pluralism and geography in Mauritius,"
      Geographical Studies (London), 5(1958), 3-19

2531 Brookfield, H. C.
      "Population distribution in Mauritius; an inquiry into the deter-
      minants of distribution in a tropical sugar land,"
      Journal of Tropical Geography, 13(1959), 1-22

9192.R4: REUNION

2532 Isnard, Hildebert
      "La Réunion: aspects de la colonisation et du peuplement,"
      Cahiers d'Outre-Mer, 3(1950), 101-122

2533 Isnard, Hildebert
        "La Réunion: problèmes démographiques, économiques, et sociaux,"
        RGA, 41(1953), 607-628

2534 Sauvy, Alfred
        "La population de la Réunion,"
        Population, 10(1955), 541-542

                        9200: SEYCHELLES

                        See 2373

                9218: COCOS-KEELING ISLANDS

2535 Smith, T. E.
        "The Cocos-Keeling Islands; a demographic laboratory,"
        Population Studies, 14(1960), 94-130

                9230: PACIFIC ISLANDS

2536 LeConte, René
        "L'émigration allemande en Océanie,"
        Mouvement Géographique, 34(1921), 505-512

2537 McArthur, Norma
        The population of the Pacific Islands
        Australian National University, Department of Geography
        Canberra, 1955

2538 Ward, R. Gerard and Moran, W.
        "Recent population trends in the southwest Pacific,"
        TESG, 50(1959), 235-240

                9280: SOLOMON ISLANDS

2539 Hogbin, H. Ian
        "The problem of depopulation in Melanesia as applied to Ongtong
          Java (Solomon Islands),"
        Journal of the Polynesian Society, 39(1930), 43-66

2540 Boag, A. D. and Curtis, R. E.
        "Agriculture and population in the Mortlock Islands,"
        Papua and New Guinea Agricultural Journal, 12(1959), 20-27

9300: NEW HEBRIDES

2541 Geslin, Y.
      "La colonisation des Nouvelles-Hébrides,"
      Cahiers d'Outre-Mer, 1(1948), 245-274

9340: NEW CALEDONIA

2542 Lenormand, M. H.
      "The population of New Caledonia and the Loyalty Islands," pp. 609-
        613 in:
      Proceedings of the 7th Pacific Science Congress, Auckland, 1949,
        Vol. 7
      Christchurch, Pegasus Press, 1953

2543 Faivre, Jean P., et al.
      La Nouvelle Calédonie; géographie et histoire, économie, démographie,
        ethnologie
      Paris, Nouvelles Editions Latines, 1955

9380: FIJI ISLANDS

2544 Derrick, R. A.
      "The people," pp. 118-145 in:
      The Fiji Islands; a geographical handbook
      Suva, Government Printing Department, 1951

2545 Campbell, Eila M. J.
      "Land and population problems in Fiji,"
      GJ, 118(1952), 476-482

2546 Ward, R. Gerard
      "The population of Fiji,"
      GR, 49(1959), 322-341

2547 Ward, R. Gerard
      "Internal migration in Fiji,"
      Journal of the Polynesian Society, 70(1961), 257-271

9400: MICRONESIA

2548 Seidel, H.
      "Die Bevölkerung der Karolinen und Marianen,"
      PM, 51(1905), 36-39

2549 Taeuber, Irene B. and Han, Chungnim C.
      "Micronesian Islands under United States trusteeship: demographic
        paradox,"
      Population Index, 16(1960), 93-115

9420:   CAROLINE ISLANDS

2550   Churchill, William
       "The peopling of Yap,"
       Bulletin of the American Geographical Society, 43(1911), 510-518

2551   Hunt, Edward E., Kidder, Nathaniel R., et al.
       The Micronesians of Yap and their depopulation; report of the
         Peabody Museum (at Harvard) Expedition to Yap Island, Micronesia,
         1947-1948
       Washington, Pacific Science Board, National Research Council, 1949

2552   Hunt, Edward E., et al.
       "The depopulation of Yap,"
       Human Biology, 26(1954), 21-51

2553   Lessa, William A.
       "Depopulation on Ulithi,"
       Human Biology, 27(1955), 161-183

9560:   SAMOA ISLANDS

2554   Durand, John
       The population of Western Samoa
       United Nations, Department of Economic and Social Affairs, Popula-
         tion Division, Population Studies, No. 1
       New York, 1948

2555   Pirie, Peter
       "The geographic implication of population growth in Western Samoa,"
         pp. 91-98 in:
       Second New Zealand Geography Conference, Christchurch, 1958, Pro-
         ceedings
       Christchurch, 1958

2556   Pirie, Peter
       The population of Western Samoa; a preliminary report based on the
         1956 census
       Canberra, Australian National University, 1960

9570:   TONGA ISLANDS

2557   Kennedy, T. F.
       "Land, food, and population in the Kingdom of Tonga,"
       EG, 37(1961), 61-71

9600:   COOK ISLANDS

2558   Johnston, William B.
       "Land, people, and progress in the Cook Islands,"
       EG, 29(1953), 107-124

9610:   FRENCH OCEANIA

2559 Teissier, Raoul
      "Etude démographique sur les Etablissements Français de l'Océanie
      de Cook au recensement des 17/18 septembre 1951,"
      Société des Etudes Océaniennes, Bulletin, 9(1953), 6-31

9660:   PITCAIRN ISLAND

2560 Hermann, Rudolph A.
      "Die Bevölkerung der Insel Pitcairn als Gegenstand wissenschaftlicher
      Untersuchung,"
      PM, 47(1901), 225-230

9700:   HAWAIIAN ISLANDS

2561 Freeman, Otis W.
      "The peopling of Hawaii,"
      Journal of Geography, 27(1928), 125-141

2562 Coulter, John Wesley
      Population and utilization of land and sea in Hawaii, 1853
      Bernice P. Bishop Museum, Bulletin 88
      Honolulu, 1931

2563 Kolb, Albert
      "Die farbige Bevölkerung der Hawaiischen Inseln,"
      Weltwirtschaftliches Archiv, 30(1942)

AUTHOR INDEX

Aagesen Aage 797, 1684, 1685, 1686
Aartsen, J. P. van 1478
Abascal Garayoa, Angel 1421, 1439
Abou El-Ezz, Mohammed 2344
Abrahamson, John D. 596
Accioly Borges, T. Pompeu 802
Acher, Gilbert 1106, 1525, 2318
Ackerman, Edward A. 36, 2158
Acsádi, György 1327
Adams, Doris G. 1933
Adams, E. 70
Adams, Georgia E. 578
Adlercreutz, B. 227
Ahlberg, Gösta 1715, 1716
Ahmad, Enayet 2006, 2023
Ahmad, Kazi S. 1944, 1945, 1946, 1964
Ahmad, Nafis 1948, 1949
Aicardi, Giacomo 1495, 1497
Aïtoff, D. 1777
Ajo, Reino 1759
Akers, Donald S. 1382
Aldama, Alvaro C.
Alers, H. J. H. 2194
Alessandri, Maria L. 1555
Alexander, Charles S. 718
Alexander, John W. 254, 418, 2062
Alexandersson, Gunnar 588, 1589
Alexandre, J. 1160, 1162
Alexandre, S. 1160
Alivia, G. 1574, 1576
Allbaugh, Leland G. 1608
Allix, André 1083, 1084
Almada, Francisco R. 629
Almagià, Roberto 20, 1473, 1487, 1489
  1491, 1557, 1585, 1613
Alsop, M. H. 2411
Alty, Stella W. 344
Alves Morgado, Nuno 2446, 2526
Ambrosius, Ernst 1222
American Geographical Society 4
Amerkhail, Najibullah 1940
Amiran, D. H. K. 1927
Amorim, Fernando B. P. de 2433
Amorim Girão, Aristides de 1456, 1457,
  1459, 1460, 1461
Anantapadmanbhan, N. 2014
Ancel, Jacques 1601
Anderle, Joseph 1834
Anderson, C. E. 1683
Anderson, Theodore R. 276
André, Jacques 1535
Andrews, John 2496

Andriot, E. 1021
Anfossi, G. 1118, 1498, 1572, 1573
Angenot, L. H. J. 1138
Anonymous 310
Anthony, Sylvia 346
Anuchin, V. A. 1848, 2101
Applebaum, William 262
Appleton, John B. 573
Appolis, Emile 1066
Arbos, Ph. 134, 1043
Arca Parró, Alberto 735, 738, 739
Ardaillon, E. 1596
Arden-Close, Charles 883
Ardissone, Romualdo 767, 770
Arditi, Nessim 780
Argentina, Ministerio de Hacienda 771
Armao, Ermanno 1606
Arnberger, Erik 1309a
Arnell, William 465
Aschmann, Homer 635
Assmann, L. 1240
Association de Géographes Français 1
Auerbach, Bertrand 1186
Auerbach, F. 173
Augelli, John P. 667, 690
Aurousseau, Marcel 42, 43
Awad, Mohammed 2343
Ayache, Albert 2301

Baal, J. van 2267
Back, C. de 2408
Backhoff, G. A. 230
Bacon, Philip 101
Badenhorst, L. T. 2281, 2412
Bainbridge, T. H. 907, 911
Baines, J. A. 1952
Baker, C. A. 2427
Baker, Colin 2421, 2429
Baker, John N. L. 1959
Baker, O. E. 199, 386, 394, 396, 400
Baker, Samuel J. K. 2359, 2362
Baldacci, Antonio 1599
Baldwin, William O. 447
Balfour, Marshall C. 2040
Ballas, Donald J. 496
Balseinte, Raymond 995, 996
Balzak, S. S. 1797
Barbieri, Giuseppe 1490
Barbour, Kenneth M. 2357a
Barclay, George 2114, 2124a, 2125
Barclay, R. S. 941

Tracey, W. R. 340
Tracy, Stanley J. 372
Träger, E.
Trewartha, Glenn T. 33, 52, 421,
  560, 1981, 2065, 2066, 2074, 2116,
  2141, 2142, 2153, 2353, 2377, 2438
Trexler, Harrison A. 521
Tricart, Jean 1181
Trifunoski, Jovan F. 1647
Troger, Ernest 1306
Troll, Carl 2277
Tronnier, R. 172
Trotter, John E. 587
Trueman, A. E. 924
Truesdell, Leon E. 422
Tsubouchi, Syoji 2172
Tschudi, Aadel B. 2163
Tu, C. W. 2052
Tuan, Chi-hsien 2124
Tufescu, Victor 1663, 1669
Tuinman, A. S. 335
Tulippe, Omer 44, 241, 1158
Tümertekin, Erol 1901
Tuncdilek, Necdet 1903
Tunkelo, A. 1754
Tverdohlebov, I. T. 1356

Ubilluz, Edmundo 741, 744
Udem, E. 1211
Ueda, Masao 2155, 2160, 2171
Ueda, Sinzo 2058
Uekötter, H. 1250
Uhlig, Carl 1259, 2378
Uhlig, Harald 1164
Uhnbom, Ivar 1726
Uhorczak, Franciszek 1379
Ul-Hasan, Reyaz 1943
Unger, Leonard 2187
U.S.S.R., Akademiia Nauk, Institut
  Nauchnoi Informatsii 8
U.S.S.R., Institut Izucheniye
  Poverchnost i Nedra 1784
United Nations, Department of
  Economic and Social Affairs
  13, 60, 102, 166, 168, 607,
  608, 698, 1870, 1873, 2235,
  2384, 2387, 2444
United Nations Educational,
  Scientific and Cultural
  Organization, International
  Committee for Social Sciences
  Documentation 7, 9, 12
United Nations, Statistical Office
  6, 10
United States, Bureau of the Census
  and Library of Congress 297, 371,
  844, 845, 2272, 2286

United States, Bureau of the Census,
  Foreign Manpower Research Office
  2041
United States, National Resources
  Committee 407
University of California, Berkeley,
  International Urban Research 129
Untilov, V. 1773
Urabayen, L. de 1425
Uribe Macip, Venus 616
Usher, Abbott P. 842

Vaganay, H. 1039
Van Aartsen, J. P. 169, 1032, 2189
Van Cleef, Eugene 331, 381, 526
Van Hinte, J. 427, 1126
Van Lohuizen, Ir. Th. K. 1125
Van Valkenburg, Samuel 864, 2247
Vance, Rupert B. 408, 487
Vanni, Manfredo 1529
Vardabasso, Silvano 1579
Varlamov, V. S. 1772
Varley, W. J. 2482
Varma, Kripa N. 2018
Vasyutin, V. F. 1797
Vaughan, T. D. 946a, 947
Vaumas, Etienne de 1906, 1910, 1911,
  1912, 1922
Vávra, Zdeněk 1362
Veen, H. N. ter 182
Velekii, S. N. 1776
Velho, Fernando 1459
Velikonja, Joseph 870
Vent, Herbert 511
Vent, P. C. de 1121, 1128
Vergez-Tricom, G. 2508
Verma, Sat D. 2019
Versantvoort, A. A. M. 2167
Verstege, J. Ch. W. 138
Veynberg, B. P. 1779
Veyret, Paul 332
Veyret-Verner, Germaine 39, 51, 55,
  81, 98, 120, 1094, 1102, 1105,
  1114
Vial, L. G. 2266
Vidal de la Blache, P. 19, 68, 60,
  1024
Vierkandt, A. 2430
Vila, Marco-Aurelio 714, 715, 719
Vila, P. 1428
Villey, Daniel 34
Vince, Stanley W. E. 888
Vincent, Paulette 1094
Visher, Stephen S. 532, 533, 534,
Vivó, Jorge A. 619
Vivó, Escoto, Jorge A. 637
Vlieland, C. A. 2216